THE POISON PATRIARCH

Also by Mark Shaw

The Reporter Who Knew Too Much
Stations Along the Way
Road to a Miracle
Beneath the Mask of Holiness
Melvin Belli: King of the Courtroom
Miscarriage of Justice: The Jonathan Pollard Story
The Perfect Yankee
Forever Flying
Down for the Count
Bury Me in a Pot Bunker
Dandelions in the Moonlight
Larry Legend
Testament to Courage

THE POISON PATRIARCH

How the Betrayals of Joseph P. Kennedy
Caused the Assassination of JFK

MARK SHAW

Skyhorse Publishing

Skyhorse Publishing books may be purchased in bulk at special discounts for sales promotion, corporate gifts, fund-raising, or educational purposes. Special editions can also be created to specifications. For details, contact the Special Sales Department, Skyhorse Publishing, 307 West 36th Street, 11th Floor, New York, NY 10018 or info@skyhorsepublishing.com.

Skyhorse® and Skyhorse Publishing® are registered trademarks of Skyhorse Publishing, Inc.®, a Delaware corporation.

Visit our website at www.skyhorsepublishing.com.

10 9 8 7 6 5 4 3 2

Library of Congress Cataloging-in-Publication Data is available on file.

Cover design by Richard Rossiter

ISBN: 978-1-5107-0419-0
Ebook ISBN: 978-1-62873-524-6

Printed in China

"The great enemy of truth is very often not the lie—deliberate, contrived, and dishonest—but the myth—persistent, persuasive, and unrealistic. Belief in myths allows the comfort of opinion without the discomfort of thought."

President John F. Kennedy

"The mission of the written word is not to buttress high policy, but to proclaim the truth."

Arthur Miller
Pulitzer Prize-Winning Playwright

Contents

Book V

Prologue

"I have news for you," the caller said in a high-pitched tone, "The President's been shot."

Gazing upward in disbelief, Attorney General Robert F. Kennedy attempted to comprehend these words as he listened carefully to FBI Director J. Edgar Hoover's voice on the telephone. It was an unusually warm, sunny afternoon in McLean, Virginia on November 22, 1963, a few minutes before two o'clock Eastern time. The attorney general had just enjoyed a swim at his Hickory Hill residence pool after spending the morning in Justice Department meetings focused on how best to continue his crusade to destroy organized crime.

Dressed in a white T-shirt and shorts, RFK asked Hoover, "Is it serious?" The answer: "I think it's serious. I am trying to get more details. I'll call you back when I find out more." Bobby covered his mouth with his right hand and returned to his wife, Ethel, and two guests: New York District Attorney Robert Morgenthau and his assistant, criminal division chief, Silvio Mollo. RFK lifted his hands to his face and mumbled, "Jack's been shot. It may be fatal."

As Ethel comforted him and the others recoiled in shock, RFK began to telephone seeking details. He finally reached Parkland Hospital in Dallas and was told that his brother was unconscious and that a priest had been summoned. Moments later, another telephone call from Hoover confirmed RFK's worst fears. "The President's dead," Hoover said without a hint of sympathy.

A few minutes later, Robert Kennedy, the second most powerful man in the country, slowly walked between the swimming pool and the tennis courts on the six-acre estate. Head down, hands in his pockets, tears welled up in Bobby's eyes with every step. Trailing at his heels was his favorite dog, Brumus, a black Newfoundland.

Robert F. Kennedy had lost a brother; the nation had lost a president. At 2:38 p.m. Central time, Lyndon Baines Johnson took the oath of office on Air Force One, still on the tarmac in Dallas, and became the thirty-sixth president of the United States.

Attempting to calm himself when he returned to Ethel and his guests, Bobby, his words barely audible, told his press secretary Ed Guthman: "There's so much bitterness; I thought they would get one of us, but Jack, after all he had been through, [I] never worried about it. . . . I never thought it would happen. I thought it would be me . . . there's been so much bitterness and hatred . . . " Later, Guthman emphasized that he was certain RFK used the word "they" and not "he," and that Bobby believed "they" might be coming after him next.

Hours later, mob lawyer Frank Ragano, the attorney for Mafia dons Carlos Marcello and Santo Trafficante and Teamsters boss James Hoffa, shared a restaurant table with his wife, Nancy, and Trafficante at the International Inn, a five-star hotel in Tampa, Florida. As related to this author by Nancy Ragano, the two were "laughing, joking, and raising glasses of champagne high in the air to toast JFK's assassination."

Why were these men celebrating? The answer may be traced to RFK's statement to Ed Guthman that Bobby believed he would be assassinated instead of his brother. But the key to understanding to whom Bobby was referring when he said "they"—as in, "*they* would get one of us"—is to focus on one cabinet appointment John F. Kennedy made shortly after becoming president. It was a decision JFK was forced to make, and one that meant his ultimate doom.

And the starting point, as unlikely as it may seem, to realizing why this decision cost JFK his life revolves around never-before-revealed information about the trial of Lee Harvey Oswald's assassin, Jack Ruby. His attorney Melvin Belli was the most famous lawyer in America, if not the world, at the time. He is also the missing link in the most scrutinized assassination investigation in five decades.

Based on these fresh disclosures, this book examines the common-sense element of motive—including focusing for the first time in any investigation or book on why Robert F. Kennedy *was not* killed in 1963 instead of why John Kennedy *was* murdered. The focus on motive makes apparent the identity of those who were behind the president and Oswald's death. Instead of conjecture, speculation, and guesswork, close scrutiny of Belli's conduct before, during, and after the Ruby trial establishes a definite connection between Oswald, Ruby, and the individual who hated the Kennedys most: the desperate man who had no alternative but to order the president's death so as to protect a multi-million-dollar empire and his very freedom.

Most importantly, for history's sake, this fresh approach, while debunking any "Oswald Alone" theory, leads to the compelling conclusion that the patriarch of the Kennedy family, Joseph P. Kennedy, bears the ultimate responsibility for the senseless death of his son, the thirty-fifth president of the United States. When the dust settled, the elder Kennedy reaped what he had sown in a scenario tantamount to a Greek tragedy with a complex moral structure where abuses of power and broken promises pervaded at every turn, culminating in betrayals, revenge, and, ultimately, murder.

BOOK I

CHAPTER ONE

The Dallas Assassinations

This book offers a completely new perspective regarding the twin assassinations in Dallas in 1963: the murders of John F. Kennedy and Lee Harvey Oswald. The underlying theory is based on close examination of fresh facts never revealed before and provides the most plausible explanation to date as to who killed President Kennedy, and why. For fifty years and counting, the truth about the Kennedy assassination has been hiding in plain sight. Even those with good intentions simply missed facts that would have led them to a simple, logical, common sense scenario regarding the events surrounding President Kennedy's death.

At times in this narrative, it may seem as if we are straying far afield from the core argument: that Joseph Kennedy bears ultimate responsibility for JFK's death. Patience is thus required in the same way that jurors must attend to details as a prosecutor progressively attempts to prove a circumstantial case. To this end, information will be presented beginning with what was known about the assassinations at the time, what was learned over the years through investigative commissions and publications, what new facts this author uncovered through substantive research, and finally what conclusions may be reached based on the body of work.

Missing links must be accounted for and explained. And in the case of the Kennedy assassination, an essential link—one connecting the man who masterminded the assassinations with those who caused them to occur through their actions—was always missing. Until now.

This said, and as unlikely as it may seem at first glance, the circuitous trail to exposing the truth about the assassinations of JFK and Oswald begins at the trial of Jack Ruby, Oswald's killer. This trial commenced at the Dallas County Courthouse in March 1964, less than four months after the twin murders. An eight-story building, constructed in 1913 by architect H. A. Overbeck in the classic neocolonial style, the courthouse stood at the corner of Houston and Main Streets in downtown Dallas. Here, a jury of Ruby's peers would decide if he was guilty of the first-degree murder of Oswald, JFK's alleged assassin, or not guilty by reason of insanity. If the former was decided based on the only live television broadcast of a murder in history, death by electrocution was the penalty.

As fifty-seven-year-old Melvin Belli stood beside Ruby in the packed courtroom, observers noted the stark differences between the two men. Though short in stature and noticeably bulky, Belli was a commanding figure with distinctive black horn-rimmed glasses and a pronounced square chin. His swept-back, wavy, silver hair exposed bushy eyebrows and a furrowed brow, belying a man oozing with confidence. When he made a point, the bombastic barrister cradled his glasses in his right hand and thrust them forward as if to say, "Now, listen closely or you'll miss something important." An *Associated Press* headline described Ruby's attorney as "Candid, Controversial, and Clever . . . " He was a headline-maker who had been the subject of a *Los Angeles Times* article by Jack Smith bearing the banner, "L.A. Watching New Court Idol Emerge."

Time magazine published an article on Belli's representation of Ruby in its December 20, 1963, issue. The byline read, "Belli For The Defense." In part, the article read, "The visitor flew in with a flourish. His pink face and silver hair gleamed above polished cowboy boots and a grand, fur-collared overcoat. San Francisco lawyer Melvin Mouron Belli had come to Dallas to defend Jack Ruby, the only man ever to ever commit a murder while the whole nation watched."

*Melvin Belli (right) and Jack Ruby during Ruby Trial—March 1964. Despite the availability
of several nationally-known criminal defense lawyers, San Francisco personal-injury
attorney Belli became Ruby's trial lawyer.   Credit: Corbis Images.*

In contrast to his attorney, the fifty-one-year-old Ruby (conflicting
records noted his age as fifty-two) had a receding hairline and bore a
smaller frame: five-foot nine and one hundred and seventy-five pounds.
To viewers in the courtroom, he seemed to have shrunk in size since
his arrest four months earlier. His face was nondescript, his expression
vacant, like that of a retired uncle whose life had passed him by. He spoke
in a high-pitched tone with a slight lisp, a trait that had led some to call
him a "sissy." His jailer, Al Maddox, told this author that Ruby was "a
used to be."

If Lee Harvey Oswald's otherwise nondescript killer possessed any distinguishing characteristic, it was his eyes. They appeared hollow, like killer's eyes. Belli, whose green eyes sparkled when he became excited, observed, "There was something about [Ruby's] eyes. They shone like a beagle's."

Time profiled the Ruby case in its January 31, 1964, issue. It featured articles previewing Teamsters union boss James Hoffa's jury-tampering trial and the designation of JFK's *Profiles in Courage* as the country's best-selling book. Included in the magazine was a description of the evidence presented during Ruby's bail hearing. It pointed out that Ruby's IQ score of 109 meant that "he tests higher in intelligence than 73% of the population."

Belli and Ruby were also profiled in the February 21, 1964, issue of *Life* magazine. Featuring the infamous and controversial photograph of Oswald brandishing his rifle on the cover, the magazine touted headlines reading, "Exclusive—Oswald Armed for Murder, In Full and Extra Ordinary Detail, The Life Of The Assassin." Below the caption, the blurb read, "As Jack Ruby Goes to Trial, Cast of Characters: How the Law Applies."

Belli, having already decided on an insanity defense, must have been pleased by the two-page vertical photograph of his client. Ruby stood, with his hands clasped in handcuffs, wearing a dark suit, white shirt, and tie. His eyes stared blankly at the reader in an eerie fashion. The photograph caption read, "As Ruby goes to trial, the question before the court: Was This Man Sane?" Readers were informed that "this extraordinary picture of Jack Ruby was taken as he was leaving jail for pretrial tests by doctors to examine the physical and mental condition of the man who shot Lee Harvey Oswald."

Belli was described as "a Californian with a fantastic record of courtroom victories." His counterpart, District Attorney Henry Wade, when asked about the insanity defense was quoted as saying, "We think it is a case of cold-blooded, calculated murder."

Photographs of Ruby included one with his sister Eva, another when he approached Oswald with murder on his mind, and a final one with two of his Carousel nightclub strippers. Scantily clad, they were positioned on both sides facing Ruby, legs and bikini bottoms in full view. A portion of the caption read: "Ruby basking in the attention of two of his strippers."

A few pages later, the "Cast of the Courtroom Drama" was presented. Belli, captured standing in his San Francisco office, was flanked by photos of the Ruby trial mainstays: D. A. Henry Wade, Assistant D. A. Bill Alexander, and presiding Judge Joe Brown. Appearing puffy-faced and wearing black horn-rimmed glasses, Wade tugged at a cigar stuffed into the right corner of his mouth. The caption mentioned that Wade's office staff had won 189 felony trials and lost only thirteen in 1963.

The photograph of Judge Brown indicated an appearance similar to that of Henry Wade except for a more bulbous nose. Jailer Al Maddox told this author the judge was "a good old country boy. Sheriff Decker liked him and if the one-eyed sheriff liked someone, then he had to be alright."

The article read in part:

> . . . Melvin Belli, chief defense counsel,
> dominates the cast of attorneys in the Ruby
> trial. Belli is known as the 'King of Torts'
> for his success in personal injury suits . . .
> Chief prosecutor Henry Wade . . . conceals
> a steel trap mind behind a cornball manner.
> Bill Alexander is a soft-spoken, but
> relentless prosecutor and cross-examiner
> in the courtroom-style of Texas-born Gregory
> Peck. The judge, Joe Brown, has 29 years'
> experience, runs a court with an easy
> Texas-style loosed rein. But he can be tough.

As jury selection approached, Belli and co-counsel Joe Tonahill, a Texan described by Bill Alexander to this author as "a big, bullfrog of a guy, a bullshit artist who liked to overpower people with his size and his voice," knew they faced a tall order. Their client had committed murder not in

front of one, two, ten or even a thousand witnesses, but millions who had
tuned in hoping to catch a glimpse of the alleged killer of their beloved
president on national television as he was being transferred from one
Dallas jail to another. Instead, they had recoiled in horror as Ruby shot
and killed Lee Harvey Oswald at point-blank range.

Oswald's death had shocked those who witnessed it, but the killing of
John Fitzgerald Kennedy had shaken the world, shaken the very core of
those who worshipped the handsome, charismatic president.

‡

The basic facts regarding the shooting of John F. Kennedy are well-known
and undisputed as is the road he took to the presidency. In 1960, by the
slimmest of margins (112,827 votes out of 68 million-plus—0.16%—303
electoral votes to 219), JFK had defeated Vice President Richard Nixon to
become president. Masterminding the election of his son from the shadows had been the Kennedy patriarch, Joseph P. Kennedy. Critics alleged
that he had manipulated the result, some used stronger language such as
"fixed," and "stolen," but, despite cries of protest from the Republicans,
no investigation of the election occurred. On inauguration day, January
20, 1961, Joe Kennedy beamed with pride, his dream of seeing a son
become president fulfilled.

Two years, ten months, and six days later, during a trip to Texas on
November 22, 1963, the president was assassinated as his limousine
passed by the Texas School Book Depository in downtown Dallas.
Arrested shortly thereafter was twenty-four-year-old Lee Harvey Oswald.
Prosecutors alleged that he had crouched in a sniper's nest he made from
book cartons on the sixth floor of the depository and aimed a Mannlicher-
Carcano 6.5-millimeter rifle out the top-floor window. When Kennedy's
limousine drove past at precisely twelve thirty in the afternoon police said,
Oswald squeezed the trigger three times in six-and-a-half seconds, hitting
the president twice and inflicting a fatal head wound. Oswald supposedly
fled the building and was captured hours later in a movie theater after
allegedly shooting and killing a Dallas police officer, J. D. Tippit. Less

than 48 hours later, Oswald himself was fatally shot by Jack Ruby as he was being transferred from police headquarters to the county jail.

‡

While Lee Harvey Oswald's motives for shooting John Kennedy and Jack Ruby's for shooting Oswald have been discussed and debated for years, there is little debate regarding Oswald's denial of guilt.

At police headquarters after his arrest, the handcuffed Oswald was told he could cover his face with his hands if he wished. To that suggestion, he told reporters, "Why should I hide my face? I haven't done anything to be ashamed of." Later, Oswald stated, "I didn't kill the President, I didn't kill nobody," at a midnight news conference at police headquarters.

District Attorney Henry Wade believed otherwise, telling reporters Oswald's fingerprints had been found on boxes in the depository where the shots were fired and on the murder weapon. Presumably to sew up the case, Wade provided details about a witness who told the authorities that after Oswald boarded a bus following the shooting, he "laughed" when told that the president had been shot. "There is no question that Oswald was JFK's murderer," Wade boasted.

When Jack Ruby had first learned the news of JFK's shooting, police said he was sitting by the desk of John Newnan, a likable advertising salesman for the *Dallas Morning News*. Ruby, a regular visitor to the newspaper who sought to impress editors and columnists with his "inside ideas for stories," discussed the appropriate copy to be included in advertisements for the Carousel and a second nightclub he owned, the Vegas Club. Satisfied with the advertisement, he wrote a check for $1.87 on his Merchants State Bank account to pay for the ads.

Moments later, at half past noon or so, a CBS News bulletin blared from a nearby television set: "Three shots were fired at President Kennedy's motorcade today in downtown Dallas." A short time later, Ruby heard Walter Cronkite, his voice quivering, announce, "President Kennedy died at 1:00 P.M. Central Standard time, two o'clock Eastern Standard time, some thirty-eight minutes ago." According to authorities, Jack Ruby then drove to his nightclub, the Carousel. Several hours later, at around midnight, Ruby headed for police headquarters where a news conference was anticipated. Ruby, packing his nickel-plated .38 pistol, was within ten feet or so of Oswald when Wade presented him to the world. An *Associated Press* photograph captured Ruby scribbling notes in the back of the room.

Questions surfaced later regarding how Ruby ended up in the Dallas Police Department basement where Oswald appeared the next morning, Sunday, November 24th. Ruby told police he drove downtown to send money to one of the strippers who worked for him via the Western Union office and then walked to police headquarters a block away. Left behind in the back seat of his white 1960 Oldsmobile was a red Dachshund named Sheba as well as a set of brass knuckles, a transistor radio, and, most interesting in view of later developments, a copy of a two-month-old *New York Sunday Mirror* article chronicling mobster Joseph Valachi's appearance before Senator John L. McClellan's Subcommittee on Investigations in early October.[1] Also discovered were copies of Dallas and Fort Worth newspapers depicting the intended route of President Kennedy's motorcade.

Wearing a dark suit, white shirt, and a silk necktie with a gold-plated tie clasp—rather formal attire for a Sunday morning trip to Western Union— Ruby had stuffed a roll of bills into one pocket totaling $2015.33. He had sixty dollars in traveler's checks as well. In his right front trousers' pocket, he carried the loaded pistol.

At 11:15 AM, Dallas homicide detectives escorted a dour-faced Oswald out of Captain Will Fritz's office door. As bright lights showered him, Oswald, arguably the most hated man in the world, smirked at three journalists who shouted questions. He was snarly and silent; beads of perspiration pockmarked his shiny forehead in the stuffy hallway. The plan, according to police, was to transport Oswald in an armored car to

---

1   Joe Valachi was the first Mafia member to publicly disclose the existence of the underworld organization, coining the phrase "Cosa Nostra" ("our thing"—a euphemism for the Italian Mafia).

the more secure county jail a few blocks away. That car was stationed in front of a ramp where policeman E. R. Vaughn stood guard.

Five minutes later, a black car driven by Lt. Rio Pierce drove up the narrow ramp as Vaughn stepped aside. Ruby later told police that this allowed him to inch his way undetected down the narrow ramp that was eight to nine feet wide. This was barely enough to permit a car to enter.

As Oswald emerged from an elevator flanked by two detectives, one journalist shouted, "Here he comes." As this point, WBAP television director Jimmy Turner swore he saw Ruby at the end of the ramp.

Oswald was handcuffed to the left wrist of detective J. R. "James" Leavelle, who wore a white suit and a gleaming white Stetson hat. Detective L.C. Graves held Oswald's left arm, but there were no officers directly in front of him. Behind Oswald's entourage, several police looked on. Eager to display the alleged killer of JFK and Dallas policeman Tippit to the world, police welcomed the swarm of reporters and photographers gathered for the photo-op.

A pivotal character in the ensuing scenario was Icarus "Ike" Pappas, one of many journalists who became well-known for their reporting of the JFK assassination. (Another was Dan Rather, whose first-rate, fast-breaking accounts of the shooting electrified the world. His sterling performance would culminate in a reporter position with CBS where he would become the network's longtime prime time news anchor.)

Pappas, later a noted reporter for CBS, but then working for *WNEW* in New York, pushed his way to a spot nearly kiss-close to the most infamous man in the world. Intent on gaining a noteworthy quote from Oswald despite the presence of more than seventy reporters and one hundred police, Pappas shoved his microphone near the accused killer. Oswald sneered as flashbulbs popped and floodlights glared in the background.

At exactly 11:21 AM, Pappas asked a question just as Jack Ruby angled in beside Pappas, just to the right of Oswald. The prisoner's bruised, unshaven face reflected his struggle with police when he was arrested. Television cameramen focused on the scene as millions of viewers glimpsed the face of the accused. They heard Pappas ask, "Lee, do you have anything to say in your defense?" It was a question Oswald never answered.

A second later, Ruby, wearing a nap-brimmed gray fedora, edged closer to Oswald. As Ruby approached, Oswald's face seemed to register a glimmer of recognition. Conspiracy buffs later alleged that Oswald, a white colored shirt peeking from under his dark crew neck sweater, recognized Ruby. Others maintained that Oswald's expression was an acknowledgment of Ruby's pistol.

Raising the weapon, Ruby extended his right arm, thrust the gun toward Oswald's stomach, and, from a distance of about fifteen inches, pulled the trigger. The gunshot caused Detective Leavelle, his eyes reflecting disbelief, to recoil in horror. Robert Jackson's Pulitzer Prize-winning photograph was taken at this moment.

Oswald moaned in anguish as his eyes looked upward, and crumpled to the ground. As the television image of the assassination spread across the planet, the black-and-white footage was accompanied by KRLD-TV reporter Bob Huffaker's commentary, "He's been shot! He's been shot! Lee Oswald has been shot by a man with a gun. There's absolute panic here in the basement of Dallas police headquarters. Detectives have their guns drawn. Oswald has been shot. No question, he has been shot."

Detective Graves freed his hand from Oswald's arm, grabbed the burly shooter, and wrestled him to the ground like a defensive lineman tackling a fullback. Graves grasped the revolver so Ruby could fire no more. By then, Lee Harvey Oswald was in cardiac arrest, with wounds to his kidneys, spleen, and aorta. The main suspect in the assassination of President John Fitzgerald Kennedy died a short time later at Parkland Memorial Hospital.

Handcuffed, Ruby was booked into jail by Al Maddox, a deputy sheriff for seven months. "I knew Jack," Maddox told this author. "When I first saw him in jail, he was barefoot and crying. He said, 'I didn't kill that man.' I said, 'Jack, we were all watching television and saw it.'"

On two days in November 1963, three men—the president of the United States, Dallas policeman Tippit, and Lee Harvey Oswald—had been murdered. One man, Jack Ruby, was left to stand in judgment regarding his responsibility for the assassination of the president's alleged assassin. When closely examined, the events surrounding Ruby's trial and the trial itself should have been an eye-opener for anyone truly interested in the truth about the Dallas killings. But it hasn't been, until now.

CHAPTER TWO

Jack Ruby and Melvin Belli

In an interview with *Time* published shortly before Jack Ruby's trial, Melvin Belli provided some insight into his client: "[Jack] Ruby is an intense, emotional man. Talking to him, the hair rose on the hackles of my neck. I felt horror, revulsion, sadness. I saw myself and millions of fellow Americans [in Ruby]."

The fifth of eight children, Ruby was born Jack Rubenstein in Chicago on March 19, 1911, or March 24, 1912, depending on which story he provided. (Dallas police preferred the latter.)

His Judaism was a source of pride for Ruby. When pro-Hitler/Nazi German Americans staged a rally in support of the Führer in Chicago, Ruby joined several friends from the Lawndale Poolroom and Restaurant who attacked the Nazi sympathizers. Later, author William Manchester wrote of Oswald's killer, "All his life Jack regarded himself as an avenger—an anti-Semitic remark set him off—and his vengeance had always expressed itself through violence. He was a direct, simple, stunted man, with a childlike inability to foresee the consequences of strenuous physical protest."

Following World War II, Ruby journeyed to Dallas to be near his sister Eva, who operated a nightclub called the Singapore Supper Club. Deciding on a future that included bright lights and dancing girls, he joined her in the business and changed the club's name to The Silver Spur Club. The nightspot gained a reputation as a "roughneck haunt"—Dallas police called it "bucket of blood"—and it eventually failed. According to Eva, who had a history of psychiatric care, her brother was so devastated that he locked himself in a motel room and threatened to commit suicide.

Strip joints became Jack Ruby's salvation, but they didn't flourish until after Ruby had tried, and failed, at several other occupations. His life changed for the better with the opening of the Carousel Club, previously known as the Sovereign. Located midway between the county jail and the police station on Commerce Street in downtown Dallas, the club was sandwiched between a parking garage and a short-order restaurant. Across the street stood the ritzy Adolphus Hotel, built by the Busch family of St. Louis.

Ruby was proud of the rectangular, lighted sign he purchased with carousel and burlesque imprinted on it. Smaller print noted girls and bar-b-q. To the left, letters spelled out the names of the featured dancers. On the Carousel's business card, the words "Sophisticated, Risqué, and Provocative" appeared in bold.

"It was a classy place," Malcolm Summers, a witness to the assassination from a location in Dealey Plaza, told a *Dallas Morning News* reporter. "Big-titty girls, all of that . . . everybody went there including [Dallas financier] Billie Sol Estes."

At times, Ruby, ever the showman, was master of ceremonies for the strip show. Entertainment columnist Tony Zoppi recalled seeing Ruby standing on stage in a large white cowboy outfit complete with a huge white hat. Zoppi later wrote that Ruby was "a born loser, a real level loser who didn't have twenty cents to his name."

Diana Hunter and Alice Anderson possessed kinder memories of the nightclub owner. They dedicated their book, *Jack Ruby's Girls*, "In loving memory of JACK RUBY, Our Raging Boss, Our Faithful Friend, The Kindest-Hearted Sonuvabitch We Ever Knew." Describing Ruby, the authors wrote, "We suppose you'd have to say he looked like a night club operator, or maybe like a gangster."

Bill Alexander, Ruby's chief trial prosecutor told this author, "I knew Ruby for ten or twelve years. He tried to keep his place clean from trouble that could cause him to lose his liquor license. Those were quite valuable in those days and Ruby sometimes called the police to have them get rid of people who were drunk or causing trouble."

From 1949 until 1963, Ruby, despite an explosive disposition, was arrested for non-violent offenses such as carrying a concealed weapon, selling liquor and permitting dancing after hours, simple assault, and ignoring traffic summons. Regardless, to prosecutors Ruby was simply a cold-blooded killer who wanted to be a big shot. After shooting JFK's alleged assassin, he certainly was.

‡

Melvin Belli was, by most accounts, an eccentric with an affection for blending fiction with fact. To many, it will be a surprise that the loquacious lawyer is considered a person of interest, a central figure in determining who was ultimately responsible for the assassination of JFK. But probing Belli's behavior before, during, and after the Ruby case is essential to any search for the truth. Clues abounded but were discarded as unimportant during the Ruby trial and in the years following the Dallas murders.

A self-styled dandy, Belli wore red silk-lined suits and calf-high black snakeskin cowboy boots at his San Francisco office. "I have a penchant for all things bright and beautiful, kinky and flawed," he told the *Los Angeles Times*, "and for good wines, great tables, wide travels, and beautiful women."

Belli celebrated his many civil court victories by raising a skull-and-crossbones pirate flag on the roof of his Montgomery Street office in downtown San Francisco. Two booming blasts from a rooftop antique ship's cannon signaled a champagne and caviar party catered for the famed attorney. A must-see stop on the Gray Line bus tour, Belli's office was a lair straight from a Dickens novel. It featured a gallimaufry of exotica including an enormous Bengal tiger-skin rug purchased from Elizabeth Taylor, a seventeenth-century globe, Nepalese tapestries, hundreds of rare books, a case of aged French Burgundy, and an eighteenth-century mahogany bar. The brick walls were dotted with signed photographs of celebrity pals Joe DiMaggio,

Hubert Humphrey, Mae West, and Frank Sinatra. A life-sized self-portrait with a distinctly Napoleonic air greeted clients and party guests.

In his prime, the lawyer who defended Jack Ruby was a larger-than-life character straight out of a Damon Runyon novel. A ladies' man extraordinaire, he married and divorced five times before his final marriage to Nancy Ho Belli. Monikered the "King of Torts" by *Life* magazine, he plied his trade and honed his lofty reputation as a plaintiff's lawyer in civil cases by being the ultimate self-promoter. Along the way, he irritated and confounded nearly every lawyer he opposed with his courtroom savvy, drew critical comments from judges for his irreverence, and alienated large corporations by winning large monetary awards against them. As a tribute to his courtroom prowess as a personal injury specialist, he named his yacht, *Adequate Award*.

Belli's client list read like a Who's Who of twentieth-century celebrities. During the decades he practiced law, Belli represented famous personalities such as actors Errol Flynn and Lana Turner; boxers George Foreman and Muhammad Ali; The Rolling Stones (Belli is prominent in the film *Gimme Shelter* which depicted the Stones disastrous 1969 concert at Altamont Speedway); evangelists Jim and Tammy Faye Bakker; comedian Lenny Bruce; Washington socialite and former wife of the attorney general, Martha Mitchell; stuntman Evel Knievel; and infamous stripper Carol Doda.

A reporter for the *San Francisco Chronicle* was puzzled by the loquacious attorney, observing, "He allows a burning ego to eclipse a first-class legal mind." Perhaps the reporter knew that when Belli entered a hotel, the first thing he did was to have himself paged ("Calling Melvin Belli, Calling Melvin Belli, Calling Melvin Belli!") on the house telephone so everyone knew he had arrived.

Without doubt, Ruby's attorney was an international personality. In later years, he appeared at White House dinners accompanied by glamorous models and as a regular on the popular *Johnny Carson Show*. This prompted one pundit to observe, "Mel [is] the real thing, a Barnum and Bailey original."

This may have been true, but one fact was certain when Jack Ruby's trial rolled around: Oswald's killer *was not* represented by a competent criminal defense attorney. Instead, by all accounts, Belli had no significant criminal trial experience of any kind, let alone experience with first-degree murder/death penalty cases or with trials where the defense of insanity was employed. This was true even through many lawyers with such experience, as we shall see, were available to represent Ruby.

To be certain, Belli's expertise at the time, as revealed to the world and all of the media covering the Ruby case in the February 21st, 1964, *Life* magazine profile (published just a month before the Ruby trial) was civil law, specifically personal injury litigation where his reputation as a plaintiff's attorney was enhanced with multi-million dollar jury verdicts. By his own admission in *My Life On Trial*, Belli chronicled landmark civil cases he filed against robust companies such as Coca-Cola (1944), Cutter Laboratories (1955), and Reynolds Tobacco (1960s) with no mention of any criminal trials, high-profile or otherwise, before the Ruby case. There were none, due to Belli's concentration on a civil practice.

During a December 12, 1963, speech by Edward Kuhn, president-elect of the American Bar Association, he made his opinion and that of the ABA crystal clear. He told reporters, "Belli is not a criminal [defense] lawyer. He will make a circus out of this case." Such a bold statement along with the *Life* magazine revelations and other similar reports should have raised red flags as to Belli's competence to handle the high profile Ruby case causing the question to be asked: Why, with all of the experienced criminal defense attorneys available to represent Ruby, facing death in the electric chair for the cold-blooded killing of the president's alleged assassin, did Ruby end up with a plaintiff's lawyer in civil cases? But no one at the time, or since, asked the question or even surface-probed this aspect of the Ruby case and its potential connection to those who masterminded the assassinations.

‡

Initially, Melvin Belli hadn't even been mentioned as possible counsel for Jack Ruby in the aftermath of Oswald's murder. Most in the Dallas legal community believed that Tom Howard, a prominent local criminal defense attorney, would represent Oswald's killer. Howard was considered a slick lawyer with more brawn than brains who had once been jailed for fighting in the courtroom. Shortly after Ruby's arrest, he visited his prospective client. Prosecutors later alleged that he suggested to Oswald's killer that he confess his guilt and say he killed Oswald "for Jackie and the kids so they wouldn't have to come to Dallas for a trial." Howard claimed that story was pure bunk.

Belli explained his link to the Ruby case in two different publications. In his 1976 bestselling autobiography, *My Life On Trial,* he alleged that Earl Ruby, to raise money for his brother's defense, agreed to syndicate Jack's life story. The promoters were Hollywood writer Billy Woodfield and the entrepreneurial businessman Lawrence Schiller, later known for penning books about O. J. Simpson and JonBenét Ramsey. Regarding the deal, Belli wrote, "They [Woodfield and Schiller] told him [Earl Ruby] that the story would be easier to sell and make more money if he [Jack] had a colorful lawyer. They suggested me."

The barrister then recounted how "in a private meeting in the kitchen of my home in Los Angeles, I told Earl my fee would be between $50,000 and $75,000." When Earl said Woodfield and Schiller were offering only $25,000 for Jack's story, Belli said, "I agreed to that figure."

Twelve years *before* authoring his autobiography, Belli told a different story. In *Dallas Justice: The Real Story of Jack Ruby,* written with Maurice C. Carroll, Belli wrote, "Three days after his brother shot Lee Harvey Oswald while a nation watched on television, Earl Ruby slipped unobtrusively into a California courtroom and watched me sum up a murder case. As soon as the session ended, a pointy-nosed, solidly-built man, his face a bit fuller than his brother Jack, walked up to me, introduced himself, and asked if I would represent Jack."

Regarding Jack Ruby's part in the hiring, Belli wrote, "It turned out that I was Jack's own choice. He had lived in San Francisco for a time, and he knew of my experience with medical cases." Regarding the fee for representation, Belli said, "Earl said he thought the case would cost $100,000 to defend. I agreed and we shook hands."

Belli swore that Earl surprised him when he informed the attorney that Jack Ruby's life story was going to be syndicated. "These plans touched off a violent argument," Belli wrote. After a shouting match, Belli added, "The upshot is that I walked out. But later Earl came to the place where we were staying in Los Angeles and we agreed to go ahead with the trial."

Two stories, two completely different explanations, each packed with contradictions triggering the question: "What is the truth?" Were Woodfield and Schiller instrumental in Belli being introduced to Earl Ruby? Could Jack Ruby's syndication rights have been more lucrative if Belli became Ruby's attorney, or was this even discussed? Was Earl Ruby's first contact with Belli in a California courtroom where Belli was summing up a murder case, if indeed there was one proceeding since Belli was specializing in civil law at the time? Did Belli really meet with Earl Ruby in the kitchen of Belli's home, argue and then make up later so Belli could go forward? Or did Belli simply make up stories as he went along, fearful someone would learn the truth about how he became Ruby's attorney?

Perhaps more importantly, how did Belli's telling conflicting stories regarding his initial representation of Ruby relate to the secret he knew about the Ruby case but would never divulge to anyone? This, unfortunately, included Oswald's assassin.

CHAPTER THREE

Jack Ruby on Trial

Because there were millions of eyewitnesses to the murder of Lee Harvey Oswald, Melvin Belli had to carefully weigh his options regarding the defense of Jack Ruby. Pleading Jack Ruby not guilty wasn't one of them. The other obvious choices were: (1) a possible plea bargain with prosecutors or (2) pleading Ruby guilty and throwing him on the mercy of the court, hoping for sympathy.

The latter strategy certainly had merit. The letters of praise Ruby received shortly after he killed Oswald, jailer Al Maddox told this author, seemed to reflect the mood of the country. Perhaps the judge would feel the same way. But Belli discarded this alternative, believing Judge Brown would show no leniency.

Any possible plea bargain was discarded, Belli later wrote, because District Attorney Henry Wade had decided that he would prosecute Ruby to the full extent of the law. In an interview with this author, Bill Alexander, Wade's chief deputy, disputed Belli's account. Alexander said that there were possible plea bargain options open but that Belli "wasn't interested."

Whatever the truth, Belli surprised both his opposition and the media at large by choosing what he called a "psychomotor epilepsy" insanity defense, alleging that Ruby, had, in effect, experienced a seizure spell at the time of the shooting of Oswald. Also called temporal lobe epilepsy, psychomotor epilepsy was characterized by the occurrence of any of a variety of auras followed by a brief loss of consciousness with accompanying repetitive, automatic movements. To Belli, who wrote later that he had learned about psychomotor epilepsy in a medical journal, this disorder apparently described Ruby's conduct, excusable, he believed, under the law. Whether a jury would agree remained to be seen.

Belli had little respect for Joe Brown. Belli believed the judge " . . . was weak and he let the District Attorney make his decisions for him, because he knew he was too ignorant of the law to make many decisions on his own." Bolstering his point about Judge Brown's lack of competence, Belli pointed out that the judge had never graduated from high school, that he attended what the barrister called "a third rate law school, practiced law for one year, became a justice of the peace, and two decades later was appointed to the criminal court." Ironically, Brown had actually supported Jack Ruby's application for membership to the Dallas Chamber of Commerce in 1959. The judge, successful in signing up one hundred new members to earn a lifetime membership, told reporters, "[I] hadn't really known him [Ruby] then."

While he regarded the presiding judge as incompetent, Belli had grudging respect for the three veteran prosecutors he would be facing. District Attorney Wade, an aspirant to a federal judgeship, led the prosecution but chief deputy Bill Alexander was lead trial counsel. Backing them up was a competent attorney sporting a recognizable name in Texas history, Jim Bowie. On occasion, when the lawyers sparred, Belli and company pronounced his name, "boy." The prosecution team returned the favor by pronouncing Belli, "Belly."

Despite facing a high-powered prosecutorial team, Belli was keen for the legal challenge. A California roughrider, he thought, could whip Texas longhorns anytime. Jack Ruby's life depended on it.

‡

"Our obligations in the Jack Ruby case were multiple," Belli later wrote. "To [our client] we owed a defense waged sincerely and strongly. To the community, we owed a disciplined, sober, complete presentation, to bare the facts, to lay to rest the rumors, and, not incidentally, to show the watching world how a defendant's rights were protected under the American legal system." This passage, written years after the Ruby trial, suggests that Belli had a sincere commitment to serving his client in a responsible, ethical, and professional manner. Evaluation of his performance after the trial raised questions as to whether he had done so.

Seymour Ellison, Belli's law partner in San Francisco, had doubts about the defense as the trial neared. He told this author: "I asked Mel what he was doing and he said, 'Cy, what greater accomplishment could there be in law than to have a man found not guilty when so many millions of people saw him do it? If I can walk the guy out, I'd be bigger than Clarence Darrow [the celebrated American attorney] ever was.'"

From that moment on, Ellison, albeit puzzled by Belli's choice of defense, believed his partner was on a mission. "It was his new Holy Grail," the lawyer said, "to get Ruby off."

‡

In an attempt to minimize the media frenzy surrounding the trial, Judge Brown and his public relations expert, Sam Bloom, maintained tight control over the granting of media credentials. Newspapers such as the *Chicago Tribune*, *San Francisco Chronicle*, and *New York Herald Tribune* were not permitted courtroom entry; they were forced to be part of a "coverage pool." Those reporters who were granted seats in the drab second-floor courtroom represented *The National Observer*, *Life*, *Time*, and the *Saturday Evening Post*, among other newspapers and magazines. This meant that the crème de la crème of the media were present to closely scrutinize every aspect of the Ruby trial. Did they do so, or did reporters at the time, and later, miss several important aspects of the case, especially those regarding Belli's representation of Ruby?

The pool of nine hundred possible jurors included a diversity of candidates. But Belli, ever the plaintiff's lawyer in civil cases despite being involved in a criminal case, was still disappointed, believing, "The whole jury [pool] looked like they came out of insurance companies. I decided if

I couldn't get warm people—waitresses, etc.—and I had to have cold fish, at least I wanted to have intelligent cold fish."

The final jury included an administrative engineer, a mother of six who was a member of the Assembly of God, a Braniff Airline mechanic, a United States postal worker who later grew a Santa Claus beard, the vice president of a chemical company who swore he hadn't seen the Oswald killing on television, and a bookkeeper who swore allegiance to the television character played by Raymond Burr, Perry Mason. With these jurors in place, the prosecution proceeded with evidence against Jack Ruby. Highlights included several Dallas police officers who swore Ruby had killed Oswald with premeditation. Crucial among them was Don Ray Archer. His testimony was particularly damaging; he spoke of Ruby's anger prior to his shooting Oswald. Archer testified, according to court records, that he was standing nearby when Ruby reached out toward the manacled presidential assassin. The police officer said of Ruby, "I saw his face momentarily . . . a split second before the shot was fired . . . I heard a phrase . . . I did make out the words . . . 'son of a bitch.'"

Worse for the defense, Archer testified that he exchanged words with Ruby in the elevator shortly after the shooting. "I said, 'I think you killed him,'" Archer said, "And he replied, 'I intended to shoot him three times.'"

Sergeant Patrick Dean, head of security for the Oswald transfer, attempted to drive a nail in Ruby's coffin. In rapid staccato, he revealed that Ruby told him he first considered shooting JFK's killer "when he saw Lee Harvey Oswald on the show-up stand." Ruby was referring to a midnight news conference held soon after he was apprehended, when Oswald was trotted out by prosecutor Wade for the world to see. If Dean was to be believed, then Ruby had formed the intent to kill Oswald two days prior to assassinating him.

‡

Jack Ruby's defense began on the sunny afternoon of March 6, 1964. Belli called several witnesses to dispute the charge of premeditation. In an attempt to establish a pattern of impulsive behavior, the attorney also provided testimony indicating Ruby's quick temper and propensity for violence.

WNEW radio reporter Ike Pappas cast considerable doubt on prosecution testimony concerning the events occurring before, during, and after the Oswald shooting. Fortunately for him, Pappas had been standing close to Oswald and was holding an expensive Swiss tape recorder as Ruby approached.

"At the time of the shooting," Pappas recalled on the witness stand, "I was holding what we call a pencil microphone. My proximity to the shooting was . . . five or six feet."

When Pappas's tape recording was played, eerie voices and sounds were heard. First Pappas was heard to ask Oswald, "Lee, do you have anything to say in your defense?" Instantaneously, the "pop" sound of Ruby's pistol interrupted any answer. Then confusion reigned.

Pleased with the answer, Belli then asked Pappas, "What did you hear?" The newsman replied, "I heard nothing before the shot," thus disputing the accounts of the police officers.

Following the prosecution's case-in-chief, Belli called to the witness stand his "dream team" of psychiatrists. Several testified, but Dr. Roy Schafer, a renowned Yale University psychologist, was the star of the show. He testified: "I determined that Ruby did have organic brain damage. The most likely specific nature of it was psychomotor epilepsy." Following up, Belli asked, "Doctor, from all of the tests . . . you have formed an opinion as to the mental state of Jack Ruby, have you not?" Schafer answered, "He has a deranged mind."

Having completed his attempt to show that Oswald's killer was a man who had experienced a seizure and, in effect, "blacked out" when he saw JFK's assassin and merely reacted with his own violence, Belli formally rested Ruby's defense on March the 11th, without putting his client on the witness stand. It was a controversial decision. A reporter, Wes Wise, had asked Ruby during the trial, "Would you like to testify?" Ruby responded, "Yes, but Mr. Belli knows better, I guess." After the trial, Ruby affirmed to the media that: "I wanted to tell my story."

Belli's decision, one that meant the jury and public at large would not hear a single word of sworn testimony from the man they most wanted to hear, caught the jury off guard as well. Jury foreman Max Causey later wrote, "The biggest shock of the trial came . . . when Mr. Belli rose to his feet and told the court, 'The defense rests' . . . I don't think we were any more surprised than the prosecution. I looked over [at them] to see what they were going to do now, and I noticed that they appeared to be taken completely by surprise."

Despite the shock, the prosecution moved ahead. After presenting several doctors who testified as to Ruby's sanity, Henry Wade said loudly, "The state rests." Belli then called in rebuttal another policeman who heard Ruby say nothing before the shooting. Wade countered with further testimony as to Ruby's competence.

Who had won and who had lost would now be determined. The clock was ticking and Jack Ruby was closer to learning his ultimate fate: whether he would be electrocuted or sent to a hospital for psychiatric treatment.

As Ruby sweated his fate, what was going through Melvin Belli's mind? Had he already "won" the case even if the verdict was guilty?

‡

Judge Joe Brown was adamant about the timeline for final arguments: "This case will go to the jury tonight and I don't give a damn what time you finish arguing it. You take as long as you want, but if we run until 9 o'clock tomorrow morning, we are going to have the arguments tonight."

At 8:04 P.M. the excitement peaked when the jury of twelve was led into the courtroom to hear the final pleas from the lawyers. Judge Brown first read the "charge" to the jury. Belli noted their reaction, recalling, "Carefully, I watched their expressions. They lit up cigarettes, then sat blank-faced through his [Judge Brown's] recitation of legal definitions of murder, insanity, proof, and evidence."

The first to rise and argue for the prosecution was Bill Alexander. He told this author, "Wade asked me to present the basic facts of the case so the rest of the prosecution's team could simply argue the merits of the allegations." Alexander first apologized for failing to protect the deceased, Lee Harvey Oswald, whom he had earlier labeled a Communist. "I'm not going to defend Oswald to you," he said, "but American justice is on trial. American justice had Oswald in its possession. Oswald was entitled to the protection of the law. Oswald was a living, breathing American citizen."

The moment he uttered these words, Alexander, in the first of many theatrical moments to come, quickly turned toward the defendant, who had shown no emotion throughout the trial, and added, "Just like you, Jack Ruby, who were judge, jury, and executioner."

Ruby flinched when the prosecutor blasted him, but Alexander wasn't through. He called Ruby "nothing but a thrill killer, seeking notoriety," and said, "Don't tell me it takes guts to shoot a man who is manacled, this is a wanton killing." He then summed up by urging that the jury inflict the death penalty since "he [Ruby] has mocked American justice while the spotlight of the world was on us."

At 11:52 P.M. Belli rose to present his final argument. He began by lavishing praise on the psychiatrists he had called as witnesses, including Dr. Schafer, reminding the jury that he had said of Ruby, "He has organic brain damage." Summing up the doctor's findings, Belli said, "So we have our diagnosis from our doctors; we have our prognosis. We know why Jack Ruby shot Lee Harvey Oswald, and we know he wasn't responsible at the time."

Belli then reminded the jurors that the Ruby case was a simple one: "We are not here to try the shooting. We are here to look into this mind with the help of our doctors."

Addressing his client, Belli then said, "Jack Ruby: This poor sick fellow—and sick he is, and you know he's sick, every one of you in your heart, every one of the twelve of you know he is sick. He is of this second class for the moment now. There cannot be any doubt that there is something wrong with Jack Ruby."

After summarizing Ruby's actions—actions, Belli maintained, that were exacerbated by the post-assassination media frenzy and the smirk on Oswald's face—Belli said, "This man does not belong in prison. Acquit him—not guilty by reason of insanity." He then added, "He is sick. Give a just and fair verdict compatible with modern science. That's what the world wants to see in justice from this community."

When Belli concluded his remarks at 12:50 AM, the jurors gazed at the famous lawyer, and at his client. Had they agreed with Belli that the accused was a sick man who should be acquitted because of his insanity? Only time would tell.

Prosecuting attorney Henry Wade's retort to Melvin Belli was short and to the point. He chastised Belli's attempts to use such fancy words as "confabulation" to confuse the jurors and then ridiculed Ruby as a man who "wanted to go down in the history books."

Challenging the jurors, Wade then asked, "What do you want the history books to say about you? Our laws are no stronger than the weakest heart on this jury." He added, "If you turn this man loose, you'd set civilization back a century. You'd set civilization back to barbarism. You'd set civilization back to the lynch laws. I ask you to show Jack Ruby the same mercy, compassion, and sympathy that he showed Lee Harvey Oswald." At 1:05 A.M. he ended his appeal by stating, "Let Communism know that we believe in the right of the law here."

By all accounts, the prosecution and defense had delivered stirring final arguments. Now twelve jurors would decide whether Jack Ruby was sent to a mental institution or electrocuted. As Melvin Belli watched the jury file out of the courtroom to deliberate, what was going through his mind? Did the outcome really matter, or had Belli succeeded with a secret plan that only he and perhaps two others knew about—a plan that, when exposed, led directly to the man ultimately most responsible for JFK's death, Joseph P. Kennedy?

CHAPTER FOUR

The Doomed Assassin

One hundred ten days after the cold-blooded murder of Lee Harvey Oswald, foreman Max Causey jotted down important issues the Jack Ruby jury needed to consider.

The first was a given: Did Jack Ruby in fact shoot Lee Harvey Oswald as charged? The second then followed in sequence: Was Jack Ruby legally sane at the time of the shooting? The third, Causey said, was, "Is Jack Ruby legally sane at the present time?" The fourth, which could only be answered if Ruby was determined to be sane when he shot Oswald: Was there malice aforethought on Ruby's mind at the time of the shooting? Using Causey's plan as a deliberation roadmap, the jurors were set to discuss all aspects of the case against Ruby.

But they didn't discuss them, at least not for very long, according to Causey's recollections. Apparently, two women jurors had slept through important medical testimony and asked that it be reread. It wasn't. Then, after minimal discussion among the jurors, an initial ballot was taken. On each of the pertinent questions—Did Ruby shoot Oswald? Was he insane when he did so? Is he insane now? Was there malice aforethought?—the jurors voted unanimously against Ruby. His conviction was assured.

Causey reported later that the only lengthy discussion among jurors had to do with the penalty: "I asked each juror to write down the sentence that he or she felt should be assessed Ruby based on the evidence that we had heard. I asked them to take their time and not to make a hasty decision since a man's life was at stake." Causey tallied the votes. Nine jurors recommended death as the penalty, two asked for a life sentence, one voted for a sentence of sixty years.

A few minutes after 11:00 AM, two hours and nineteen minutes after Causey was selected as foreman (not all spent deliberating), the vote was unanimous: Jack Ruby was a dead man. He just didn't know it yet.

The jurors were somber as they filed into the courtroom and took their seats without glancing in Ruby's direction. Even though his expertise was civil law, Belli knew what this meant. He turned to his client, put his hand on his shoulder, and whispered, according to his later writings, "It's bad. Take it easy. We expected it all along and we tried this case for an appeal court. We'll make it there. I'll stick with you." Only half-hearing Belli's words, Ruby's face was ashen, any hope of freedom dashed.

The regimen called for the foreman to hand the verdict form to bailiff Bo Mabra, who in turn handed it to Judge Brown. After shuffling through the pages and reviewing it, the judge read the words aloud without expression, "We the jury find the defendant guilty of murder with malice, as charged in the indictment, and affix his punishment at death." The judge then quickly asked, "Is this unanimous? So say you all? Please hold up your right hands." All twelve jurors raised a hand.

The crowd appeared dazed, confused as to how to react. There was no eruption of cheering and no sobbing. Reporters scurried to write their stories, each hiding any emotion behind blank faces. Ruby's sister Eileen, tears welling in her eyes, and his brother Earl bowed their heads. Ruby himself appeared dazed, a look of puzzlement and confusion apparent on his face. Had he really heard the words "affix his punishment at death"?

Ruby was encircled by sheriff's deputies and hustled out of the courtroom. Belli, his face flushed with anger, stood and screamed, "May I thank the jury for a victory for bigotry and injustice." He added, "American justice has been raped." The next morning, a *Dallas Morning News* headline read: "Ruby Draws Death Penalty; Belli Flays Jury Verdict, Pledges Appeal Outside City."

After the verdict, Belli visited Ruby in his cell. The conversation was short and sorrowful. Belli later wrote that Ruby said, "That's all right, Mel. Next time you try it the same way. You're the one I've always had the most confidence in." They wouldn't see each other again for months. When they did meet again again, it was a boiling hot day in August 1964. Belli's recollection of his famous client was most vivid. "Jack's skin was flabby," he wrote, "It no longer had the taut tone that his constant calisthenics had maintained even during the long imprisonment leading up to the trial. His hair was wispy and there were sores on his scalp; he had been pulling hair from his head."

After the perfunctory exchange of pleasantries, Belli recalled that Ruby startled his attorney with a question. "Mel," he asked, "Do you think I'm crazy?'" Belli's answer: "What could I say to this poor shrunken man? I lied [and said] 'Jack, I don't know. I do know you need some treatment.'"

When the two faced each other for the final time, Belli recalled the moment: "Jack stepped forward and gave me a strange handshake, a sort of secret grip of some sort I assumed. That pathetic gesture was his last that night. He was led away, back to his floodlit mattress in the metal corridor of the brutally hot jail with the guards to watch him."

‡

On March 19, 1964, the headline of the *Dallas Morning News* read: "Jack Ruby Fires Belli as Chief Defense Counsel." Quoted in the article was Ruby's sister Eva, who said that the Ruby family was "dissatisfied with the defense presented by Belli and expressed shock at the tirade he delivered after Saturday's verdict." Eva accused Belli of being interested in "promoting only [his] personal fame and fortune." She added that a January 22nd letter to Belli signed by Jack Ruby, "tried to engage Belli in disagreement over tactics employed by the lawyer and that Belli bitterly opposed and forced himself on Ruby. . . . " Jack Ruby's brother, Hyman, assaulted Belli in the newspaper article stating, "[Belli] never consulted us about anything regarding the case . . . I had the feeling he was evading the whole family."

Hyman also said that Jack had told him, "Belli [is] more interested in making a circus and condemning Dallas than representing me, his client."

Ultimately, Jack Ruby's conviction was overturned. On October 5th, 1966, the Texas Court of Criminal Appeals ruled, among other matters, that the judge's denial of the change of venue motion was a reversible error. They ordered a new trial be held away from Dallas. Judge W. T. McDonald, after discussing the machinations of emotion seething in Dallas after JFK's murder, wrote: "Against such a background of unusual and extraordinary invasions of the expected neutral mental processes of a citizenry from which a jury is to be chosen, the Dallas County climate was one of such strong feeling that it was not humanly possible to give Ruby a fair and impartial trial which is the hallmark of American due process of law." No date for a new trial, to be held in a venue outside of Dallas, was set.

Three attempts at suicide failed, but Jack Ruby did not live long enough for his new trial. He died of lung cancer on January 3, 1967—ironically, at Parkland Hospital, where both John F. Kennedy and Lee Harvey Oswald had been declared dead.

On January 7, 1967, 1,139 days after Ruby assassinated Lee Harvey Oswald, Ruby was laid to rest next to his mother, Fannie, and father, Joseph, in Westlawn Cemetery on Montrose Avenue in Chicago. His guilty verdict overturned, Jack Ruby technically died an innocent man. More importantly, based on fresh information never revealed before, he died without knowing several critical facts about his trial lawyer. These included the truth as to why Belli had come to represent him, the complete story regarding a messy encounter Belli had with Judge Brown *before* the Ruby trial, and Belli's failure to disclose certain salient facts regarding his relationships with dangerous men linked to Ruby. He also died without knowing the real reason behind Belli's ill-fated psychomotor epilepsy insanity defense.

To the general public, the media, the Dallas legal community, the Ruby family, and Belli's law partners and colleagues, Belli had lost the case of a lifetime. But to another group of people—specifically those who had worried about what Ruby might have revealed during the trial—there was a feeling of jubilation. Ruby hadn't been given the opportunity to take the stand in his own defense. Better still, Belli had portrayed Ruby as a lunatic whose credibility was shattered.

To this group of people, the clever Belli was a hero. He had done his job by executing one of one of the most elaborate ruses ever perpetrated in a courtroom. While doing so, he had kept others from discovering who, ultimately, was most responsible for the death of John F. Kennedy.

BOOK II

CHAPTER FIVE

The Government Investigations

If focusing on Melvin Belli and the Jack Ruby trial will provide key factors toward finally discovering the truth about the Dallas assassinations leading to Joe Kennedy as the one most responsible for President Kennedy's death, how and why did the fresh information this book will reveal escape attention for fifty years and counting? One reason: while the facts were hiding in plain sight, every investigative body, and the author of every book written about the Dallas killings simply looked in the wrong direction since each focused on why JFK *was* killed instead of why Bobby Kennedy *was not*. To prove this point, we begin with what was known about the assassinations at the time before turning to what was learned through the years.

An executive order signed by President Lyndon B. Johnson on November 29, 1963, established the infamous Warren Commission "to investigate the assassination . . . of John Fitzgerald Kennedy, the 35th President of the United States." The commission was directed to "evaluate all of the facts and circumstances surrounding the assassination and the subsequent killing of the alleged assassin and to report its findings and conclusions to the President."

Its blue-ribbon members included Supreme Court Chief Justice Earl Warren, Congressman Gerald R. Ford, and former CIA Director Allen W. Dulles. Bolstering their efforts was the work of federal agencies including the Federal Bureau of Investigation and the Secret Service, with the former conducting more than twenty-five thousand interviews and reinterviews. Summing up their duties, the Commission reported that it "has functioned neither as a court presiding over an adversary proceeding nor as a prosecutor determined to prove a case, but as a fact-finding agency committed to the ascertainment of the truth."

The Commission's final report contained this conclusion: "*The Commission has found no evidence that either Lee Harvey Oswald or Jack Ruby was part of any conspiracy, domestic or foreign, to assassinate President Kennedy.*" Summarizing its findings, the Commission reported that there was (1) "no evidence that anyone assisted Oswald in planning or carrying out the assassination," (2) "no evidence that Oswald was involved with any person or group in a conspiracy to assassinate the President," (3) "no evidence to show that Oswald was employed, persuaded, or encouraged by any foreign government to assassinate President Kennedy," (4) "no evidence to support the speculation that Oswald was an agent, employee, or informant of the FBI, the CIA, or any governmental agency," (5) "no direct relationship between Lee Harvey Oswald and Jack Ruby," and (6) "no evidence that Jack Ruby acted with any other person in the killing of Lee Harvey Oswald." Based on these findings, the Commission wrote that, "On the basis of the evidence before the Commission it concludes that Oswald acted alone."

‡

To bolster this proclamation, a report section titled "Possible Conspiracy Involving Jack Ruby" was added after describing Ruby's murder of Oswald: "Almost immediately, speculation arose that Ruby had acted on behalf of members of a conspiracy who had planned the killing of President Kennedy and wanted to silence Oswald." Jack Ruby's life is then chronicled with details provided, among others, as to family background, mental history, work history, his move from Chicago to Dallas, his operation of both the Carousel and Vegas nightclubs, his associations with various persons in the Dallas area and around the country, his activities prior to the assassination of JFK, and his actions before and after shooting Lee Harvey Oswald. Two paragraphs focus on questions regarding an alleged conspiracy:

> Aside from the results of the Commission's investigation reported above, there are reasons to doubt that Jack Ruby would have shot Oswald as he did if he had been involved in a conspiracy to carry out the assassination, or that he would have been delegated to perform the shooting of Oswald on behalf of others who were involved in the slaying of the President. By striking in the city jail, Ruby was certain to be apprehended.

> An attempt to silence Oswald by having Ruby kill him would have presented exceptionally grave dangers to any other persons involved in the scheme. If the attempt had failed, Oswald might have been moved to disclose his confederates to the authorities. If it succeeded, as it did, the additional killing might itself have produced a trail to them. Moreover, Ruby was regarded by most persons who knew him as moody and unstable—hardly one to have encouraged the confidence of persons in a sensitive conspiracy.
> Based on the investigation reviewed in this chapter, the Commission concluded that there is no credible evidence that Lee Harvey Oswald was part of a conspiracy to assassinate President Kennedy. Examination of the facts of the assassination itself revealed no indication that Oswald was aided in the planning or execution of his scheme . . . Nor did the Commission's investigation of Jack Ruby produce any grounds for believing that Ruby's killing of Oswald was part of a conspiracy.

A third paragraph noted those who had supported the findings:

> The conclusion that there is no evidence of a conspiracy was reached
> independently by Dean Rusk, the Secretary of State, Robert S.
> McNamara, the Secretary of Defense, C. Douglas Dillon, the
> Secretary of the Treasury; *Robert F. Kennedy* [emphasis added],
> the Attorney General, J. Edgar Hoover, the Director of the FBI,
> John A McCone, the Director of the CIA, and James J. Rowley,
> the Chief of the Secret Service, on the basis of information
> available to each of them.

‡

Also included in the final report was a section detailing Jack Ruby's life titled: "Possible Underworld Connection." It began, "The Commission has investigated Ruby's possible criminal activities, looking with particular concern for evidence that he engaged in illegal activities with members of the organized underworld or that, on his own, he was a promoter of illegal endeavors."

Among the twenty-seven pages of information in an appendix, only two short paragraphs were devoted to discussion of Ruby's "underworld ties." Most prominently mentioned were Ruby's Dallas association with Paul Roland Jones, a narcotics dealer, his partnership in the Vegas Club with Joe Bonds, who had a criminal record, his affinity for "card playing and horse racing," and his friendship with "several professional gamblers." It was also noted that he "visited Cuba at the invitation and expense of Lewis McWillie, a professional gambler."

Despite the minimal information, paragraph three of this section read, "Based on its evaluation of the record . . . the Commission believes that the evidence does not establish a significant link between Ruby and organized crime. Both State and Federal Officials have indicated that Ruby was not affiliated with organized crime activities. And numerous persons have reported that Ruby was not connected with such activity."

In addition to its depiction of Jack Ruby's "underworld ties," the Warren Commission investigated links between Ruby and the Dallas police. In a subsection under "Police Associations," the report presented three paragraphs with the first beginning, "Although the precise nature of his relationship to members of the Dallas Police Department is not susceptible to conclusive evaluation, the evidence indicates that Ruby was keenly interested in policemen and their work."

Details included statements such as "Jesse Curry, chief of the DPD, testified that no more than 25 to 50 of Dallas's almost 1200 policemen were acquainted with Ruby," "there is no credible evidence that Ruby sought special favors from police officers or attempted to bribe them," and "Ruby regarded several police officers as personal friends, and others had worked for him."

An appendix explained the "Polygraph Examination of Jack Ruby": "As early as December 1963, Jack Ruby expressed his desire to be examined with a polygraph, truth serum or any other scientific device which would test his veracity." Once legal challenges and questions regarding Ruby's mental state had been addressed to permit a test, the report noted that one was scheduled for July 18, 1964. The session was held at the Dallas County jail. Administering the test was FBI Special Agent Bell P. Herndon, a polygraph expert.

Fifty-six questions were asked of Ruby, among them: "Did you know Oswald before November 22, 1963? Did you assist Oswald in the assassination? Are you now a member of the Communist Party? Are you now a member of any group that advocates the violent overthrow of the United States Government? Did you shoot Oswald in order to silence him? Did you first decide to shoot Oswald on Saturday night? Is everything you told the Warren Commission the whole truth? Did any foreign influence cause you to shoot Oswald? Did you shoot Oswald because of a labor union influence?" and "Did you shoot Oswald because of any influence of the underworld?"

To all of these questions except the one relating to whether he told the Warren Commission the truth Ruby answered, "No." Regarding evaluation of the veracity of his answers, the report explained that, "An accurate evaluation of Ruby's polygraph examination depends on whether he was psychotic." A discussion was then initiated about whether a medical diagnosis by Dr. William R. Beavers that Ruby was "a psychotic depressive" meant the test results would be invalid. The potential for this having occurred prompted FBI Director J. Edgar Hoover to opine that, "In view of the serious question raised by Ruby's mental condition, no significance should be placed on the polygraph examination and it should be considered non-conclusive as the charts cannot be relied upon." Commenting on Hoover's opinion, the report stated, "The Commission did not rely on the results of this examination in reaching the conclusions stated in this report."

The Commission also did not reach its conclusions based on testimony from Melvin Belli. He was never called as a witness despite being in the thick of the Ruby case. Commission legal counsel G. Robert Blakey told this author, "Belli was interviewed but that went nowhere."

‡

Despite the "case closed" findings of the Warren Commission that no conspiracy existed on any level, during the mid-1960s and throughout the first half of the 1970s, various assassination "experts" and authors presented new facts regarding the tragic 1963 Dallas events. Each added a viewpoint supplementing new information, with several at odds with the Commission's report.

Among the publications were Melvin Belli's two books, *Dallas Justice* (1964) and *My Life on Trial* (1976), and two others of interest to anyone paying attention since they dealt with Belli and the Ruby case: *The Trial of Jack Ruby* by John Kaplan and John R. Waltz (1965), and Garry Wills and Ovid Demoris's book, *Jack Ruby* (1968).

Wills, later a professor of history emeritus at Northwestern University, and Demoris, a United Press International reporter during the trial, provided a deeper glimpse into Jack Ruby's persona and background without focusing exclusively on the trial itself. One of the few to touch on the Ruby/Belli relationship, the authors wrote, "If Belli was intrigued by Ruby, he intrigued Oswald's killer. When Belli appeared in the Dallas jail in his resplendent tailoring, he seemed the embodiment of all things Ruby admired—bantam-cock of a man, nearly as short as Jack, but with a creamy head of hair, with a fortune in clothes on his back, a gallery of 'names' for friends, a poly-syllabic uninterruptability an earthy charm. [It was] a mirror where plump short unimpressive and tongue-tied Jack Ruby was put magically face to face with the plump short impressive 'Great Mouthpiece.'" The authors said Belli told them it made [Ruby] feel good that "I not only knew my law but was a sharp dresser and a great cocksman."

Based on their observations, the authors believed that the loquacious Ruby had the perfect set of attorneys, writing, "With his champions flanking him—on one side Belli, who looks like a pugnacious Liberace; [on the other] Joe Tonahill, a mild bulldog blimp drifted off from some Macy's parade."

Kaplan and Waltz's book, published three years earlier, detailed the Ruby trial while presenting objections to Belli and his representation of Ruby. Calling Belli "loud and pushy," the authors echoed Dallas jailer Al Maddox's comment to this author that mail received favored a light sentence for Ruby. Kaplan and Waltz wrote, "After all, Jack Ruby had killed the man who had committed one of the most wanton and frightful crimes of the century. A friend of Howard's [lawyer Tom Howard] who was a member of the grand-jury panel had taken an informal poll of two hundred citizens of Dallas concerning the sentence Ruby should receive." The results, the authors reported, were "seven to one for a light sentence" with "almost half . . . [feeling] Ruby should receive no punishment at all." These statistics caused Kaplan and Waltz to question why Belli, after, as they alleged, his ill-advised "psychomotor" defense collapsed during testimony, decided to "make it clear during his final argument that there was only one proper disposition of Jack Ruby's case: he must be acquitted outright, on grounds of insanity." The authors added, "Over and over again Belli informed the jurors there was no middle ground, no room for compromise."

Summing up, Kaplan and Waltz wrote, " . . . of all the tactical mysteries of a mysterious trial, probably the two greatest occurred in Melvin

Belli's final argument." In addition to the apparent error regarding the potential for a compromise verdict, the authors alleged that "the second, and probably the greatest, mystery of the case was why Belli did not ever try to talk the jury out of imposing the death penalty on his client." This was accurate since Belli did not ask for mercy for Ruby during his closing statement.

Disgruntlement with Belli's handling of Ruby's case, the authors alleged, had been seeping to the surface throughout the trial. They reported, "The entire Ruby family had been watching the proceedings carefully and they did not like the way things were going . . . they had observed what appeared to them as a succession of prosecution victories and defense defeats." The result: "Jack, his brother Earl, and his sister Eva decided that they wished Belli to have the aid of a criminal lawyer more experienced" than Belli's current co-counsels including Joe Tonahill. But when the suggestion was made to Belli, he reacted with "a burst of invective" and the matter was dropped. When Belli next saw Ruby in the courtroom, he chastised his client for believing that he needed help, "Belli would have none of this; he asserted that he had the case won . . . and that he would 'walk' Ruby out" [of the courtroom]."

Though the details of Ruby's trial were well-chronicled, these authors had, like other authors, taken Belli's entry into the Ruby case and his insanity defense at face value, never realizing that investigating Belli would have reaped benefits beyond their imagination. They were simply reporters regurgitating surface facts, and never grasped the full extent of Belli's secret, his intended dual-purpose game plan. Instead, they focused solely on his performance surrounding Ruby's defense. That they never investigated further, perhaps to the extent of investigating Belli himself so as to garner answers to questions they had raised, was predictable, but, for history's sake, unfortunate. Belli had gotten a pass from them, from the Warren Commission, from anyone searching for the truth about the assassinations.

More than ten years after the *Warren Commission Report* was issued, the true impetus for revisiting the Dallas tragedies occurred when the House Select Committee on Assassinations (HSCA) was convened in 1976 with its comprehensive report issued *three* years later. For months it labored through secret sessions inspecting evidence and listening to witness after witness describe every nuance of the JFK and Oswald killings. The result of the Select Committee probe was an unanticipated bombshell: members determined that there *was* a conspiracy to assassinate JFK. Some specifics were left to the imagination of the public, but there was little doubt that "lone assassination" theories regarding the killing had been debunked.

Among the conclusions was the belief that "a high probability" existed that at least two gunmen fired a total of three shots at the president, the second and third striking him, and the third being fatal. The committee further believed that Kennedy "was probably assassinated as a result of a conspiracy" but was "unable to identify the other gunmen or the extent of the conspiracy." It discounted involvement in the conspiracy by the Soviet government, the Cuban government including anti-Castro groups, and the Secret Service, FBI, and CIA.

The report also concluded, "that the national syndicate of organized crime, as a group, was not involved in the assassination of President Kennedy, but that available evidence does not preclude the possibility that individual members may have been involved." While condemning the protection afforded Kennedy by government agencies, the report questioned whether investigation into the possibility of conspiracy was "inadequate."

Important to assessing the historical events in Dallas were the Select Committee's raising new questions concerning Jack Ruby. Deciding there was much more complexity to the man, the congressmen investigated him thoroughly. A foreword to their report read: "Early in its investigation, as soon as it was realized that a plot of elements of organized crime in the United States to assassinate President John F. Kennedy warranted serious consideration, the committee decided to assemble the most reliable information available on the subject. The focus was to be primarily on the history of organized crime; the impact of the Kennedy administration's campaign against it . . . possible links of Lee Harvey Oswald and Jack Ruby with underworld figures; and the development of new evidence or leads." Added to the mix a few lines later was the bold statement: *"A major reason for suspecting conspiracy was Oswald's murder by Jack Ruby* [emphasis added]."

The Committee's portrayal of organized crime in America was chilling. Detailing the presence of gangsters in the United States since the late nineteenth century, the report stated that by 1960 organized crime was flourishing. Attempting to combat its influence were Senator John F. Kennedy and his brother Robert, purportedly to "get even" for mobsters having impinged on the success of their father, Joseph Kennedy. Much of Kennedy's fortune, the report stated, stemmed from bootlegging, but mob boss Frank Costello's operation cut into Kennedy's share of the profits. Now it was payback time, so the Kennedy brothers planned to attack organized crime with a vengeance. The report noted that when RFK became attorney general, "as a first step, [he] dramatically expanded the number of attorneys in the Organized Crime and Racketeering Section of the Justice Department." He also "put together a list of 40 organized crime figures who were targeted for investigation." On that list were Tampa don Santo Trafficante and New Orleans don Carlos Marcello.

‡

The *HSCA Report* detailed how federal investigators had penetrated the mob through the efforts of a snitch named Joseph Valachi. A narcotics pusher, he turned against his brethren while facing a murder charge for beating a fellow prisoner to death. Under terms of an immunity agreement, Valachi became a star witness against the Mafia and much was learned about the inner workings of the organization.[2]

An FBI internal memorandum included in the report indicated how dangerous the underworld was as of May 1963, six months before the JFK assassination. It stated, "The Mafia [La Cosa Nostra] represents one of the most ruthless, pernicious, and enduring forms of criminality ever

---

2   In Dallas, the report stated, one man was paying attention to Valachi's turncoat performance: Jack Ruby. Following his arrest for killing Oswald, the newspaper article detailing Valachi's exploits, as noted, was discovered in the trunk of Ruby's car.

to exist in the United States. The viciousness and the effectiveness of the Mafia stems from its conspiratorial groups of Sicilian-Italian hoodlums, its adherence to a code of secrecy and silence, and its use of intimidation, violence, vengeance, and murder."

The report's "Attitude toward the Kennedy's: Before and After," included an analysis of mob disapproval of the Kennedys. Typical threats included those of Willie Weisburg, an associate of Philadelphia crime boss Angelo Bruno: "See what Kennedy done. With Kennedy, a guy should take a knife, like one of them other guys, and stab and kill the [obscenity] where he is now . . . I mean it. This is true. Honest to God . . . I hope I get a week's notice. I'll kill. Right in the [obscenity] in the White House. Somebody's got to get rid of this [obscenity]."

The report detailed a taped conversation of Chicago mobster Sam Giancana. Discussing JFK's propensity to play golf, Giancana, the report stated, "suggested putting a bomb in his golf bag, and they all laughed." When mafiosi Stefano Magaddino and brother Peter spoke on October 31, 1963, the conversation as noted in the report was, "[JFK] should drop dead. They should kill the whole family, the mother and father too. When he [JFK] talks, he talks like a mad man. . . . "

Among the Mafia figures who had incurred RFK's wrath, Carlos Marcello was number one on the list. Even before he became attorney general, the report concluded, Kennedy planned to deport the mafiosi. RFK "ordered the Justice Department to focus on him, along with other figures such as Teamsters president Hoffa, and Chicago Mafia leader Sam Giancana."

Little known was Marcello's attempt to make peace with the Kennedys. The report detailed efforts by Santo Trafficante to intercede on Marcello's behalf with Frank Sinatra, a friend of the Kennedys and Trafficante. A wiretap conversation between Philadelphia mobster Angelo Bruno and Russell Bufalino, an underboss in Pennsylvania, disclosed that Sinatra discussed Marcello with RFK. The effort backfired, and Robert Kennedy intensified his efforts to nab the Mafia chieftain.

True to his word, on April 4, 1961, the report stated, RFK had overseen the abduction of Marcello in New Orleans. When the don walked into the INS to report as an alien, agents arrested and handcuffed him, whisked him off to a waiting plane, and dumped him unceremoniously in Guatemala City. The next day, a smiling RFK took credit for the deportation while Marcello and his powerful allies vowed revenge, dubbing the incident nothing less than a "kidnapping." Two months later Marcello, seething over the actions of his mortal enemy RFK, was smuggled back into the country. The government struck back, filing charges alleging conspiracy in falsifying a Guatemalan passport and perjury, as well as hitting Marcello with an $835,000 tax evasion indictment.

Among Marcello's threats against the Kennedys, the report stated, were words uttered in September 1962 during a mob confab at a plantation owned by Marcello near New Orleans. Relying on informant Edward Becker, a Las Vegas private investigator with access to Marcello, Ed Reid, former newspaper editor and author of *The Grim Reapers: The Anatomy of Organized Crime in America* told the Committee of Marcello's overall disgust for the Kennedy infiltration of the Mafia "brotherhood" based on his conversations with Becker. "It was then that Carlos's voice lost its softness, and his words were bitten off and spit out when mention was made of . . . Robert Kennedy, who was still on the trail of Marcello. 'Livarsi na petra di la scarpa,' Carlos shrilled the Mafia cry of revenge: 'Take the stone out of my shoe.'" Marcello added, "Don't worry about that little Bobby son of a bitch. He's going to be taken care of." Reid then related that Becker told him that Marcello "knew that to rid himself of Robert Kennedy, he would first have to remove the President. Any killer of the Attorney General would be hunted down by his brother; the death of the President would seal the fate of the Attorney General."

Reid noted, "No one at the meeting had any doubt about Marcello's intentions when he abruptly rose from the table. Marcello did not joke about such things. In any case, the matter had gone beyond mere 'business;' it had become an affair of honor, a Sicilian vendetta." Again relying on Becker's eyewitness account, Reid told the Committee that Marcello "had begun to plan a move. He had, for example, already thought of using a 'nut' to do the job." The report noted that a year and a half before

Reid's book was published, the FBI was aware of the Mafia meeting and Marcello's threats when Reid showed agents his manuscript.

When the Select Committee interviewed Becker, he informed them that his account "is truthful. It was then and it is now." He told investigators he knew Marcello through business colleague Carl Roppolo, adding that when Marcello discussed killing JFK he also stated that "his own lieutenants must not be identified as the assassins and that there would thus be a necessity to have them use or manipulate someone else to carry out the actual crime."

Carlos Marcello appeared before the Committee in January and denied Becker's account. He swore he had never threatened RFK or JFK. In the paragraphs under "Analyzing the Evidence," the Select Committee denounced the FBI for failing to properly investigate Becker's allegations. It did not discount the statements alleging Carlos Marcello threatened to have the president killed.

‡

The Select Committee also investigated the background of Lee Harvey Oswald to discover whether Oswald could have been the "nut" Carlos Marcello referred to. Nineteen pages of the report looked into the Oswald/organized crime potential, many focused on the relationship of JFK's assassin to David Ferrie, described in the report as "a private investigator and even, perhaps, a pilot for Marcello before and during 1963." The report also stated that Oswald and Ferrie knew each other through service in the Civil Air Patrol and various acquaintances.[3] Ferrie was also linked to Marcello's attorney, G. Wray Gill, while admitting, according to the report, "his association with Marcello and . . . personal contact with the syndicate leader in the fall of 1963" to the extent of being "present with

---

3   John Canal's book, *Silencing The Lone Assassin* (2000), provided an eyewitness, John Ciravoli Jr., who swore both he and Canal attended a CAP meeting with Ferrie and Oswald in 1955. Alongside the account was a photograph depicting ten "soldiers" around an outdoor luncheon table near Alexandria, Louisiana. Second from the left stood David Ferrie while Ciravoli stood to the left and in front of a thin Oswald, clad in T-shirt and jeans.

Marcello at the courthouse in New Orleans" on November 22nd, the day JFK was killed.[4]

More background information about Oswald was presented, but the Committee then focused on Melvin Belli's client, Jack Ruby. When they were through comparing his version of killing Lee Harvey Oswald with new information surfacing during its investigation, the Committee basically called Ruby a liar.

The report began by inspecting Ruby's relationship with law enforcement and public officials. Summations included the belief that Ruby was "a police buff, had great respect for authority." The report said Ruby alleged that he never gave money or presents or did favors for officers except for whiskey at Christmas. The report disagreed with his assertions, noting several instances where Ruby bought drinks, permitted sexual favors, and allowed police officers to be bouncers in violation of departmental rules.

The Select Committee report branded Ruby, described by Detective A. M. Eberhadt as knowing "just about everyone on the police force," a "fink." It stated that he was an informant to the police who was known as "quite reliable."

The quid pro quo for Ruby was avoiding arrest. Even when he was, the charges were usually dropped. "Ruby seems to have been able to avoid minor legal and criminal difficulties, difficulties which should have followed from Ruby's violent behavior," the report stated.

Access to police was easy for Ruby, the Select Committee believed. "Ruby was seemingly able to enter DPD [Dallas Police Department] headquarters unnoticed and unchallenged, as was dramatically illustrated during the assassination weekend, when he was seen within and around headquarters several times on Friday night and Saturday, and of course, on Sunday morning in the DPD basement."

---

4 G. Robert Blakey, counsel to the Committee, believed evidence pointed toward Oswalds' complicity in the assassinations. He told ABC News in November 2003, "I can show you that Lee Harvey Oswald knew from his boyhood days forward, David Ferrie, and that Ferrie was an investigator for Carlos Marcello on the day of the assassination [of JFK]. I can show you that Oswald, when he grew up in New Orleans, lived with the Dutz Murret family [one of Oswald's uncles] and that Murret was a bookmaker for Carlos Marcello. . . . Could he be induced to kill the president for organized crime reasons unknown to him? I think the answer is yes and compelling."

The Committee investigated Ruby's story regarding his entry into that basement. Utilizing a detailed drawing, the report attempted to reconcile Ruby's version with facts stated by those on the scene when Oswald was shot. It could not.

The most compelling witness quoted by the Committee was patrolman Roy Vaughn, assigned to guard the Main Street ramp. The report summary read: "Even when [Vaughn] stepped away from his position to assure the police car [one leaving the basement] safe ingress to the street, he was still able to see the ramp, and saw nobody go down it at that time." Regarding his account, the *HSCA Report* stated, "Patrolman Vaughn's assertion has not changed in fifteen years. He was deemed truthful in a polygraph given several days after the Oswald shooting. . . ."

After discussing the potential that Ruby was permitted entry through "an alley door," the Committee report stated, " . . . The timing was so perfect that it made it difficult to accept *mere coincidence,* [emphasis added] and it is unlikely that Ruby entered the basement without some sort of assistance. This might have been in the form of knowledge of the Oswald transfer plans, direct help in entering the basement, or direct help in both entering and shooting Oswald."[5]

In a further attempt to unlock the mystery of Jack Ruby's participation in a conspiracy, the Committee delved into his association with organized crime figures. While doing so, it denounced the Warren Commission for its inability to gather any semblance of the facts surrounding Ruby's background both in Chicago and Dallas. Most compelling was this statement in the report: "The committee also established associations between Jack Ruby and several individuals affiliated with the underworld activities of Carlos Marcello. Ruby was a personal acquaintance of Joseph Civello,

---

5 Interviewed by this author about the "ramp" question, Al Maddox, the jailer who booked Ruby after he shot Oswald, said he asked Ruby about his entry. "He told me he came down the ramp," Maddox said. When asked if he believed other police officers might have aided Ruby's entry through a stairway, Maddox said, "Would you admit it if you let Jack Ruby down the ramp?" Author William Manchester certainly didn't accept the Ruby story regarding his entry, writing, "Ruby's presence in the basement is utterly confounding. To some it will remain forever mystifying, to others it will always provide positive proof of police collusion in a complex conspiracy, and even those who have sifted all the evidence are left a vague impression of a Houdini effect."

the Marcello associate who allegedly headed organized crime activities in Dallas."[6] A report footnote, after identifying Joseph Campisi as an "organized crime figure" in Dallas, confirmed that "Ruby visited Campisi's restaurant on the evening of November 21st and that Ruby was visited in jail after the shooting of Oswald by Campisi and his wife. Further, Campisi acknowledged a long-standing business and personal relationship with Marcello."

‡

Surfacing in the report was Los Angeles record producer Michael Shore, president of Reprise Records, a company owned by Frank Sinatra. Shore, the report stated, was not only a friend of Earl Ruby, but Chicago-based Irwin Weiner, a prominent underworld bondsman who was closely associated with such men as James Hoffa and Sam Giancana. According to law enforcement files, Weiner had served as a key functionary in the relationship between the Chicago Mafia and various corrupt union officials, particularly while Hoffa was president of the Teamsters union.

The report stated: "Shore attended school with Weiner and Ruby and he and Weiner have been involved in a number of business transactions." Weiner, the report added, recalled that Michael Shore discussed with him the search for an attorney for Jack Ruby after the Oswald shooting. Weiner said Shore told him "that he [Shore] had arranged with Earl to try to get him some legal help in." Further, Weiner quoted Shore as saying, "There was an attorney in San Francisco that I knew and Earl wanted to hire him. I forget his name." Prompted later with the question, "Was his name Melvin Belli?" Weiner responded, "That is his name."

Despite this revelation, the Committee never called Belli as a witness. Once again, the chance to learn more about the circumstances surrounding Ruby's assassination of Oswald, how Belli became Ruby's lawyer, and why he had utilized a highly criticized trial defense had been lost. And with it, the opportunity to probe deeply into whether Belli's links to

---

6　The US Senate Permanent Subcommittee on Investigations Report, filed July 30, 1964, stated that Civello controlled "all rackets in Dallas and the vicinity."

Michael Shore, connected as he was to Irwin Weiner, who was connected to members of organized crime as well as James Hoffa, prompted more investigation of Ruby's attorney.

Unfortunately, Belli, the man of secrets, was the forgotten man during the HSCA's investigation. They had missed the obvious, missed the opportunity to understand how Belli was a key figure in identifying those that the Committee could not identify regarding who had killed the president and why. Like others who had diligently probed the assassinations, they did not realize they were oh-so-close to solving what became known as the greatest murder mystery in history. The truth had been at their fingertips but without what we shall call "The Belli Factor," that truth was hidden from view.

CHAPTER SIX

Theories Abound

In 1978, during the time when the House Select Committee on Assassinations was investigating the JFK and Lee Harvey Oswald killings, the most thoroughly researched book about Jack Ruby was released. If anyone had been paying attention to the potential that Melvin Belli was a critical link to those most responsible for the JFK and Oswald assassinations, they certainly would have discovered clues pointing in that direction.

Titled *Who Was Jack Ruby?* (later issued as *The Ruby Cover-up*), author Seth Kantor's book was designed to tell the "inside story of Ruby" like no book before it. For the most part, Kantor, an award-winning journalist with the *Dallas Times Herald*, offered new facts about Ruby, including a chronicle of his early days in Chicago, foreshadowing what the HSCA report revealed one year later.

Although other authors had hinted at such a possibility, Kantor was arguably the first author to propose that Lee Harvey Oswald had been killed for less than obvious reasons. According to Kantor, the plan to *silence* Lee Harvey Oswald could only have been carried out by one man: Belli's client, Jack Ruby.

Working backwards to link Ruby to the Kennedy assassination, Kantor, a former reporter for Scripps Howard who was an eyewitness to the Ruby trial, portrayed in-depth the man Melvin Belli learned to know, the one whose involvement in the JFK and Oswald murders was shrouded in mystery.

The road map to Ruby's mind began with the realization that Oswald's killer was much more involved with the underworld and as an informant for the FBI and local police than previously understood. To that end, Kantor wrote, "Ruby had been a two-way informer between the police and the hoods [Mafia] on a number of levels—double agent among the chasers and the chasees." He added, "Ruby had been an FBI contact in 1959 . . . [but his] hidden relationship with the FBI was not made public by FBI director J. Edgar Hoover until several years after the Warren Commission Report was published."

Addressing Oswald's killer's popularity with police, Kantor said Earl Ruby witnessed it firsthand. When Jack invited him along to police headquarters to "see some of my friends," Earl told Kantor, "It was 'Hi Jack, Hi Jack, Hi Jack' all the way down the hall" as they encountered officers.

Kantor alleged that the nightclub owner gave officers money on occasion and free admission and drinks when they visited his nightclubs.[7] Ruby's Carousel employees Diane Hunter and Alice Anderson confirmed police contact with the Carousel. "It's been reported that the Dallas police hung out at the Carousel. . . . Why, of course they did. There were cops there every night . . . off-duty, sure. Jack always sold them beer for 40 cents a bottle while everybody else paid 60. They even brought their wives."

Supplementing Kantor and Maddox's observations is a video produced shortly after Ruby assassinated Oswald. One of several available on YouTube, including trial verdict coverage and an interview with Jack Ruby under the banner "The Trial of Jack Ruby – Relssagen – Mod Jack Ruby" (see www.youtube.com/watch?v=7RSZDmlSr3o), an unidentified newsman questions prosecutor Henry Wade. Regarding Jack Ruby's appearance at the midnight press conference where Oswald appeared, the newsman is heard saying, "I thought [Ruby] was a detective. He seemed like he was all

---

7   Al Maddox, the jailer who "booked" Ruby following the Oswald killing, confirmed police payoffs to this author. "I used to go in there," Maddox said, "Ruby 'comped' all the police. They all owed him."

over the place." Wade then admits he saw Ruby inside police headquarters as well.

Prior to the assassinations, Ruby, according to Kantor, made a telephone call that would prove significant in light of Belli's behavior at trial. After contacting an exotic dancer named Jada, Ruby called a stripper named Candy Barr. Ruby, attempting to improve business, begged both Jada and Candy to dance at the Carousel. Barr could not perform due to restrictions with court-ordered probation, a fact that will prove quite relevant when this author later discloses the details of what led to Barr's probation in the first place.

Money was always a concern to Ruby, which Seth Kantor believed to be one motive for killing Oswald. Tracing the steps Ruby took immediately prior to his shooting of JFK's killer lent credibility to that claim, since Ruby, according to Kantor's research, admitted he owed nearly $40,000 in excise and income taxes as of June 1963. Negotiations with the mob to provide the funds failed, Kantor reported.

As Kennedy's fateful visit neared, Ruby's financial situation drastically improved according to Kanter's research. Belli's client told his tax attorney, Graham Koch that he had secured "someone" to pay off his liabilities. A bank officer said Ruby suddenly possessed $7,000 in cash.

HSCA legal counsel and author G. Robert Blakey did not pinpoint the source of the cash, but alleged Ruby's strong ties to the underworld. These included the Campisi brothers and Joseph Civello, a Mafia family chieftain in Dallas. Both were linked to Carlos Marcello. Blakey also stated that Ruby "was open to being used in an underworld operation. Organized-crime figures had motive to kill the President; in Oswald, they had the means to kill him. When Oswald neither escaped nor was killed in flight, they were presented with a motive to silence him." Concluding, Blakey said Ruby's conduct "at least established that he was an available means to affect Oswald's elimination."

Author David Scheim echoed Blakey's conclusions based on comments attributed to West Coast Mafia don Johnny Roselli. Scheim reported that Roselli told Congressional investigators, syndicated columnist Jack Anderson, and other members of the media, "Ruby was one of our guys and had been dispatched to kill Oswald." Quoting Roselli's further admissions to Anderson, Scheim wrote, "When Oswald was picked up, Roselli suggested, the underworld conspirators feared that he would crack and disclose information that might lead to them. . . . So Jack Ruby was ordered to eliminate Oswald." Scheim believed Roselli paid for breaking the Mafia code of silence when his dismembered body was discovered in a fifty-five-gallon oil drum floating in Miami's Dumfounding Bay.

In fact, anyone with the belief that Ruby's killing of Oswald was simply happenstance must dwell in the world of coincidences to the extent that Belli's client had *just happened* to wear a suit and tie on a Sunday morning to send a telegram instead of his usual casual wear, *just happened* to have a wad of cash on him when all indications were that he was flat broke, and *just happened* to drive to the Western Union office a few minutes after eleven o'clock, an office that *just happened* to be three hundred fifty feet from police headquarters. Ruby, according to this version, then *just happened* to see the gathering crowd, *just happened* to walk down there, and *just happened* to amble down the ramp when no one else was able to do so except for police officers. Curiously, he also *just happened* to be close by when Oswald was being led out of the elevator, and seeing him, then *just happened* to be able to gain clear entry to JFK's assassin. He then *just happened* to shoot him without any preconceived plan to do so. This way, JFK's alleged assassin *just happened* to be silenced forever.

‡

Jack Ruby's actions, and more importantly, his words following the Oswald shooting stretched in all directions. While being thrown to the floor, Ruby, according to Seth Kantor and police records, said to men he knew to be detectives, "Hey, you guys know me, I'm Jack Ruby."

When Carousel comedian Wally Weston visited Ruby in his cell, Oswald's killer appeared frightened. He said to Weston, Kantor reported, "Wally, they're going to find out about Cuba. They're going to find out about the guns, find out about New Orleans, find out about everything."

To add to the intrigue, Ruby provided a statement that chilled anyone who witnessed the tape of his remarks, recorded shortly before the Warren Commission finished interrogating him. The words were spoken slowly and methodically, as if scripted. Standing before what appeared to be a court railing, his arms gesturing as he spoke, Ruby said in an eerie tone:

The world will never know the true facts of what occurred.
My motives. I'm the only person in the background that
knows the truth pertaining to everything relating to my
circumstances. The people who have had so much to gain
and had such an ulterior motive to put me in this position
I'm in will never let the true facts come above board to the
world. [preserved at www.youtube.com/watch?v=7RSZDmlSr3o]

Ruby's words to the Warren Commission, connected with those above, added to the intrigue:

Chief Justice WARREN: The President will know everything
that you have said, everything that you have said.

Mr. RUBY: But I won't be around, Chief Justice. I won't
be around to verify these things you are going to tell the
President.

Mr. TONAHILL: Who do you think is going to eliminate
you, Jack?

Mr. RUBY: I have been used for a purpose, and there
will be a certain tragic occurrence happening if you don't
take my testimony and somehow vindicate me so my people
don't suffer because of what I have done.

Chief Justice WARREN: But we have taken your testimony.
We have it here. It will be in permanent form for the President

of the United States and for the Congress of the United States, and for the courts of the United States, and for the people of the entire world. It is there. It will be recorded for all to see. That is the purpose of our coming here today. We feel that you are entitled to have your story told.

Mr. RUBY: You have lost me though. You have lost me, Chief Justice Warren.

Chief Justice WARREN: Lost you in what sense?

Mr. RUBY: I won't be around for you to come and question me again.

Later in his testimony, Ruby continued to request a lie detector test. Chief Justice Warren promised him one only to hear Ruby say, "Gentlemen, my life is in danger here," and then, "I may not live tomorrow to give any further testimony."

Despite Ruby's confusing words, when the Warren Commission finally issued its report in September 1964, it stated that Oswald *and Ruby* had acted alone. Curiously, former President Gerald Ford, a member of the Commission, told the History Channel in 2001, "We said we found no evidence of a conspiracy. We didn't say there was *no* conspiracy."

CHAPTER SEVEN

Frank Ragano's Story

In 1994, JFK assassination "experts" who had researched or written about the Dallas killings were blindsided by a new book. Its different slant to the assassinations impacted every theory, whether involving a conspiracy or not. The impact of this book should not be underestimated since, when melded into fresh information about the twin assassinations revealed here, the allegations presented make perfect sense toward assessing ultimate responsibility for John Kennedy's death in the direction of his father Joe.

Thirty-one years following the Dallas killings, Charles Scribner's Sons published the bestseller *Mob Lawyer* by underworld attorney Frank Ragano and *New York Times* reporter Selwyn Raab. To their credit, the duo not only revealed fresh information about Melvin Belli's involvement in the Jack Ruby case but also the possibility of Belli's being part of a cover-up following the twin assassinations.

Unlike any book where secondary sources were the norm, Ragano was a primary source, a true eyewitness to history, a crafty, courtroom-savvy, Florida-based criminal defense attorney who had represented a mind-boggling, dangerous triumvirate: Teamsters boss James Hoffa and mobsters Santo Trafficante and Carlos Marcello. Bolstering Ragano's claims was coauthor Raab, a *New York Times* award-winning reporter who had covered the Mafia for more than twenty years. If Raab's credentials were impressive, so were those of Nicholas Pileggi, who wrote the book's foreword. The author of such bestselling books as *Wiseguy* (adapted into the film *Goodfellas*) and *Casino*, Pileggi noted in his foreword that Ragano's revelations were a "bonanza" and that he was "the invisible link between the mob, corrupt politicians, crooked businessmen, and powerful labor leaders like [James] Hoffa," whom Ragano represented for more than fifteen years.

With Raab, the respected journalist by his side to keep him "honest" thus providing credibility (Raab required Ragano to produce corroboration for anything he alleged including hotel and dinner receipts for dates Ragano met with Hoffa and his underworld clients), Ragano weaved a story that spanned his early days to the time when he became arguably the most famous "mob lawyer" in the world.

What Ragano had to say about Jack Ruby, Melvin Belli, and the Ruby case in *Mob Lawyer* was preceded by startling revelations regarding responsibility for JFK's assassination beginning with the initial connection between Kennedy and Tampa-based Santo Trafficante in 1957 when Kennedy was a senator. According to Ragano, Trafficante and a Cuban casino partner, Evaristo Garcia, arranged for JFK to frolic with three sexy young Cuban prostitutes at the Commodoro Hotel in Havana. When Kennedy accepted the invitation for a sex party, Trafficante and Garcia positioned themselves in front of a two-way mirror and watched. Their only regret, they said later, was that they hadn't photographed Kennedy in action.[8]

The two mobsters lost respect for Kennedy. "From their viewpoint," Ragano wrote, "an official like Kennedy, who publicly preached law, order, and decency and secretly took bribes or slept with prostitutes, was a rank

---

8   John Kennedy's presence in Cuba during 1957 is confirmed through FBI files. The bureau noted that one of the reasons for his trip was to visit Florence Pritchett (wife of Earl Smith, the Ambassador Extraordinary and Plenipotentiary to Cuba), with whom JFK had a long-standing love affair.

hypocrite who deserved no esteem." Ragano added that Trafficante "knew [Kennedy] to have been sexually profligate in Cuba and considered him a hypocritical phony unworthy of being president. He was contemptuous of [John and Robert] for harping about law-and-order-issues, which he interpreted as cheap political pandering." Ragano called Trafficante's distaste for both Kennedys "intense and unmistakable," an attitude Trafficante's brother in crime, Marcello, shared. This was based, Ragano stated, on Robert Kennedy having deported Marcello to Latin America.

By 1963, Ragano had risen to prominence, representing not only Trafficante and Marcello, but also Teamsters union boss James Hoffa regarding legal matters based on RFK's efforts to imprison Hoffa for corruption. Besides being impressed with Ragano's work as a trial lawyer, Ragano suspected Hoffa chose him to ensure access to underworld figures if the need arose. It would.

Regarding James Hoffa's behavior just prior to the assassinations, Ragano wrote, "Hoffa hated the Kennedys as much as the two mobsters [Trafficante and Marcello] did. In the first months of 1963, Jimmy was consumed by the prospect of looming indictments and his animosity toward the Kennedys. A day rarely went by without him unleashing his customary obscenities at 'Booby,' his unflattering sobriquet for the attorney general."

Ragano's entry into Hoffa's world began in June of 1961, but the union leader became aware of the attorney's prowess through his representation of the mobster Trafficante, a close friend of mob-connected singer Frank Sinatra, a friend of the Kennedy family. According to various sources, Tampa-born Trafficante rose through the Mafia ranks under his father's tutelage until he joined forces in the 1940s with infamous gangsters Meyer Lansky, Frank Costello, and Lucky Luciano to set up casinos in Cuba. During Trafficante's stay in Cuba, he operated the Sans Souci and the Casino International gambling operations and was also a behind-the-scenes partner in several other casinos.

Trafficante also had interest in restaurants in the Ybor City district of Tampa, Florida, but his bigger interests were focused on gambling. This caused him to be convicted for running illegal bolita lotteries. He was imprisoned until the Florida Supreme Court reversed his conviction. While attending the infamous "Apalachin" Upstate New York meeting of fifty-six known gangsters in 1957, Trafficante was arrested again, but later released. Suspicion arose that the mild-mannered mafiosi masterminded New York City's Park Sheraton Hotel barbershop killing of arch-rival Murder, Inc. chief Albert Anastasia, but no charges were ever filed.

Trafficante's various legal problems had caused him to land at Frank Ragano's doorstep. When the attorney gained an acquittal for the mobster on a tax evasion charge, Hoffa was impressed by the result. He contacted Ragano after being indicted in June of 1961 for racketeering in connection with a retirement home project near Cape Canaveral.

From word one, Ragano said the two men discovered a common enemy: Robert F. Kennedy. Ragano's apparent distaste for RFK ("[Bobby's] an arrogant son of a bitch"), cemented a bond with Hoffa; who also detested the attorney general.

Hoffa had opposite feelings toward Santo Trafficante. "He's a classy guy," he told his lawyer, according to Ragano, "I'd like to meet him." Informed of the accolade, Trafficante returned the favor: "Tell Jimmy that I consider him a friend and that I hope he considers me a friend. If there is anything I can do for him I would be glad to do it." Ragano and Trafficante, the lawyer alleged, then agreed that when they met, they would call Hoffa, "Maretuzzo," Sicilian for "Little Hammer."

Before the retirement home case was completed, Hoffa was indicted in Nashville, Tennessee for violating the Landrum-Griffin Act that forbade union leaders from accepting payoffs from employers in return for sweetheart contracts. The trial resulted in a hung jury, and jury tampering was suspected. During the trial, Ragano impressed Carlos Marcello, the feared New Orleans don and a close friend of Trafficante's. Within months, Ragano added Marcello to his client list. This occurred, Ragano said, after he impressed the "Big Daddy in the Big Easy," Ragano's nickname for Marcello, with his savvy handling of a pending Louisiana indictment against Hoffa.

After a dinner in March 1963 attended by Ragano, Trafficante, and Marcello, the mob lawyer quoted Marcello as saying, "It's a goddamn shame what the Kennedys are putting Jimmy [Hoffa] through." "Yes,"

Trafficante agreed, "If Kennedy hadn't been elected, Jimmy never would have been indicted."

In between sips of steaming coffee, Marcello continued the discussion, saying, "You, Jimmy, and me are in for hard times as long as Bobby Kennedy is in office. Someone ought to kill that son-of-a-bitch. That f_____ Bobby Kennedy is making life miserable for me and my friends. Someone ought to kill *all* of those Kennedys."

Later that evening, Ragano wrote that Trafficante mentioned his distaste for the Kennedys due to their hypocrisy. "Here's this guy, Bobby Kennedy, talking about law and order, and these guys made their goddamn fortune through bootlegging," he said in a reference to Joseph Kennedy's past bootlegging operations. Trafficante then added, according to Ragano, "Bobby Kennedy is stepping on too many toes. Che [Trafficante's nickname for Ragano], you wait and see, somebody is going to kill those sons-of-bitches. It's just a matter of time."

Ragano wrote that JFK's fate was debated in front of the mob lawyer in March 1963. This occurred, Ragano's wife Nancy confirmed to this author, in Hoffa's suite at the Edgewater Beach Hotel in Chicago. Among those attending, in addition to Ragano, were Hoffa, attorney Bill Bufalino, and Joey Glimco, head of Chicago cabdrivers' Local 777.[9]

Amid a rigorous gin rummy game, Glimco, who had battled RFK during a Senate hearing on racketeering, blurted, according to Ragano, "What do you think would happen if something happened to Bobby Kennedy?" Buffalino retorted, " . . . John Kennedy would be so pissed off, he would probably replace him with someone who would be more of a son-of-a-bitch than Bobby."

Ragano wrote that the thought lingered in the smoke-filled room for a few seconds until James Hoffa spoke up. "Suppose something happened to the president, instead of Bobby?" he said. Buffalino answered, "Lyndon Johnson would get rid of Bobby."

9 Also in attendance, Nancy Ragano told this author, was Frank "The Irishman" Sheeran, a trusted Hoffa Teamsters official who confirmed the meeting to author Charles Brandt in the 2005 book, *I Heard You Paint Houses: Frank "The Irishman" Sheeran and the Inside Story of the Mafia, the Teamsters, and the Last Ride of Jimmy Hoffa.*

"Damn right he would," Hoffa exclaimed, "He hates him as much as I do. Don't forget, I've given a hell of a lot of money to Lyndon in the past."

In May of 1963, two months after Hoffa's comment, the union leader was indicted for jury tampering in Chattanooga. And months later, as noted, he was indicted in New Orleans. The charges, Ragano wrote, escalated the harsh feelings Hoffa, and by extension how Trafficante and Marcello felt about RFK and the president.

Evidence of Hoffa's personal hatred for Robert Kennedy surfaced shortly thereafter. According to Ragano, RFK had agreed to be present during a meeting in Washington DC when prosecutors were to deliver documents critical to Hoffa's prosecutions. The union boss accompanied his attorneys, but when they arrived, RFK was absent.

Hoffa fumed at the slight while Ragano sifted through the documents. Forty-five minutes later, the attorney general sauntered through the door accompanied by a large dog on a leash. "Where the hell do you get off keeping me waiting while you're walking your f____ dog," Hoffa roared, "I've got a lot of important people to see."

Kennedy ignored the testy words, spouting, "I'm in charge, not you." Without hesitation, Hoffa lunged at Kennedy, and started choking him. "You son of a bitch," he screamed. "I'll break your f____ing neck. I'll kill you."

Ragano swore he and his colleagues had to pry Hoffa's fingers from RFK's throat. Seconds later, the attorney general, without so much as a word, marched out of the room, dog in tow. Ragano's wife Nancy corroborated the story by telling this author that when Ragano met her at the Miami airport that evening, he was "visibly shaken" by the encounter. She added, "[Frank] thought Hoffa was going to kill Kennedy."

Hoffa's frame of mind, Ragano reported, was "unpredictable." Nancy confirmed this state of mind, telling this author the Teamsters boss "had begun to lose it [since] Bobby Kennedy was getting to him." Ragano believed that "after his encounter with RFK, Jimmy was increasingly distraught, his temper at a lower-than-usual flashpoint."

A subsequent July 23, 1963, meeting with Hoffa at his Chicago headquarters caused Ragano to realize that his client had passed the talking stage. When they were alone in the hotel dining room, the mob attorney recalled, "Jimmy drew his chair close to mine and in a muffled voice asked when I intended to see Santo and Carlos."

Ragano answered that he was leaving that evening for New Orleans to meet both men. Hoffa's face lit up, "The time has come for your friend and Carlos to get rid of him, kill that son-of-a-bitch John Kennedy."

"For a second I thought I had misheard him," Ragano recalled, "And I was unable to conceal the astonishment that he must have read in my face. But he stared penetratingly into my eyes, with a fiercely determined gaze."

According to Ragano, Hoffa then said, "This has got to be done. Be sure to tell them what I said. No more f_____ around. We're running out of time—something has got to be done." Nancy Ragano told this author that Ragano later told her, "Hoffa had lost control, lost his mind," all the while making light, Nancy said, of "what had occurred since he was troubled by what had happened in Dallas and was trying to shed the guilt he felt over being the go-between for Hoffa with Marcello and Trafficante."

Regardless, Hoffa's directive dictated that Ragano inform Trafficante and Marcello of Hoffa's order. Duty bound, the lawyer said he did so during a meeting at the Royal Orleans Hotel. When Hoffa was mentioned during conversation, Ragano uttered in a whispered tone, "Maretuzzo [Hoffa's code name] wants you to do a little favor for him. You won't believe this, but he wants you to kill John Kennedy."

Ragano, who described the atmosphere as "icy," said there was dead silence at the table as Trafficante and Marcello exchanged glances. "He wants you to get rid of the President right away," Ragano added, unaware that Marcello, as we shall learn, possessed similar notions.

Exactly four months later to the day, John F. Kennedy was assassinated in Dallas. Ragano wrote that shortly after he heard the news, he was summoned to the telephone where he heard Hoffa's excited voice. "Did you hear the good news?" Hoffa blared, "They killed the son-of-a-bitch bastard."

That evening Ragano and Trafficante enjoyed dinner at the International Inn in Tampa. Regarding the encounter, Ragano wrote, "A smiling Santo greeted me at the table. 'Isn't that something, they killed the son-of-a-bitch,' he said, hugging and kissing me on the cheeks. 'The son-of-a-bitch is dead.'" While toasting the momentous occasion, Trafficante added, "This is like lifting a load of stones off my shoulders. Now they'll get off my back, off Carlos's back, and off [Hoffa's] back."

Nancy Ragano told this author she approached the corner table that evening only to see Ragano and Trafficante, normally a quiet, well-mannered man who seldom laughed, celebrating by "lifting glasses of champagne high in the air, toasting JFK's death while laughing and joking. I couldn't comprehend what was occurring and was disgusted by the irreverent behavior. I said 'Frank, you can't mean that.' He said he did." Nancy informed this author that she put down her drink and left the restaurant in a huff. So upset with Frank over his conduct and despite the fact that she loved him, Nancy said she ended the relationship: "I did not speak to Frank for six months. The incident was like something out of a horror movie. I am still horrified when I think of it."

Despite Ragano's calling Trafficante a "refined gentleman" most interested in gambling and real estate, and Marcello resembling "a harmless elf who excused himself from staying out late because his wife might worry if he got home after 10:00 PM," the mob lawyer concluded the two men were "uniquely capable of arranging the murder of a president." This was true since their minds "performed unscrupulous and daring gymnastics that could befuddle and outmaneuver the best police and intelligence agents in the country." Ragano believed this was especially true of Trafficante, since "his criminal organizational skills bordered on brilliant."

‡

Mob Lawyer's startling revelations caused assassination experts to reconsider their theories by probing whether what Ragano had divulged was indeed true. But while doing so, no one paid any attention to other disclosures regarding Jack Ruby, Melvin Belli, and the Oswald/Ruby murder case. Like those who had primarily focused on who killed JFK and why, these experts never followed up on Ragano's words of warning. Recalling them and the context within which they were offered provides understanding about why the relationship between Ruby and Belli is critical to discovering who was most responsible for the assassinations, with Ragano, as unlikely as it may seem at first glance, as the conduit to uncovering facts and drawing conclusions never considered before.

In 1966, just three years after the Dallas killings, Ragano sued *Time* magazine for libel in connection with a photograph at the La Stella Restaurant in New York City published under the banner, "Top Cosa Nostra Hoodlums." The photograph was taken the same week thirteen mobsters, including Trafficante, Marcello, Joseph Columbo of the Columbo crime family, co-bosses of the Genovese family, and Aniello Delacroce, a Gambino family underboss, had met at the restaurant with Ragano and Marcello's New Orleans attorney Jack Wasserman. The reason, according to Ragano: "Some New York mobsters were trying to poach on the action in New Orleans . . . and Carlos was ready to resist intrusions by outsiders." The mobsters, murderers, and racketeers all were arrested by police for "consorting with known criminals."

While on bond, and awaiting grand jury appearances, Ragano, Wasserman, Marcello, Trafficante, and other crime family members had another lunch at La Stella. The famous photograph depicting Ragano and Trafficante raising their glasses in a mock toast toward the cameraman, while Marcello looked on, had been published in *Time*. Insulted by the magazine caption intimating that Ragano was a member of the Mafia, he demanded a retraction. This was denied, and Ragano sued *Time* for 2.5 million dollars.

The restaurant incident was confirmed to this author by Nick Pileggi, then a journalist at the AP who was writing a story titled "Little Apalachin Mob Meeting." During a break from covering a grand jury hearing focused on the mobsters including, according to Pileggi, "Carlos Marcello, his brother Joseph, Trafficante, Mike Miranda of the Genovese crew, and others I can't remember," Pileggi and a photographer visited "La Stella on Queens Boulevard." Pileggi said he was the one who asked for the photo that led to the libel lawsuit.[10]

---

10 Describing Marcello, Pileggi told this author, "[He] was the least friendly. He didn't smile. He didn't do anything. He was expressionless. Short. Round. Hard as a Civil War

To pursue his claim, Ragano could have hired any one of many noted lawyers in the libel field. Instead, he hired Melvin Belli, arguably the most famous attorney in the world at the time, but one who specialized in personal injury litigation, a far cry from a libel case. Ragano never divulged why he hired Belli, but what he had to say about Jack Ruby's attorney in *Mob Lawyer* more thirty years after the Dallas assassinations was alarming. Unfortunately, no one, especially those still attempting to probe the truth about the JFK and Oswald deaths, paid attention to the explosive allegations. They should have.

In his book, Ragano recalled interaction with Santo Trafficante regarding the hiring of Belli, the veracity of which was confirmed to this author by Ragano's widow, Nancy. One steamy Florida afternoon, Ragano wrote, his ears perked up during a conversation with Trafficante when the aging mobster's face became rigid at the name "Belli." Trafficante said, "[Belli's] a great lawyer. I'm surprised he would take your case." Moving closer, Trafficante in a soft but stern voice added, "whatever you do, don't ask him about Jack Ruby. Don't get involved. It's none of your business."

Heeding the warning, Ragano wrote that he never questioned Belli about his representation of Ruby during the *Time* magazine case or later when they became social friends. This was because, he explained, "Santo cautioned me several times in the late sixties to avoid talking with Melvin Belli about Jack Ruby's reasons for murdering Lee Harvey Oswald. At the time, I trusted Santo and believed he was looking out for my interest. More likely he was fearful that Mel might inadvertently say something that would lead me to connect Santo or Carlos to the conspiracy [to assassinate JFK]." Regardless, Ragano believed there was an unrevealed, "mysterious connection between Ruby and Belli" never revealed, "that [Santo] felt, for my own good, I should not learn."

These unforgettable words regarding what Santo Trafficante said to Ragano were disregarded, lost amidst the strong, headline-making allega-

_____

cannon ball." Regarding the difference between Trafficante and Marcello, Pileggi added, "Trafficante was a second generation Mafia boss; he was elegant. Liked opera, etc. Marcello was of the immigrant generation. Tough. Impossible to seduce and the kind of Sicilian mafiosi you didn't want to turn into an enemy."

Mob Lawyer Frank Ragano (right) and Melvin Belli (center)—1966. Even when it was reported that Mafia don Santo Trafficante, one of Ragano's clients along with Carlos Marcello and James Hoffa, warned Ragano, "Whatever you do, don't ask Melvin Belli about the Jack Ruby case, it's none of your business." Questions about Belli's representation of Ruby went unanswered.   Credit: Tampa Tribune.

tions that Hoffa, Trafficante, and Marcello were behind JFK's murder. But close inspection in light of new facts uncovered about Belli trigger the requirement that the assassinations be reconsidered to discover how "The Belli Factor," the inclusion of Ruby's lawyer into any discussion of the Dallas killings and beyond, impacts the truth. Before doing so, it is important to assess Ragano's credibility to pinpoint whether his words in *Mob Lawyer* ring true.

John H. Davis, author of *Mafia Kingfish*, wrote of the mob lawyer's claims in *The Kennedy Contract: The Mafia Plot to Assassinate the President*. First, Davis interviewed Nicholas Pileggi, who as noted, wrote the foreword for Ragano's book. Pileggi, Davis wrote, said that Ragano first sent him his book manuscript in the fall of 1991 seeking editorial advice. After speaking with Pileggi at length about Ragano's story, Davis wrote, "Pileggi told me that he believes Ragano is 'absolutely credible.'" To bolster Pileggi's assertion, Davis then quoted G. Robert Blakey, the former counsel to the HSCA: "He [Blakey] told me that he believes Ragano's story is the 'most plausible and logical explanation' of the assassination."

Regarding Ragano's story of the Hoffa/Marcello/Trafficante link to JFK and Oswald's death, Davis pointed out that the mob lawyer "went public" with his allegations in 1992, two years before *Mob Lawyer* was published. This, Davis believed, refuted allegations that Ragano was "puffing smoke in order to sell books." Frank's widow, Nancy Ragano, agreed with Davis, telling this author that the idea for a book was actually hers: "Frank kept a lot of scrapbooks and pictures and I felt he had lived a lot of history. He never had time to do anything with a book, but then health problems began and he decided to write. I suggested a book about his trials since he had a gift for selecting and reading juries."

As the book idea progressed, Nancy told this author she was surprised at what she learned about her husband. "I had some suspicions," she said, "but I learned many things I did not know as Frank began to unburden himself of what had occurred in his life. After many years of marriage, he confessed many things to me, some that were surprising and shocking." One involved Santo Trafficante: "With him things happened that had many double meanings," she told this author, "To me, Santo was a kind man, a friend, a nice man, a father-figure. Then I saw things about him on television and newspapers and learned the truth, but I still could not believe he had done the things they accused him of doing." This reminded her, she said, of why she believed her husband about what Trafficante had said to him regarding Belli. Nancy thought "Trafficante's words of warning" was "history repeating itself" since "Frank had expressed a similar sentiment ('It's none of your business') before she met Trafficante for the first time." When Nancy pressed him as to why regarding both warnings, she told this author he said, "End of conversation." She added, "This caused me to wonder what Frank really knew about Belli's complicity in the assassination cover-up."

If Nancy had doubts about Trafficante, she had no doubts about why the book was written. "Frank had much to tell, and it *was* part of history," she told this author, "He knew the Teamsters had used him as a go-between with the mobsters. He had been burdened with this for a long time and wanted to rest in peace." As for the veracity of what her husband wrote, Nancy was certain "it happened." She was impressed, she said, with collaborator Selwyn Raab's tenacity in demanding that Ragano produce documentation for certain matters including events with Hoffa. "Frank did not make this up," she emphasized.

Regarding his thoughts about Ragano, author Davis wrote, "I was impressed with Frank Ragano when I first met him and his wife and found nothing in their attitude or demeanor that told me they were not sincere." The author added, "The allegation of Frank Ragano now has an impressive list of supporters, House Assassination chief counsel G. Robert Blakey, writers Nick Pileggi and Jack Newfield, and former Kennedy aides Frank Mankiewicz, Adam Walinsky, and Richard Goodwin."

During an interview with this author, Selwyn Raab explained, "Frank's general reputation among the law faculty in Tampa and Florida was mixed and I described it that way [in the book] without superfluous comments from people refusing to be identified. For what it is worth, often when dining or in public places with Frank, judges and lawyers would seek him out in complimentary style. Most, however, ducked being quoted on the record. I therefore blended the pejorative with the kudos in describing the mixed sentiments about him and let his record speak for itself."

Raab added, "If I had been dubious about his account of relaying a message from Hoffa to Trafficante and Marcello about a hit on Kennedy, I would not have included it [in the book]. Frank had the records of hotel stays and diaries of dates with Hoffa in Washington and with mobsters in New Orleans. [This] is no absolute proof the Mafia had a hand in Kennedy's assassination, but it is indisputable that they profited from it since Bobby was now powerless."

Raab's comment was made without his having knowledge of "The Belli Factor." Others who decided they would attempt to debunk Ragano's story suffered a similar fate, but it did not keep them from blasting away at the mob lawyer's allegations. Despite Ragano's claims, Jack Ruby's lawyer was still the forgotten man. No one wanted to pay attention to why probing Belli and the Ruby case was the missing link to connecting the dots regarding who was most responsible for JFK's death. This was the unfortunate state of affairs even though Ragano's strong words about Belli ("Whatever you do, don't ask him about Jack Ruby. Don't get involved. It's none of your business.") should have ignited a full-blown investigation of Ruby's attorney by those interested in the truth about the assassinations. The words didn't.

CHAPTER EIGHT

Attacking Ragano

When Frank Ragano initially splashed his accusations about a Hoffa/ Marcello/Trafficante link to JFK's assassination to the media in January 1992, reaction was mixed. Upon the release of *Mob Lawyer* two years later, doubts would intensify from every direction concerning his allegations against the three men, triggering neglect of anything Ragano wrote about Melvin Belli.

On January 16, 1992, the *Tampa Tribune* included a story by reporter Tim Collie under the banner, "Lawyer Links Mob, Hoffa to JFK Slaying," Collie wrote, "Amidst a resurgence of interest in the assassination of President John F. Kennedy, a prominent Tampa attorney says he may have carried the order to kill the president between two major figures he represented." Collie added, "Putting a new spin on an old conspiracy theory, Frank Ragano told the *New York Post* this week that he believed he carried an assassination order from Teamsters union leader Jimmy Hoffa to Tampa-based crime kingpin Santo Trafficante Jr. and New Orleans mob boss Carlos Marcello in early 1963." The story further noted that Ragano described himself as an "unwitting intermediary" in the equation. Collie said Ragano "would be willing to testify under oath before a government panel." Journalist Collie also wrote that Ragano was in New York "hunting for a publisher for his autobiography he hoped to publish in March

[1993].'' Ragano, Coole reported, said the book was to be entitled, *The Price of Loyalty.*

In tandem with fellow *Tribune* reporter Neil King Jr., Tim Collie had written about Santo Trafficante in 1992. Under the headline, "The Tampa Connection," the journalists dubbed Trafficante "The Tampa Godfather." They chronicled his associations with mobsters Meyer Lansky, Carlos Marcello, and Sam Giancana. Regarding Trafficante's link to JFK's death, the reporters wrote, "Law enforcement agents who spent years trying to snare Trafficante doubt that the smart and wily gangster would have risked killing a US president. They point to the Trafficante mystique—a quiet, unassuming profile of a man who kept his friends close, but his enemies closer." Collie and King Jr. then added a caveat, "The assassinations of two Trafficante enemies, Albert Anastasia in 1957, and [Johnny] Roselli, in 1976, followed closely visits from the Tampa mafiosi himself."

Two weeks after his revelations to the *New York Post*, Ragano made more headlines—ones he did not relish. Under the banner, "Lawyer in Kennedy Controversy Faces Hearing," the *Tampa Tribune* detailed that Ragano "faced disbarment proceedings in an unrelated case." Prior to being disbarred due to a client dispute, Ragano agreed to retire from the practice of law.

In 1993, Ragano spoke about his Mafia ties in an interview with Michael Browning, a reporter for the *Miami Herald*. Ragano told Browning, "I made a devil's bargain, and I have to live with it the rest of my life," a reference, Browning said, to Ragano's representation of Trafficante and James Hoffa. Ragano then added, "I just hope to devote my remaining years to warning other young lawyers not to make the mistakes I made."

Nancy Ragano told this author it took her time to forgive Frank for not telling her the truth about Trafficante. "Frank tried to be something other than what he was," she said, "He was not honest with me. When he finally confessed everything to me it was similar to when Santo finally confessed to him about his participation in the JFK assassination. I was upset but then I forgave Frank for what he did."

As the wife of the mob lawyer, Nancy said she paid a price. At one point when Frank was under investigation by the FBI, Nancy told this author she "was tailed and forced to endure surveillance vehicles outside her living room window. Neighbors shunned me," she recalled, after agents visited them in search of information about Frank and her.

When Frank Ragano died in May 1998, several colleagues and associates spoke about the controversial lawyer. "He was gutsy," Boston lawyer Paul Antinori told the *Tampa Tribune*. "[Ragano] was known for the courage he displayed in the courtroom. He never shied away from risky cases. He had a brilliant legal mind."

Turning toward the dark side of Ragano, Tampa attorney Manual Machin told the *Tampa Tribune*, "Among local attorneys, Ragano had a reputation as being a lawyer who could not be trusted. And in his old age, he became a bit of a story teller." Asked about Ragano's proclamations in his book, Machin stated, "If true, they were a blatant violation of the lawyer-client privilege, even though his client, Trafficante, was dead. It was like a priest writing about his confessionals."

‡

In 1992, author Gerald Posner had discounted theories that James Hoffa, the Mafia, or anyone else had ordered the murder of President John F. Kennedy when he proposed the latest of the "Oswald Alone" theories. Based on this foundation, he instantly became an authority, the loud voice crying "foul" regarding any and all of Frank Ragano's allegations in *Mob Lawyer* two years later.

Addressing Ragano's public version of the events unfolding before JFK's death in *Case Closed*, Posner recalled the 1967 interview Ragano had with the FBI when he failed to mention the Hoffa/Marcello/Trafficante scenario. Posner also stated that Ragano's new version of the alleged plot to kill JFK first appeared immediately after the release of Oliver Stone's film *JFK* in 1991. "There is no corroboration for his [Ragano's] new tale [in *Mob Lawyer*]," Posner summarized.

Posner disregarded Ragano's explanation for his decision to explain his side of the story in *Mob Lawyer*. In the epilogue to the book, Ragano wrote, "Several factors kept me from immediately revealing Santo's . . .

disclosures. No man wants his family and friends to regard him a mindless dupe or a villain for being Hoffa's courier. . . . Most of the principals in the Kennedy assassination and Hoffa's murder are dead. Time is running out for me, too. Before I go, I feel compelled to provide a full account of my knowledge of how the Mafia arranged the death of John Kennedy. . . ." Regarding his motives, Ragano wrote, "Do I have all the answers? Of course not. But I represented and knew three significant suspects in the Kennedy assassination. . . . My information about their actions and words will add to or help to correct the historical record."

Despite Ragano's words, his story continued to be bombarded with allegations of untruth. Echoing Gerald Posner's attacks on Ragano's story, but with much more emphasis, was former Charles Manson prosecutor and bestselling author Vincent Bugliosi. In his 2007 book, *Reclaiming History: The Assassination of President John F. Kennedy*, he presented his arguments for the "Oswald Alone" theory, believing no conspiracy was evident.

After the book was released, JFK assassination experts packed the airwaves with opinions about Bugliosi's theories, pro and con. Regarding Frank Ragano and his claims, Bugliosi was highly critical of the mob lawyer and everything about him. This was predictable since if Ragano was telling the truth, Bugliosi's theories weren't credible.

Proclaiming himself meticulous in his research, in a tome stretching to more than sixteen hundred pages, Bugliosi began his questioning of Ragano's allegations by stating, "Since trial lawyers, as Ragano was, live in a world of lies, either by their client or by their opposition, one would think Ragano would be capable of a better lie than the one he told in his 1994 book, *Mob Lawyer*." Lumping Ragano in with others who advocated conspiracies, Bugliosi charged that they were "within the grasp of, or flirting very heavily with, psychosis." The former prosecutor then pegged Ragano as having "made up his story for his own self-aggrandizing reasons."

To make the point that Ragano's version of events was faulty, the former prosecutor attempted to prove Ragano wrote conflicting accounts of Marcello and Trafficante's roles in JFK's death with the insinuation that Ragano was a liar of the first degree. Bugliosi asserted that Ragano had first admitted that the two men were very cautious, "two prudent godfa-thers," and that the idea they could be involved in JFK's assassination was absurd before proclaiming that they were in fact vital participants in the Dallas killing. This inconsistency, Bugliosi boasted, confirmed his belief that it was ridiculous to allege that any mafiosi would execute a plan to kill the president. He also chastised Ragano for suggesting that Marcello and Trafficante would do so as a favor to James Hoffa.

Two problems exist with Bugliosi's argument. First, when Ragano referenced his disbelief that Marcello and Trafficante "would dare to get involved in a plot against the president," Ragano was stating his belief at the time, one altered later when he realized, "Now the facts and clues that I had subconsciously suppressed for more than two decades could no longer be ignored: Carlos, Santo, *and Jimmy* [emphasis added] undoubt-edly had roles in Kennedy's death: they had planned to murder him and they used me as an unwitting accomplice in their scheme." There was thus no conflict in Ragano's statements; they simply referenced different time periods, one made before the other occurred.

Second, close examination of Bugliosi's argument indicated appar-ent disregard for the accuracy of Ragano's words, as a deft prosecutor tends to do to make the facts fit the argument he is making. To this end, Bugliosi failed to mention that early in Ragano's book, the full quote was: "Now the facts and clues that I had subconsciously suppressed for more than two decades could no longer be ignored: Carlos, Santo, *and Jimmy* [emphasis added] undoubtedly had roles in Kennedy's death: they had planned to murder him and they used me as an unwitting accomplice in their scheme." Conveniently, the name "Jimmy" was left out of the Ragano quote Bugliosi included in his book. Why this occurred was not explained, leading one to speculate that Bugliosi simply did not want to suggest that Hoffa and the two mobsters were in any way connected since this was inconsistent with Bugliosi's theories that no conspiracy could have possibly existed.

Bugliosi's next attack on Ragano was to question why the mob lawyer would expose himself to potential prosecution for being part of the conspiracy to kill JFK by admitting in *Mob Lawyer* his participation, through giving the "kill JFK" message from Hoffa to Marcello and Trafficante. Bugliosi criticized Ragano by alleging that the attorney would be setting himself up for prosecution as an accessory since no statute of limitation prevented such charges, ones that could result in the death penalty.

Bugliosi also believed that Ragano understood that "a bullet in the head is the customary penalty for violation of omertà the Mafia's code of silence," indicating that the former prosecutor apparently believed Ragano would be assassinated, apparently by mobsters with a grudge to bear. This argument was most difficult to understand since any mafiosi associated with crime in the 1960s was most likely dead, and modern-day underworld figures weren't concerned about something occurring four-plus decades earlier. This meant the threat of repercussion to Ragano was virtually impossible, undermining another theory Bugliosi had about why Ragano's story was untrue.

Summing up, Bugliosi concluded that none of this made any difference since Ragano was a boldface liar. The former prosecutor asserted that Ragano wrote what he did to get back at Trafficante after he refused financial help when Ragano lost his legal license and couldn't make a living. But the former prosecutor had forgotten that Ragano, whose second son's godfather was Trafficante, represented the underworld boss in a federal racketeering case and attended the mobster's funeral after the money squabble, indicating there was no ill-feeling between the pair.

Moving forward in every direction to discredit Ragano, the prosecutor turned author, while admitting that Trafficante was dead when *Mob Lawyer* was published (thus causing no taint on his reputation), decided a second reason as to why Ragano squealed on Trafficante, Hoffa, and Marcello was that Ragano wanted to stimulate book sales. Bugliosi said Ragano enjoyed the limelight while pointing out that it had taken the mob lawyer thirty years to come up with what Bugliosi called "a whopper" of a story.

Apparently satisfied he had assaulted the personal side of Ragano to the core, Bugliosi moved on to the mob lawyer's allegations about Jimmy Hoffa's potential participation in the JFK assassination by making what was a startling admission. After once again criticizing Ragano's version of events as fiction, Bugliosi wrote: ". . . it is *pretty well accepted* [emphasis added] that Hoffa, though never ordering, at least discussed the possibility of murdering his chief nemesis, the president's brother, RFK." Such a revelation, it would appear, was completely in line with Ragano's story that while the hated one was truly Bobby, killing Jack made much more sense in terms of rendering RFK, the "chief nemesis," powerless. Bugliosi's admission, that Hoffa did in fact discuss the potential to kill RFK, bolsters Ragano's story instead of undermining it. The former prosecutor's words also point toward the need to consider why RFK *was not* killed instead of why the president *was*, a focus separating this author's book from every other one ever written about the assassinations.

To prove the "Oswald Alone" theory his book advocated, Bugliosi stated that other than Oswald, whom he called "a virtual madman," no one else would have the audacity to kill the president. Since no one other than a "madman would do so, Bugliosi believed that if the mob really wanted to "get [JFK's] brother, Robert Kennedy, off its back," one who had put "unprecedented heat on organized crime," it would have focused on the fact that "President Kennedy was a hound dog when it came to women, continuing his indiscriminate liaisons with women through his one thousand days in office." Apparently Bugliosi imagined some sort of blackmail scheme would have been more appealing to those intent on eliminating JFK than the efforts of a rifleman shooting the president while he was riding in a convertible, which was exactly what occurred.

Of note is the former prosecutor's mention of the mob's need to "get [JFK's] brother, Robert Kennedy, off its back" since RFK had put "unprecedented heat on organized crime." But Bugliosi apparently never considered whether Bobby's pursuit of the Mafia was the true motive for killing the president.

Unlike Vincent Bugliosi, author David Kaiser, a professor at the Naval War College, wasn't as quick to dismiss Frank Ragano's allegations. In his 2008 book, *The Road to Dallas*, Kaiser first noted "Attorney General Robert Kennedy's unprecedented, all-out effort to put the

American mob out of business." The particulars: "That effort included intensive surveillance and harassment of Sam Giancana in Chicago, similar treatment for [Santo] Trafficante in Tampa and Miami, and a three-year effort to deport Carlos Marcello, who had two direct links to Lee Harvey Oswald."

Kaiser wrote that Robert Kennedy's other key target was "Jimmy Hoffa of the Teamsters Union, who had close business ties with Giancana, Marcello, and Trafficante, and shared a lawyer, Frank Ragano, with Trafficante." Without a whisper of dissent, Kaiser then detailed how "Ragano delivered a message from Hoffa to the two mob bosses: that it was time to execute the contract on President Kennedy." Summing up conclusions based, in part, on his belief in Ragano's story, Kaiser wrote, "The killing of President Kennedy, followed by the resignation less than a year later of Robert Kennedy as attorney general, seriously curtailed the government's effort to clean up organized crime—just as it was intended to do."

Kaiser noted that Trafficante's hatred of RFK stemmed from the attorney general's enlistment of the IRS to inspect his finances. The result: "The US Attorney in Tampa filed a complaint [in 1962] against Trafficante and three of his brothers, alleging specifically that Santo owed more than $46,000 in taxes." Kaiser said Trafficante wanted to "sue the government for libel," but Ragano talked him out of it. Kaiser then related Ragano's story from *Mob Lawyer* regarding preliminaries to the plot to kill JFK. He did not question Ragano's disclosure that he was the go-between for Hoffa, Trafficante, and Marcello regarding Hoffa's order that the president must be assassinated.

Utilizing Ragano's story with belief that it was credible, Kaiser set out a logical scenario for the assassination of JFK. He wrote, "In the fall 1963, the outlines of a conspiracy among members of organized crime to kill President Kennedy were becoming clear. It involved three of Robert Kennedy's principal targets, Santo Trafficante, Carlos Marcello and Jimmy Hoffa."

To aid his theory, Kaiser presented facts regarding the links between Hoffa, Trafficante, and Marcello. He wrote, "Frank Ragano made it very clear that Marcello and Trafficante were depending on Hoffa for a steady stream of loans from the Central States Pension Fund."[11]

While Kaiser had connected Hoffa, Marcello, and Trafficante based on their "business" dealings, the author had neglected another mafiosi with interest when probing the JFK assassination—infamous Los Angeles gangster Mickey Cohen. When his involvement is probed, the need for an even closer focus on Melvin Belli is required, one leading straight ahead toward Joseph P. Kennedy's complicity in the death of his son John, the president.

11 This flow of funds is confirmed by Hoffa's Teamster friend Frank "The Irishman" Sheeran in Charles Brandt's 2004 book, *I Heard You Paint Houses*. He was quoted as saying, "Jimmy's cut was to get a finder's fee off the [loan's] books. He took points under the table for approving the loans. Jimmy helped out certain friends like Russell Bufalino, or New Orleans boss Carlos Marcello, or Florida boss Santo Trafficante. . . . they would bring customers [for the loans]."

BOOK III

CHAPTER NINE

A Lighter Shade of
Gray

For five decades and counting, no one has cared, no one has believed that focusing on Melvin Belli and the Jack Ruby case could have made any difference in the search for truth regarding the twin assassinations.

How do we know? Because during official investigations including the Warren Commission and House Select Committee on Assassinations hearings, and in their reports, and in over *two thousand* books written about one of history's most significant events, any probe, even a surface one, of Belli and his representation of Ruby is simply left out of the picture, or considered a side issue to be handled with a light touch.[12] Significantly, neither the *Warren Commission Report* nor the *HSCA Report* bothered to include Belli in its findings. All but a few authors ignored Belli completely, despite writing perhaps as many as a million pages about the assassinations, causing any conclusions on their part to be vastly inadequate.

In *The Plot to Kill the President* (1981), arguably the finest book written about the assassinations, authors G. Robert Blakey and Richard Billings

---

12 This includes the assassination investigation by New Orleans District Attorney Jim Garrison in 1966. Author Joan Mellen's book, *A Farewell to Justice* (2007), which revisits Garrison's probe, contains no references to Melvin Belli.

dedicated nine pages out of nearly four hundred to Belli and his representation of Ruby. To their credit, in a chapter entitled "Jack Ruby: His Role Reconsidered," Blakey and Billings at least regurgitated the evidence the HSCA had considered regarding how Belli became Ruby's attorney in the first place. This meant there was interest in this issue, as well there should have been.

Blakey and Billings explained: "How Melvin Belli, a nationally known trial lawyer, was brought in to handle the Ruby defense, was a matter of some dispute. We heard a report that Seymour Ellison, a lawyer associated with Belli, got the phone call from 'a Las Vegas attorney' who said, 'Sy, one of our guys just bumped off the son of a bitch that gunned down the president. We can't move in to handle it, but there's a million bucks net for Mel if he'll take it.'"

The authors explained that Ellison did not recall who telephoned him; but no matter, his version of what occurred conflicted with Belli's, providing a clue for others to follow. This was the version where the famous attorney, said, Blakey and Billings recalled, that Earl Ruby "watched Belli sum up a murder defense in a Los Angeles courtroom and he asked him to take the case." Blakey and Billings then related the story that Earl Ruby had told them regarding his considering and then rejecting all Texas attorneys, and even famous ones such as Jake Erlich and Charles Bellows. This led Earl, the authors wrote, to contact Michael Shore, "a friend in Los Angeles," previously noted as being involved with Frank Sinatra's Reprise Records. Shore, the authors said, contacted Billy Woodfield, and he is the one who suggested Belli.

Blakey and Billings then recalled that "Belli told us he was Jack Ruby's only choice, and he said [Jack] Ruby told him he had 'checked him out.' We [the HSCA] were led to believe that Belli, who had probably come to his attention by representing a mobster and a stripper, was, in fact, Jack Ruby's first choice." Little did the HSCA know, as will be explained, that they had landed on a gold mine regarding many facets of the JFK and Oswald assassinations when they mentioned "a mobster and a stripper." Unfortunately, the Committee never followed up on what it had uncovered. Neither did Blakey or Billings or any other authors despite the obvious discrepancies in Belli's stories as to how he became Jack Ruby's lawyer.

To his credit, Vincent Bugliosi attempted to assess Belli's importance to the assassination scenario. Before tackling Belli's involvement in the Ruby case, Bugliosi criticized anyone who had proposed a conspiracy theory through their writings. He accused the authors of such books of distorting the truth with "their fanciful theories" and the fact that they "twist, warp, and distort the evidence, or simply ignore it." In the forty-six-page introduction to his book, Bugliosi *praised* the *Warren Commission Report* while downgrading the *HSCA Report*, stating that JFK "was probably killed as a result of a conspiracy."

While Gerald Posner brushed aside the mention of Belli in *Case Closed*, Bugliosi apparently decided he had to include Belli in the mix since it was obvious to him, as it should have been to the Warren Commission, the HSCA, and every author with interest in the truth about the assassinations, that Belli was at the center of the storm as Ruby's attorney, a pivotal player in any assassination probe. Therefore, Belli appeared frequently in *Reclaiming History*. But when he did, Bugliosi chose a convenient and deadly weapon to discard "The Belli Factor": another type of assassination—character—while playing loosely with some facts regarding Belli's actual entry into the Ruby case.

Instead of focusing on the important "why" involved with Belli's representation of Ruby in the main text, Bugliosi included, toward the end of the book almost as an afterthought, a short section of "bookends" chronicling "The Murder Trial of Jack Ruby." Here, Bugliosi's intent was to concentrate on Belli's quizzical defense of Ruby, and criticize his strategy. For at least doing so, he should be commended.

Bugliosi initially explained an important fact—perhaps one more important than he realized—that Belli was, at the time, a specialist on personal injury law, not criminal law but this did not concern the former prosecutor. Despite this knowledge, Bugliosi simply moved on to mention that Tom Howard, a Dallas defense attorney, was Ruby's initial counsel and that Howard wanted to employ a dual-purpose defense, one stipulating that Ruby was "emotionally unstable" while throwing him on the witness stand to plead for mercy. This would have resulted, Howard believed, in the jury wanting to "pin a medal on Jack" for killing Oswald. The result, according to Bugliosi's perception of Howard's defense strategy: perhaps a few years in prison at the worst. Next, Bugliosi reported that the Jack Ruby family didn't believe Howard had the credentials to represent Jack, and thus retained Belli on December 10, 1963. This was an important fact, but not as critical as probing further *why* Belli became Ruby's lawyer, something Bugliosi avoided despite having access to Belli colleagues, friends, and legal associates, including Seymour Ellison, concerning this aspect of the Ruby case.

Bugliosi, who had confused the dates Belli actually entered the Ruby case, focused on the Belli representation itself by attacking his courtroom strategies. Readying his assault on Belli—dead, and thus unable to defend himself—Bugliosi began by launching into a long paragraph, with inclusion of a footnote, characterizing Belli as "flamboyant," "married six times," and, as noted, "primarily a civil not a criminal lawyer." This was old news, but without further ado, Bugliosi moved into the case against Ruby. It was complete with facts about the trial atmosphere, the "imaginative defense" Belli decided to employ proving that Ruby was "temporarily" insane at the time of the Oswald shooting, the medical evidence presented, and jury selection after Judge Joe Brown denied Belli's motion for a change of venue. Criticizing Belli, he then called the famous lawyer's case "an extremely anemic defense," one doomed because no jury could disregard Ruby's guilt unless it was shown that he was insane at the time of the shooting. Since Belli didn't achieve this based on an incompetent defense, Bugliosi suggested, the guilty verdict was predictable.

Continuing to assault Belli's handling of the Ruby case, and to gain a sense of why the jury acted as they did in ordering him to be put to death, Bugliosi interviewed Ruby trial assistant prosecutor Bill Alexander for *Reclaiming History*. According to Bugliosi, Alexander told him the jury didn't favor Belli because of his lofty attitude and harsh remarks about Dallas. In addition, Belli's demeanor, flashy dress, and attitude were turnoffs. In a dandy of a conclusion, Alexander added, "The jury wasn't sentencing Jack Ruby, they were sentencing Melvin Belli."

Delving further into the reasons behind the verdict, Bugliosi presented quotes from "acclaimed journalist" Murray Kempton, a distinguished journalist and columnist and Pulitzer Prize winner in 1985. Kempton apparently told Bugliosi that Belli presented what amounted to no defense and the jury disliked Belli more than they did his client.

Having castigated Belli as being basically incompetent, Bugliosi then repeated a quote by former Belli partner Seymour Ellison that Belli was obsessed with being as famous as Clarence Darrow by gaining an acquittal for Ruby. Bugliosi commented, "Then Belli committed the ultimate sin of a trial lawyer, putting his interest before that of his client, particularly serious when Belli was playing with Ruby's life."

Apparently believing that Belli was only interested in winning so as to be compared with the great lawyer Darrow, Bugliosi never considered that Ruby's lawyer may have had other motives as to why he handled Ruby's case as he did, why he put "his interest" before his client's. Instead, he simply berated Belli's efforts, and left it at that.

‡

Since Vincent Bugliosi is the only author to date to spend considerable time chronicling Belli's conduct before, during, and after the Ruby trial, what did he miss that might very well have caused him to further investigate whether Belli had ulterior motives while defending Ruby? Based on the wealth of information about Belli available, he missed a great deal, but two omissions stand out.

Checking Bugliosi's book index, there is the absence of two names he either intentionally failed to include, or simply disregarded as being unimportant when it came to Belli and his conduct during the Ruby trial. One is Candy Barr, the infamous Dallas nightclub stripper and exotic dancer, and the other is Los Angeles-based mobster Mickey Cohen. Through each, clues exist permitting a better understanding of Belli and the Ruby case.

Even though these two were eyewitnesses to history, each was overlooked by not only Bugliosi but every journalist covering the Ruby trial, every assassination author and expert, and every investigation into the JFK and Oswald assassinations for five decades and counting. Certainly the truth was there for all to see, but those intent on discovering the truth were simply focused on other matters they considered more important surrounding the assassinations especially since the focus, the *only* focus, was on why JFK was killed. Later, the HSCA investigators were on the right track, aware as they were of two people, "a mobster and a stripper," who could add critical information about the assassinations. But the "mobster and the stripper" were not named, resulting in a dead end regarding any connection between the mobster, the stripper, and anyone associated with the two assassinations, including Melvin Belli.

The trail to uncovering Belli's true motives during the Ruby case thus requires a new line of thinking, that of combing the Dallas newspapers and any other sources *prior* to the assassinations to search for fresh information providing clarity about Belli's interaction with the Texas legal system, or Texas in general, *before* he agreed to defend Ruby. Interviews with any of those who interacted with the San Francisco barrister would then supplement whatever information was garnered from old newspaper clippings. These represented primary source material since they were published in close proximity to the Dallas tragedies.

Ironically, or perhaps not, in light of Belli's fascinating lifestyle and his known reputation as ladies' man, the key to understanding how he appeared on the Dallas legal scene begins with the story of the stripper, Candy Barr. Focusing on her may at first glance seem a waste of time when the ultimate goal of this book is to indicate how the betrayals of Joseph P. Kennedy caused the assassination of JFK. But as we shall learn, Barr is a key element in this search for the truth, one unlikely at first glance which may be why no one has ever noted a connection with the stripper to new information about Belli's possible motives for representing Jack Ruby, as well as other matters critical to understanding the Dallas events. Why? Because tracing Barr's footprint through the late 1950s and early '60s by way of newspaper accounts of her legal travails causes several names to

Candy Barr (right) and Joan Collins—1959. Striptease queen Candy Barr, sweetheart of gangster Mickey Cohen, a client and close friend of Melvin Belli's, helps actress Joan Collins rehearse for the 20th Century Fox production of Seven Thieves. *When Barr was imprisoned for Dallas narcotics violations, Cohen hired Belli as Candy's appeals lawyer before the Ruby case. Credit: Corbis Images.*

surface, many of whom played a significant part in the assassinations and the Ruby trial.

Barr was born Juanita Dale Slusher in Edna, Texas. She alleged molestation at age nine after her mother died. At 16, Juanita said she was forced to act in a pornographic film, *Smart Aleck.* Juanita then became a cigarette girl and exotic dancer. Because she enjoyed eating chocolate, she picked the stage name, "Candy Barr." She ended up in Las Vegas as a stripper making more than $2,000 a week, a huge sum during the mid-1950s.[13]

From Las Vegas, it was on to Los Angeles where Barr danced at the Largo on Hollywood's Sunset Strip, a notorious playground that gangsters like Mickey Cohen frequented. Returning to Dallas, she was a dancer at two clubs located near Jack Ruby's strip joints. By then, Barr had become quite well-known for her striptease act, one during which she dangled a Stetson from her left breast.

Beginning in January 1956, *Dallas Morning News* ads promoted Barr's appearances at the Jack Ruby's Colony Club as the "Sugar and Spice Girl." She was still appearing there when a *Morning News* front page headline read, "Charges Filed on Candy Barr." The story reported that Barr was charged with attempted murder less than six hours after police found her estranged husband Troy Phillips Jr. lying by the front door of her apartment, shot in the abdomen. Further details disclosed that Barr had shot him after he threatened to beat her up. Subsequently, police and the DA's office, headed by future Ruby prosecutor Henry Wade, apparently believed Candy's story, and the charges were dismissed.

Barr's life as a celebrity stripper continued to flourish until at the height of her popularity in late 1957 she was arrested on a charge of possession of narcotics. She swore a "friend" left the marijuana in question with her, but police did not buy this story.

At trial, Judge Joe Brown, the very same one later to preside over the Jack Ruby case, denied the defense any opportunity to prove police entrapment when he refused testimony regarding the identity of a police informant. During final argument, prosecutor Bill Alexander, later chief trial prosecutor at Jack Ruby's trial, told the jury during final argument, "[Candy] may be cute, but under the evidence, she's soiled and dirty." Barr was convicted, and a jury of eleven men and one woman fixed her punishment at fifteen years in prison despite her having no previous criminal record.

---

13 To indicate Candy Barr's popularity during her performing days, *Playboy* magazine listed her in 1999 as one of the twentieth century's most desirable women.

On April 27, 1959, two additional names appeared for the first time in *Morning News* accounts that would later connect to the Dallas assassinations more than four years later. The headline read, "Candy Given Aid in Fight" with the text noting "Dallas strip teaser Candy Barr got added help over the weekend in her fight to reverse a narcotics conviction and 15-year prison term. Former Los Angeles mobster Mickey Cohen announced in Las Vegas, where Candy is appearing in a show while free on $15,000 appeal bond, that he has retained a lawyer to fight the case. Cohen declared that he has hired San Francisco Atty. Melvin Belli to take the appeal to the United States Supreme Court, United Press International reported."

Four days later, a story detailing a mix-up regarding the dancer's bail bond began, "The former Dallas nightclub performer had the backing of onetime Los Angeles mobster Mickey Cohen, who professed his love for Candy and indicated he would propose to her. The chubby Cohen went to jail to see Candy and fired a 2-page telegram to Judge Joe Brown [asking for Candy's release]." Despite Cohen's intervention, Candy's appeal failed, and finally, on October 14, 1959, a *Dallas Morning News* headline read, "Judge Will Order Candy to Prison in Two Weeks." This order resulted from a Texas Supreme Court ruling which turned down her appeal. One note of interest appeared in the story: "Candy . . . was not available for comment. Her attorney, Melvin Belli, also could not be reached."

Unfortunately for Candy, all appeals were unsuccessful, and she finally entered Goree State Farm for Women in Huntsville, Texas to begin her long prison sentence. Later, the *Morning News* listed Candy's legal case as one of the top stories of 1959, indicating the strong notoriety she received across Dallas. She also made the pages of *Time* magazine for the world to see under the "Milestones" section where it was noted that "Married. Juanita Dale Phillips (Candy Barr), 24, a Las Vegas stripteasor sentenced to 15 years on a narcotics conviction whose unsuccessful US Supreme Court appeal was financed by Mickey Cohen."

When Barr's parole finally was approved by Governor John Connally, she was freed after serving three years and ninety-one days. She married and divorced before finally settling in a small Texas town. Bill Alexander told this author Barr called him for advice from time to time attempting to stay free from trouble that would land her back in prison.

All told, from the mid-fifties until her parole, Candy's name appeared in more than six hundred *Dallas Morning News* articles, many of them front page news. This meant that Judge Brown, prosecutors Henry Wade and Bill Alexander, and Jack Ruby, who operated his Dallas nightclubs during this time, were aware of Candy and her trials and tribulations. In fact, positive proof that Ruby knew of Barr was acknowledged by his attempting to hire her as late as December 2, 1963, less than two weeks *after* Ruby had assassinated Lee Harvey Oswald. A *Dallas Morning News* article headlined "Candy Spurns Ruby's Offer," read in part, "Former stripper Candy Barr . . . got a job offer from Dallas burlesque show operator Jack Ruby, her parole officers said over the weekend."

The parole officer added that, "Ruby talked with Candy Barr . . . about the possibility of getting parole restrictions lifted to let her be a stripper again. She turned him down, he said," meaning that Ruby apparently talked to the newspaper reporter. No details were given as to how "Ruby talked with Candy" since he was in jail at the time with no hope of being released on bail. This account is debatable, but that was the report, with no follow-up on how Ruby was able to speak to Barr appearing in further newspaper editions.

Later, it was divulged that Candy had become close to Ruby, and considered him a true friend when, after her prison release, he learned of her decision to raise dogs through a breeding business. To help her out, Ruby drove to Edna, Texas, where Candy lived, with the gift of two dachshund breeding dogs to help her get started. In the book *Candy Barr*, author Ted Schwartz quoted Barr several times regarding her relationship with Ruby. They included, "Jack Ruby was so taken with Juanita . . . that he began acting like her big brother," and further, "Dear Jack . . . he brought me several presents . . . two of them were AKC dachshunds . . . he also brought me an air conditioner . . . and then he gave me $50."

The Barr/Ruby relationship was confirmed on November 25, 1963, one day after Ruby killed Oswald, when Barr was mentioned in a *Dallas*

Morning News article comparing Oswald and Ruby. Among the observations: "Sunday's tragedy was played by men of opposite characters. Lee Harvey Oswald killed from a hiding place. Jack Ruby stepped before the cameras of a nation to cut down Oswald. Ruby was known as a loud-mouthed, good-natured heavyweight with many friends. Oswald was a sullen figure with a narrow group of acquaintances. Oswald dripped with political venom. Ruby would rather talk about baseball." Near the end of the article, the reporters noted, "[Ruby] gave a puppy to Candy Barr, [a] well-known Dallas stripper who worked a few doors down from Ruby's strip club." She also told the reporters of a telephone call she received shortly before the JFK assassination: "It was a call that Juanita would barely remember because it did not seem all that important at the time. [Ruby] was trying to get in touch with Mickey Cohen or some other mobster. Ruby was certain that Juanita would know [how]." How Ruby was able to call Barr and why Ruby wanted to contact Cohen is unknown, but author John H. Davis pointed out that "Ruby often boasted of his friendship with the legendary Mickey Cohen and took pride in the fact that he had had an affair with a woman [Barr] who had been engaged to the Los Angeles mobster."

Certainly the FBI knew of Candy Barr's relationship with Ruby. According to Davis, "It was no more than ten hours after Ruby's shooting of Oswald that the FBI came to interrogate Juanita concerning her part in an alleged plot to kill the president. The interrogation went on hour after hour."

Ruby trial chief prosecutor Bill Alexander was aware of the Ruby/Barr/Belli/Cohen connection telling this author, "I understood that Belli had told Cohen that he, Belli, could fix the Barr case through Judge Brown." The judge had acknowledged both Cohen and Belli in his book, *Dallas and the Jack Ruby Trial*, noting, "My first contact with Melvin Belli . . . had occurred five years [before the Ruby trial]." He then added, "When a Dallas bondsman went off [Candy's] bond, and a warrant went out for Candy's arrest, her gangster boyfriend, Mickey Cohen, telephoned me. I refused to talk to him."

To date, with the exception of one book noted below where a sliver of information is included, none of the above has ever been revealed, the absolute proof positive that Melvin Belli was known to Judge Brown, prosecutors Henry Wade and Bill Alexander, and by reference, and most important, Jack Ruby. The latter is critical in lieu of later disclosures by Ruby that he had no knowledge of Belli before he was hired, a certain falsehood due to Ruby's awareness of Barr's legal woes, ones where Belli represented her at the behest of Mickey Cohen, amidst the widespread media attention given to Barr's legal travails in the very city where Ruby lived, *before* the Ruby trial. Cementing this revelation is Jack Ruby's own words, noted above, to Candy Barr when he called her after shooting Oswald: "[Ruby] was trying to get in touch with Mickey Cohen or some other mobster."

Without doubt, Judge Brown, Wade, Alexander, and Ruby also knew that Belli represented one of the most dangerous men in America at the time, the gangster Cohen. It is also revealing that no journalist covering the Ruby trial, according to an exhaustive search of Dallas newspaper files, noted any of these connections during the Ruby trial, and no author or investigative body ever checked to see if such connections might exist. Why this is so remains a mystery but is perhaps understandable due to the clever Belli's deft ability to hide a secret, to shift attention away from him and his shady dealings with Cohen, connected as the mobster was to the same dangerous men who later surrounded Frank Ragano at the La Stella restaurant in New York City in 1966. These included Tampa don Santo Trafficante and New Orleans don Carlos Marcello.

‡

After Jack Ruby was arrested for killing Lee Harvey Oswald, articles in the *Dallas Morning News* shed light on Melvin Belli. One piece should have raised the proverbial red flag, causing reporters to stand at attention and probe further into Belli's possible ulterior motives for representing Ruby. Under the banner "Belli flashy in Dress, Colorful in Everything," the first paragraph read, "He fooled the nation's top attorneys by introducing mobster Mickey Cohen as an expert on income taxes [at the ABA convention in Miami]. He carries a wine-red Italian velvet briefcase and wears black boots when he strides into a courtroom. He buys his suits a half dozen at a time on London's Saville Row. This is Melvin M. Belli, the portly 55-year-old lawyer who will serve as chief defense attorney for Jack Ruby."

As the date for the Ruby trial neared in March 1964, the *Morning News* once again featured an article on Ruby's attorney under the head-line, "King of Torts Has Flair for the Colorful," noting, "His clients have included Mae West, gambler Mickey Cohen and Beverly Aadland, Errol Flynn's protégé."

Interestingly enough, if authors such as Gerald Posner and Vincent Bugliosi, each of whom left Barr and Cohen out of their books, and others pursuing the truth about the assassinations had checked Belli's 1964 book, *Dallas Justice*, they would have learned about his representation of Candy Barr, and in turn, about a rather startling development occurring *before* the Ruby trial. Here Belli acknowledged his representation of Barr by telling the following story: "Everybody in Dallas knows the story about Judge Joe B. Brown and Candy Barr, the striptease. Big city in size, small town in outlook, Dallas knows a lot about the lives of its public people, and the Candy Barr story was always the first thing you heard when you mentioned Judge Brown." Belli then added, "The striptease dancer was brought into Judge Brown's court on a narcotics charge. Soon, the story goes, he called a recess, invited her into his chambers, and talked her into posing for pictures. . . . " Regarding his knowledge of Candy, Belli wrote, "Furthermore, I had represented Candy Barr on appeal of her conviction, and I had sent Judge Brown a telegram in connection with it, I recalled, that was about as vituperative as you can get this side of libel. 'I remember you,' he said when we first met in connection with the Ruby case. 'You once sent me a [nasty] telegram.'"

Belli may have believed the judge held no grudge, but he could not be certain of this as the Ruby trial proceeded. At no point does Belli ever admit disclosing this information, potentially damaging, to Ruby, or his brother Earl, whom Belli said had hired him to represent Jack. This meant that Belli, by keeping a stilted relationship with Judge Brown secret, had violated legal ethics by being less than honest with his client.

If a State Bar Association had gotten wind of Belli not alerting Ruby to Judge Brown's possible bias in light of Belli sending him a "nasty telegram," the famous lawyer would have been subject to disciplinary action or even disbarment.

‡

To the authors' credit, a glimpse of the above information, but only a glimpse, connecting Belli to Cohen and to Barr appeared in the book *The Plot to Kill the President* by G. Robert Blakey and Richard N. Billings. Without fully realizing it, as Blakey basically admitted to this author, the two were close to learning the truth about Belli and his strange entry into the Jack Ruby case. They simply did not go far enough with the probe based on the clues that the HSCA had found during its investigation of the twin assassinations.

Recall that Blakey and Billings mentioned being led to believe that Belli had been Ruby's first choice as his attorney since Belli "had probably come to [Jack Ruby's] attention by representing a mobster and a stripper." Who were the authors referring to? As confirmed by Blakey to this author, none other than Mickey Cohen and Candy Barr.

This is also evident since Blakey and Billings chronicled the relationships Barr and Cohen had, beginning with the statement: "Ruby liked to tell friends that he knew Mickey Cohen, the West Coast hoodlum. He also knew Juanita Dale Phillips, a stripper whose stage name was Candy Barr." The authors then recalled how Belli represented Barr during the marijuana possession appeal prosecutor Bill Alexander noted before.

Regarding the connection between Ruby and Cohen, the authors wrote, "We could not be certain Ruby knew Cohen, who also grew up in Chicago, *but he admired him and tried to emulate him* [emphasis added]." Blakey and Billings then added, "Dean Jennings who was the AGVA (The American Guild of Variety Artists) branch manager in Dallas in 1956 and 1957, said Ruby 'was somewhat of a tough guy' who often appeared to be acting out a 'junior version of Mickey Cohen.'"

Deciding to pursue the "follow the money" theory many detectives use to solve crimes, Blakey and Billings wrote, "We [HSCA] made an effort to examine the financing of Ruby's defense, through Earl Ruby, who handled the money, but he apparently did not keep adequate records." Summing up, Blakey and Billings wrote, "We found it difficult to believe that Belli did not receive a substantial fee for his defense of Ruby." Whether he did, or not, remains a mystery, since bank records have long been destroyed.

Regarding what occurred at trial concerning Ruby's not testifying, Blakey and Billings challenged readers to ponder certain scenarios. They first noted that "Ruby did not take the stand in his trial. Belli would not let him," before concluding that, "The murder of Oswald had all the earmarks of an organized-crime hit, [including] an action to silence the assassin, so he could not reveal the conspiracy."

During an email exchange with this author, it became apparent that Blakey's knowledge of the new evidence uncovered by this author regarding "The Belli Factor" permitted him a stark realization. He concluded that if the HSCA had gone a step or two further and followed up on Belli's connections to Mickey Cohen and Candy Barr, and had noted Jack Ruby's knowledge of Belli through his friendship with Barr and Belli's representation of her during her Texas appeal, the commission may have very well decided that Belli's appearance in the Ruby case merited closer inspection. But, according to Blakey, the HSCA never fished in that direction, never headed down the Cohen to Barr to Ruby to Belli path. Regardless, Blakey told this author, "Based on the new information you have revealed, the possible connection between Jack Ruby's lawyer and the mob is certainly there. This sheds light on one of the darker questions about the assassinations."

If reporters covering the Jack Ruby case had uncovered Melvin Belli's representation of Candy Barr, realized that she was gangster Mickey Cohen's girlfriend, and then followed-up to discover that Belli was not only Cohen's personal lawyer but also a close personal friend, what conclusions could have been reached? As noted, common sense dictates that a warning sign would have appeared, causing members of the media to scream, "Wait a minute, why is the attorney for one of the most notorious mafiosi in the country, one connected to the very same men Attorney General Robert Kennedy is pursuing at the time, representing Jack Ruby?" But no one did, then or since.

CHAPTER TEN

Mickey

The *Dallas Morning News* articles could have been the starting point if someone had looked into the Mickey Cohen/Melvin Belli relationship and how it might affect a search for truth about the assassinations leading to Joseph P. Kennedy's doorstep, but there was no shortage of information about the infamous mobster. Author Brad Lewis dubbed him "a little man with a larger-than-life presence."

Cohen was the same underworld figure of whom Lewis wrote, "he was the most social of any mobster in history, he bridged the gap between Hollywood, Las Vegas, and Washington . . . he had the ear of many powerful people, including Richard Nixon, Reverend Billy Graham, and *Washington Post* columnist Drew Pearson." During the 1940s and '50s, reporters and authors who later wrote about the Ruby trial would have discovered that Cohen roamed Los Angeles as a cult hero. Formerly a bodyguard to Benjamin "Bugsy" Siegel, a textbook sociopathic killer, Cohen was described by former FBI Agent Bill Turner as the Los Angeles "front man" for powerful Mafia don Meyer Lansky, the Russian-born organized crime figure who along with Charles "Lucky" Luciano created a national crime syndicate. "We know because we wiretapped Cohen's telephones," Turner told this author.

Cohen was first arrested at age *nine*, for bootlegging. An amateur fighter, he was a bulldog of a man, who sported a receding hairline, a large, sloping nose, and deep-set eyes. During the late fifties full-length articles in the *Saturday Evening Post, Life, Look* magazine and newspapers across the country as well as an appearance on *The Mike Wallace Interview* and at a highly-publicized event at New York City's Madison Square Garden with Billy Graham made Cohen a household name.

If one of the journalists covering the Ruby case, or for that matter, any reporters or authors since, had made the Candy Barr to Cohen to Belli to Ruby connection, they could have easily discovered curious facts about the dangerous mafiosi through one man who had paid close attention to Cohen, none other than Robert Kennedy. RFK, citing "our investigation," wrote about the infamous mobster in his 1960 bestselling book, *The Enemy Within,* noting that, "Hoodlums [like Cohen] living reputable lives in Los Angeles have major vice and gambling holdings in the Midwest. They seek to corrupt and do corrupt public officials to an alarming extent." RFK also accused Cohen of tax evasion noting he reported income of only $1,200 in 1956 and $1,500 the next year with the explanation by Cohen that his lavish lifestyle ($275 for silk lounging pajamas, $25,000 for a specially built bulletproof car and at one time had 300 different suits, 1,500 pairs of socks and 60 pairs of $60 shoes) stemmed from loans from friends. Having RFK single Cohen out for special mention in *The Enemy Within* to the extent of disclosing what the mobster spent for pajamas must have been a personal affront, an embarrassment to the LA don.

Mickey Cohen's link to New Orleans Mafia don Carlos Marcello was unchallenged. In his autobiography, Cohen wrote, "[Marcello] is a beautiful person, a real gentleman who would break his nuts to do good for you or anyone he feels is right."

Cohen and Marcello had crossed paths in 1959 during the McClellen Congressional Hearings when the committee, investigating organized crime, subpoenaed both (a photograph taken depicts a dour-faced Cohen sitting across from the dour-faced "racketeer" Marcello, who is wearing sunglasses). The inquisitor for the committee was Robert Kennedy, of whom Cohen wrote in his book, "Senator McClellen only opened his mouth a very few times. But Bobby Kennedy, this snotty little guy, questioned like an out-and-out punk. . . . If you really want to get down to it, he didn't know his ass from a hole in the ground."

By all accounts, Cohen and RFK became bitter adversaries during the hearings. After Bobby kept badgering Cohen about his decision to take the Fifth Amendment and not testify, and whether a gentleman, which Cohen claimed to be, would do such a thing, he asked the suspected mobster, "What's the meaning in the underworld or the racket world when somebody's 'lights are to be put out?'" A smirk on his face while butchering the English language with nearly every breath, Cohen replied, "Lookit, I don't know what you're talking about. I'm not an electrician." He then wrote, "Boy, he [RFK] got hot as a pistol. He starts to come down off the podium where he was sitting with all them senators."

Cohen wrote that McClellen grabbed Kennedy before he could do so. "If he had come down there, there would have been a real Hey, Rube! in that joint. I would have torn him apart, kicked his f____ head in," Cohen stated. Author Tere Tereba wrote that RFK's near-attack of Cohen was because "Kennedy could not countenance being derided by a contemptuous California mobster. By the time the hearings were over, Bobby Kennedy had become a national figure. He also had created a personal enemies list: Jimmy Hoffa, Carlos Marcello, and Mickey Cohen."

Later, Cohen said RFK was responsible for the mobster's income tax evasion charges. Actually, Cohen was convicted twice. The first time he was transported to McNeil Island where he spent, as Cohen bragged, "Three years, eight months, and sixteen days." The second imprisonment was more prohibitive. He served ten years of a fifteen-year sentence, the majority at Alcatraz. Cohen alleged the "Rock," America's Devil's Island, which he dubbed a "crumbling dungeon," was "only for personal enemies of Bobby Kennedy."

When Alcatraz closed, Cohen, the leader of what jokingly was referred to as "the Mickey Mouse Mafia," worked in the same electrical shop at the Atlanta Federal Penitentiary earlier inhabited by Vito Genovese, Don Vito of *Godfather* fame. When an unstable inmate named Estes McDonald bludgeoned Cohen's head with a three-foot, lead conduit pipe on August

14, 1963, Melvin Belli was summoned. He represented his friend in a lawsuit against the federal government for $10,000,000, winning a $110,000 judgment. Tax authorities promptly confiscated the bounty, which Belli wrote in *My Life On Trial,* "included my fee," claiming it was due for back taxes.

When the friendship began between the infamous mobster and the famous lawyer was unclear, but Belli had first represented Cohen in the late 1950s. This occurred when Cohen cold-cocked a federal narcotics officer named Chappell who suspected the gangster was dealing drugs.

‡

Regarding Belli, Mickey Cohen wrote in his autobiography, "Attorney Melvin Belli and I were very good friends." Describing the scene at a Los Angeles hangout called Rhondelli's, which he co-owned, Cohen said, "We had a very fine restaurant there. Errol Flynn, Melvin Belli would be there. Liberace and his brother."

The San Francisco barrister returned the favor praising Cohen. "Was Cohen a crook?" he asked rhetorically in *My Life on Trial.* "On many counts," he answered, "I'd put Cohen up against the high priests and hypocrites in the ABA or some of the fixers in certain Washington law firms who never go to court. . . . I would have put Cohen up against J. Edgar Hoover himself. And certainly Richard Nixon."

Though Cohen was a convicted felon, and considered one of the most feared men in the country, Belli had a soft spot for the man. "To me," Belli wrote, "Cohen wasn't a 'pug ugly.' He was a gentleman of great courtliness and charm who was doing the best he could with the lot he had been given in life. . . . "

Displaying his affection for, and approval of Cohen, Belli and wife Joy, according to Belli's autobiography, let the gangster babysit for their six-year-old son Caesar while they were living in a home above Sunset Strip in Hollywood. Guests, including newspaper tycoon Randolph Hearst, were visiting when suddenly at the top of the stairs stood Mickey Cohen with little Caesar behind him. As the child shouted sounds emulating the firing of a gun while sticking a banana in the mobster's back, Cohen yelled, "Don't shoot, don't shoot." Belli began laughing, but several of the guests, he said, quickly darted out the door at the sight of the underworld figure.

‡

No truer portrayal of the Mickey Cohen that Melvin Belli chose to befriend, and represent, exists than the one painted in Cohen's FBI file. *Seventeen hundred and fifty-five pages* in length, it covered Cohen's life from the first day he received a parking ticket. From there, the "notorious and well-known LA racketeer" who was "considered to be the key underworld figure in LA," was being investigated for, among other crimes, extortion, gambling, kidnapping, narcotics, prostitution, armed robbery, shylocking, and murder. His arrest record stretched from 1933 and reached nearly every major city in the US including Los Angeles, Chicago, Albuquerque, Wichita Falls, New York City, Tampa, and Miami. Gangster tie-ins included Bugsy Siegel and Jack Dragna as well as John Stompanato, actress Lana Turner's boyfriend who was stabbed to death by her daughter. From June 1959 on, bureau mention of Belli's close friend would feature the words, "COHEN HAS KILLED IN THE PAST AND SHOULD BE CONSIDERED ARMED AND DANGEROUS."

To be certain, Cohen's celebrity was well-known across the country, including Dallas after Cohen appeared, the report stated, "on *The Mike Wallace Interview* ABC-TV" on May 19, 1957. Wallace described Cohen as a "colorful and notorious gangster who was convicted of income tax evasion."

The FBI report stated that during Cohen's incarceration at the Atlanta Federal Penitentiary in June 1963, the mobster spoke, appropriately enough, to the visiting Robert F. Kennedy, whose awareness of Cohen was well-documented in his FBI file. The entry explained, "While the A.G.'s group passed that part of the prison wherein subject [Cohen] was working, Cohen stepped out of line and spoke for approximately 30 seconds to the Attorney General. This conversation involved merely a remark or two on the part of Cohen and a reply from the Attorney General." Author Brad Lewis presented a different version believing that RFK sought Cohen's assistance in providing "extensive information about syndicated crime, and hoped to make Mickey an informant." To intimidate him, Lewis wrote, RFK, with reporters' cameras zooming away, cornered Cohen as he was stepping from the shower and asked, "How the hell are ya gonna live fifteen years in this goddamn chicken coop?" Cohen's face soured but he disregarded the remark and walked away.

According to the FBI file, a definite link between Cohen and Marcello was established. After the gangster served 10½ years of the fifteen-year income tax evasion sentence with release occurring in early January 1972, it was disclosed that Cohen, in ill health but able to celebrate with others at a "release party," visited several "mineral baths" in Hot Springs, Arkansas. According to the file notes, Cohen "called Carlos Marcello in New Orleans" and "planned to see Marcello in New Orleans before returning to Los Angeles." A later entry related, "[Cohen] in the company of an unknown individual, visited the office of Carlos Marcello, New Orleans LCN (La Cosa Nostra) boss and spent approximately an hour with Marcello. Marcello reportedly gave the subject $3,000 in cash which, according to the source, was not a loan."

Two questions appear considering the FBI notation. First, why did Cohen make the very first stop after his victory party a trip to see the New Orleans don instead of returning to his Los Angeles home or flying to another part of the country? Second, if the money was "not a loan," and a payment of sorts according to the FBI, then what was the payment for, since Cohen had been in prison for so long?

Certainly these questions may not be answered with certainty, but since Cohen made it a priority to see the New Orleans don first after the victory party, the long-standing friendship with Marcello Cohen alluded to in his autobiography was confirmed. This means that despite being in prison, Cohen, who also wrote in his autobiography, " . . . we went to New Orleans and I met Carlos Marcello. We talked about old times, among other things," had ready access through either telephone or intermediaries to contact Marcello or be contacted by him when an attorney was required to defend Ruby.

Regarding the $3,000 payment (worth nearly $20,000 in modern-day value) with perhaps more to come, common sense dictates that at least the possibility exists that Cohen may have been rewarded for his access to his friend and attorney, Melvin Belli at the time of the twin assassinations. If so, could this explain how Belli was actually brought in to represent Jack Ruby instead of Belli's conflicting accounts? The meeting between Cohen and Marcello, and the $3,000 payment having been

Carlos Marcello, Vincent Marcello, and Mickey Cohen at the 1959 McClellan Committee hearings. When committee counsel Robert Kennedy badgered Carlos Marcello, Cohen, and others during the hearings, RFK triggered hatred that would escalate towards retaliation against JFK four years later. Credit: Associated Press.

made certainly lends credence to the connection of Marcello to Belli through Cohen, a significant fact never probed before. Questioning the time lapse between the assassinations and when Cohen received this payment, more than eight years, is valid, but paying Cohen earlier when he was in prison made little sense. Linking Cohen to Marcello had been confirmed through author John Davis who had written, " . . . one of [Robert] Kennedy's most determined enemies was Los Angeles organized crime boss Mickey Cohen, who had links to Carlos Marcello . . ." He added, "[Marcello] had remained on friendly terms with West Coast mobster Mickey Cohen since the days when he and Cohen had sat together at the witness table during one of the McClellan Committee hearings on organized crime in 1959."

Cohen's FBI file also revealed another exchange of money that must have occurred when Cohen returned to Los Angeles shortly after meeting Marcello. A January 27, 1972, file entry noted that Cohen "received $25,000 from Frank Sinatra and that Sinatra promised Cohen additional money if he needed it." Answers as to why Sinatra, connected previously to Michael Shore through Sinatra's company, Reprise Records, paid Cohen are unknown but it may be recalled that Shore is the one who said he contacted Belli on behalf of Earl Ruby.

These facts throw another question into the mix: Is it possible that Sinatra was adding money to Cohen's bank account (nearly $137,000 in modern-day value) in addition to that supplied by Marcello for Cohen's work in aiding the cover-up years earlier through Belli's entry into the Ruby case? Is it also possible that Cohen, who resumed his friendship with, and representation by Belli, passed along part of the money Sinatra gave him to Belli, due him for representing Ruby? Efforts to confirm that this may have occurred are impossible since no records exist and any witnesses are dead, but in 1972, Belli continued to operate out of a Los Angeles office in addition to the one in San Francisco.

Mickey Cohen's connections to Belli were strewn throughout the gangster's FBI file. In 1959, entries confirmed that Cohen was in Las Vegas "accompanied by an attorney from San Francisco by the name of Melvin Belli, who arranged for Cohen to register as an ex-convict."

Another entry details Cohen's telephone calls, under surveillance, to "Melvin M. Belli, 8334 Marmont Lane, Los Angeles, California OL 6-664." This same entry reported, "Melvin Belli, mentioned previously, was owed a substantial sum of money by Cohen for legal matters he had handled for him." Later, Belli would be denoted, "a well known San Francisco attorney, who is better known for his work in the civil field," a reminder that Belli was not practicing criminal law when he accepted Ruby's representation.

Belli and Cohen's relationship went way beyond "attorney/client." Author Brad Lewis observed, "Belli and Mickey were real pals, socialized regularly, had many laughs together, and shared the same cynical world outlook." Lewis pointed out that Belli and Cohen, along with a future Israeli prime minister, met regularly to discuss various topics including the Kennedys. Then they would "adjourn to the home of Melvin Belli."

Ever the actor, the publicity hound, Belli actually flaunted his relationship with Cohen as was noted in a *Dallas Morning News* article. According to Belli's FBI file, at an ABA convention held in Miami in 1959, just four years before the Dallas assassinations, Belli introduced a "tax expert" as Professor Julian O'Brien of Harvard University. The "professor" proceeded to lecture the attendees with what Belli described as "an amusing pastiche which ended with altogether fitting proportion, "My advice to you guys is, 'Pay your taxes.'"

Duly impressed, the delegates to the convention began to discuss "Professor O'Brien's" speech that evening. As noted, they were shocked when they discovered that it wasn't a Harvard professor who had spoken to them but Mickey Cohen, the same mobster who had been charged with tax evasion. The *New York Times* chronicled the story under the banner, "Mobster's Lecture Embarrasses Bar." After detailing Cohen's appearance to discuss "tax evasion and other criminal cases," the reporter wrote that immediately after speaking, Cohen was questioned by detectives regarding the murder of Fred Evans, a gangster in Chicago.

Certainly Belli, as evidenced by this public prank with a noted killer, enjoyed the spotlight, enjoyed his relationships with those like Cohen who had broken the law. Belli either rationalized their behavior, and the physical harm they had caused, or simply relished being in the company of mobsters. Due to such behavior, doesn't common sense dictate that when a lawyer was needed in Dallas shortly after the assassinations to represent Jack Ruby, Melvin Belli was the logical, or more likely, the only choice by those who had masterminded the assassinations, those with links to the man ultimately responsible for JFK's death, Joseph P. Kennedy?

CHAPTER ELEVEN

Melvin Belli and
the Mob

Since the connection between Mickey Cohen and Carlos Marcello is well-established, one must focus on the Belli/Cohen relationship to realize the true story as to how and why Belli became Jack Ruby's attorney. This relationship is discoverable since, like his pal Cohen, Belli had an FBI file that is most revealing, one packed with information confirming Belli's reputation as not only a rebel who defined the word "antiestablishment," but also his close association with underworld figures including Cohen.

The two-inch thick, six hundred-plus page dossier provides insight into the mindset of an attorney who had the guts and savvy to take on any foe considered worthy. For this reason, by September 1959, four years *before* the Dallas assassinations, the FBI had been closely monitoring Belli. This was reflected in a United States Government memorandum: "The director has instructed that our San Francisco Office keep alert for any violation of law by Belli in view of his questionable record. Attached is a brief letter to San Francisco with appropriate instructions."

Unfortunately, the entire text of the instructions was marked out for security reasons, but the incident precipitating this memo concerned

Belli's shenanigans with mobster Mickey Cohen at the ABA convention in Miami.

On March 18, 1960, Belli's antics warranted an eight-page FBI account of his personal life. The report told of his marriages to date, his most famous cases, a recap of the Cohen incident in Miami, and Belli's defense of Cohen's girlfriend Candy Barr in Dallas. This meant the FBI had knowledge of Belli's representation of Barr and the links to Cohen *before* the Ruby trial. If anyone in the bureau including J. Edgar Hoover investigated why the gangster's lawyer was now Jack Ruby's lawyer, there is no mention of it in the file; this leads to the common sense notion that the bureau either ignored the connection or missed it completely. If they had followed up, perhaps the bureau would have investigated further and landed on the plausible Cohen/Marcello link noted before causing them to ask the question: Is it possible that Cohen and Carlos Marcello could have been involved in JFK's death? But focused as they, and Hoover were, as we shall learn, on the "Oswald Alone" theory for a variety of reasons, no follow-up was carried out.

‡

Since Melvin Belli died in 1996, he may no longer defend his actions in the Jack Ruby case. How he acted and what he said to friends, legal colleagues, and family, and wrote in his books are thus the only witnesses to his behavior with regard to the historic events that took place in 1963/64. They must be evaluated based on the facts as they are known, including: background information provided in his FBI file; his conduct before, during, and after the trial; relevant statements by those connected to the JFK and Oswald assassinations; and various clues left behind during the remaining years of his life.

As the Warren Commission, the HSCA, and the authors of every book written to date on the JFK assassination failed to discover, Melvin Belli was a bona fide Mafia wannabe. One interesting clue: Belli actually called director Francis Ford Coppola to request a screen test to play the role of Don Corleone in the epic film *The Godfather*. When Marlon Brando was chosen, Belli sulked for days with disappointment.

Belli was also a great admirer of the mob's rigid rule of honor, omertà, the "code of silence." It was based on a Belli staple—loyalty—which included, when appropriate, keeping one's mouth shut, not an easy assignment for a blabbermouth like him. During a six month friendship with the famous lawyer in the mid-1980s and while researching this author's book, *Melvin Belli: King of the Courtroom*, for publication in 2007, this author witnessed firsthand the common knowledge that Belli was quite verbose with everyone he met. Interviews of people who knew him best, for this book, confirmed that Belli loved to tell stories whether the stories were true or not. Above all, he loved the limelight and was a braggart of the first degree.

Belli, in effect, was a Mafia groupie who held court in his San Francisco lair like he *was* Don Corleone. To substantiate the claim, one only has to consider the words of Belli's chauffeur and close friend Milton Hunt. He told this author, "The whole Belli office was like something out of Chicago gangster movies." Having visited that office several times during the 1980s while working with Belli on a television series, this author may vouch for Hunt's claim.

To ingratiate himself with the mob, which he loved more than any woman, Belli hobnobbed with Mafia family characters from coast to coast. While it is easy to brush by the famous names like they are characters out of a novel, the fact remains that Belli represented and became friends with dangerous men who exhibited violence similar to the gangsters portrayed in the hit television series *The Sopranos*.

Among Belli's friends, clients, and associates were thugs, scam artists, blackmailers, arsonists, strong-arm bullies, thieves, extortionists, and mobsters like Mickey Cohen. In fact, those who failed to investigate Belli's background in connection with the representation of Jack Ruby may have been deterred by having fallen under the spell of the larger-than-life personas of the criminals he represented or befriended. Bottom line: Belli loved those who thumbed their nose at any authority, especially the ones who got away with it. One could speculate that Belli may have had just this thought in mind regarding his representation of Ruby, especially since he was denounced by the legal establishment from start to finish.

Little did they know of secret motives, ones never discovered, permitting him to hoodwink those who weren't clever enough to see through his true intentions at the Ruby trial.

Milton Hunt, who, along with longtime secretary Joyce Revilla, knew more about Belli than anyone, told this author his boss was "enamored" of the mob and other corrupt individuals. Revilla backed up this claim, telling this author, "Mr. Belli would never say anything bad about the Mafia. Or his friend Mickey Cohen. He represented Phyllis McGuire, who was the girlfriend of [gangster Sam] Giancana of Chicago. And one time, we talked about the restaurateur who had a great business and then ended up in a burger joint. When I asked him what happened to the guy, Mr. Belli gave me the impression that the Mafia had been on his tail." These remarks by Revilla regarding Belli's knowledge of the Mafia echo another by a Belli associate who wished to remain anonymous: "Mel was intoxicated with the Mafia," he told this author, "He loved the power, the money, the irreverence they had for authority just like he did."

Former Belli legal associate John O'Connor, responsible for revealing the infamous "Deep Throat," Mark Felt, and coauthor of *A G-Man's Life: The FBI, Being 'Deep Throat,' and the Struggle for Honor in Washington*, acknowledged to this author Belli's interaction with Las Vegas mobsters. O'Conner also witnessed Belli's representation of Andy Gatusso, a beer distributor from Chicago whom O'Conner believes may have been referred by the "San Mateo boys." Mocking the deep voice and Eastern accent of a typical mobster, O'Connor said Gatusso, who always denied he was Mafia, told Belli, "'Hey, I just want to make a living. Tell them I just want to make a living.' Next thing I knew, Mel made the problem, whatever it was, go away." Later, O'Connor told this author, "Mel was tight with Mickey Cohen and talked about him all the time. He certainly was one with connections [to the underworld] and my understanding was that he was approved as 'okay' by the mob."

"Belli loved for people to *assume* he was connected to the underworld," Milton Hunt explained to this author, "And he was. For some time, Mel was what I would call an unofficial member of the San Mateo mob. He never went to court for them, but he was certainly an adviser."

Daughter Jeanne Belli said the attraction to mobsters was easy to understand. "He loved the fact that they got away with things," she told this author. Belli's private investigator Jim Licavoli, aware that his boss's bookkeeper had ties to the Bonanno crime family, told this author, "Mel loved the mob and they loved him."

To Belli, Las Vegas was the Mafia playground, one he visited whenever possible. Bob Lieff, a former partner of Belli's, recalled that his famous colleague received first-class treatment no matter where he traveled in Vegas. "His connections were very extensive," Lieff told this author.

Seymour Ellison, the former partner who accompanied Belli to Las Vegas on several occasions, mirrored private investigator Jim Licavoli's statement verbatim. He told this author, "Mel loved the mob and they loved him."

Attorney Gary Logan, who represented Michigan investors when they bought the Aladdin Hotel, partnered with the Belli firm on several aviation cases. He was also co-counsel with Belli on the infamous "Angel of Death" case involving grisly murders committed by Michael Lane.

Logan recalled Belli's energy and the celebrity status that the seventy-three-year-old barrister enjoyed in Las Vegas. "Mel was sharp as ever then," he told this author, "going on all twelve cylinders. He was witty and had that wry sense of humor. I also recall how much he loved being around those associated with organized crime. He enjoyed their company and they basked in his glory since everyone in Vegas knew who Mel Belli was."

In early 1972, Lieff witnessed firsthand mob violence regarding those who crossed them. He also confirmed Belli's "connections" to these same underworld figures. This occurred during a divorce case Lieff handled with Belli in Las Vegas. Opposing counsel was Lou Weiner, whom Lieff told this author had affiliations with mobsters, including the notorious Bugsy Siegel. According to Lieff, Weiner and Belli were fast friends. Lieff said, "I remember that Lou had a copy of one of Mel's books behind his desk. It was autographed."

Lieff recalled that before he traveled to Las Vegas, he was warned by his local counsel to stay away. The next day a witness in the divorce met his maker when the Cadillac he was driving blew up. When Lieff told Belli about the case, one dripping with mobsters, Lieff said Belli laughed off the incident, telling him, "next time you're in Vegas, rent a motorcycle."

Belli's flip comment underscored his belief that friendship with dangerous mafiosi was ethically and morally correct. Perhaps this is why so many neglected to take the relationships seriously. And why so many never connected Belli to those who had masterminded/orchestrated the assassinations of John Fitzgerald Kennedy and Lee Harvey Oswald.

‡

While evidence that Belli was connected to Mickey Cohen, Candy Barr, and Jack Ruby was a given based on associations before, during, and after the Ruby case, linking Belli to any logical suspects in the killing of the president was not possible until 1994 when *Mob Lawyer*, written by Frank Ragano, was published. Delving more thoroughly into what James Hoffa, Carlos Marcello, and Santo Trafficante's attorney wrote about Belli, some of which has already been presented, indicates the definite link that was hiding in plain sight until the mid-nineties.

In his book, Ragano chronicled how Belli was hired to represent the mob lawyer in a civil lawsuit against *Time* magazine for libel. The allegations related, as noted, to a photograph the magazine published depicting Ragano next to several known mafiosi including Carlos Marcello. Ragano believed he had been libeled when the photograph caption indicated he was part of the Mafia as well.

Ragano wrote that during a delay before his May 1971 trial, Belli and Ragano, at Belli's urging, visited New Orleans. Ragano said District Attorney Jim Garrison was prosecuting Clay Shaw for his role in the JFK assassination. Belli knew Garrison and secured front row seats in the courtroom. For three days, he and Ragano watched the action.

One evening, Ragano swore, Belli, Ragano, Garrison, and female companions, including Nancy Ragano, dined at the famous Antoine's Restaurant. Belli, according to Nancy, inquired about James Hoffa, Santo Trafficante, and especially Carlos Marcello. Marcello, Garrison commented, was "highly respected" in New Orleans. Nancy was more interested in Belli's strange behavior. She told this author that "he walked into the kitchen and made us all go with him. Then he picked up a huge bowl of salad and began shaking it in the air with some spilling over on the floor." This bizarre conduct coincided with her feelings about Belli: "He was a real character. Mel thought he could do anything he wanted to at any time he wanted to because he was Melvin Belli and nobody could say anything. I was disgusted with his behavior. Maybe he was just too smart for his own good; brilliant, but eccentric."

In 1969, Ragano's friendship with Belli had been so solid that he had played host to Belli on a deep-sea fishing trip aboard a forty-foot schooner. It slept six and was owned by Jimmy Hoffa's Teamsters union. Hoffa was in prison at the time, but Ragano said, "[T]he vessel was at my disposal; all I had to provide for a day's outing was food and drinks."

Nancy Ragano recalled the fishing trip less for the fish caught than Belli's escapades with a curvy figure doll imported from San Francisco. "[Belli] proudly introduced her as having posed nude in a recent *Playboy* centerfold," Ragano wrote.

Months before the *Time* magazine verdict (Ragano, as a public figure charged with proving *Time* acted with "actual malice or reckless disregard," lost the case) the relationship between Ragano and Belli flourished. In early 1971, Seymour Ellison told this author he and Belli were Ragano's guests at the Super Bowl in Miami. They were two of 79,204 fans in the Orange Bowl who watched the Baltimore Colts defeat Tom Landry's Dallas Cowboys, 16-13. "Frank didn't show up," Ellison recalled, "but Mel and I had great fun."

Frank Ragano was amazed at Belli's inquisitive nature regarding mob figures. He wrote, "Keenly interested in organized-crime figures, Mel would never hear enough about Santo and other mafioso whom I had represented or encountered." Recalling other conversations, Ragano stated, "During the week we spent in New Orleans, Mel, who delighted in recounting stories of bruising battles in court and his legal jousts, never mentioned his most important contest, the Jack Ruby trial. Heeding Santo's admonition, I never raised the subject."

Nancy Ragano confirmed to this author Belli's fascination with the Mafia and her husband's suspicions regarding Belli's complicity in the assassination scenario. "What I recall was that Santo cautioned both Frank and me (we were going out on Hoffa's yacht for deep-sea fishing with Mel) not to talk to Mel about certain things. Frank never knew why he could not speak about Jack Ruby with Mel and I would not even attempt to guess at it." She added, "Actually, Mel was fascinated with members of the Mafia and asked question after question about certain alleged Mafia members and how well did Santo know them. I remember Frank changing the subject many times because he couldn't figure out what Mel's angle was in asking about them. I remember Frank telling Santo about the people that Mel asked about."

Frank Ragano's final note in *Mob Lawyer* regarding the Belli connection to the Kennedy assassination scenario appeared in the book's epilogue. While detailing his strongest reasons for connecting Hoffa, Trafficante, and Marcello to Lee Harvey Oswald and to the killing of President Kennedy, Ragano listed as "Point Number Seven" mentioned before: "Santo cautioned me several times in the late sixties and early seventies to avoid talking with Melvin Belli about Jack Ruby's reasons for murdering Lee Harvey Oswald . . . he was fearful that Mel might inadvertently say something that would lead me to connect Santo or Carlos in the conspiracy." The mobster's realization that Belli was a blabbermouth must have concerned both men. But Belli knew the penalty for breaking the loyalty oath of omertà. This is why he never discussed the Ruby case with anyone, perhaps fearful that he might become a victim like Oswald and Ruby.

‡

Asked whether linking Hoffa, Marcello, and Trafficante through Ragano to Cohen, Ruby, and finally to Belli made sense to him, Seymour Ellison, who was squarely in the middle of Belli's participation in the case, told this author, "It does. Mel loved Frank Ragano. Frank had unbelievable connections with the Teamsters and the mob and could really make things happen. He was like a shadow character. He lived life his own way. Mel liked that."

Ellison told this author that Ragano's connections gained him a powerful reputation. "Frank was the type of guy who could spit in the face of a highway patrolman," Ellison said, "and before they could arrest him he'd have the cop transferred to the deepest, darkest part of the world."

In Louisiana, Ellison witnessed Ragano's connections to the underworld. "We were in New Orleans for an ATLA Association of Trial Lawyers of America convention," Ellison said, "Mel took me to Mosca's, a restaurant outside the city [that was a reputed mob hang-out]. 'Frank [Ragano] has set up everything,' he told me, 'There will be more beautiful women, all available, than you've ever seen in your life.'" Belli was right, Ellison said: "Frank joined us later; and the girls, there were dozens of them all around. He was a true wise guy. I'd call him a schnora."

The restaurant Ellison described enjoyed a rich, if somewhat dubious history. In 1989, author John T. Davis wrote, "When Carlos would arrive at Mosca's usually accompanied by five or six of 'his people,' the whole place would turn into 'kind of a celebration.' Carlos would be greeted as if he were a king. Plates of steaming hot spaghetti with clam sauce would start streaming out of the kitchen in a steady procession accompanied by bowls of salad, loaves of Italian bread, and bottles of white wine."

While Mosca's was a Marcello favorite, he also frequented, according to author Davis, mobster Sam Saia's Felix Oyster Bar where Lee Harvey Oswald and his uncle Dutz Murret worked in 1963. Two doors down from Felix Oyster Bar was La Louisiana, owned by Marcello.

Interestingly enough, Belli, who discussed freely his association with Mickey Cohen in his autobiography, neglected to mention his friendship with, or the representation of, Ragano in the book. Belli also did not reference Santo Trafficante or Carlos Marcello despite his continuing curiosity about these dangerous men and other underworld figures. Why hadn't he done so?

CHAPTER TWELVE

Melvin Belli as Jack Ruby's Lawyer

Having detailed with accuracy Melvin Belli's ties to the underworld, both through his friendship with, and representation of, Mickey Cohen and Frank Ragano, the logical question to ask is how this fresh information impacts questions surrounding Belli's representation of Jack Ruby. And why inspection of the true reasons for that representation helps uncover the strategy employed by those who masterminded the assassinations, using Belli to their best interests and not Ruby's. This, in turn, continues the path toward indicating the plausibility of Joseph P. Kennedy's culpability in the death of JFK.

When it came to *how* and *why* Belli was retained, the truth became murky since Belli, as mentioned, apparently wanted the world to believe one of two stories that he told the press and later embellished upon in both *Dallas Justice* (1964) and *My Life On Trial* (1976). In the former, Belli swore that Earl Ruby had watched him perform in a "California courtroom" and "sum up a case" before asking Belli to represent Earl's brother. In the latter, Belli said Billy Woodfield and Lawrence Schiller, attempting to sell Jack Ruby's story, suggested Belli to Earl before the two men agreed to Belli's representation, and settled on a fee of $50,000 to $75,000, at Belli's Los Angeles home.

Certainly the discrepancy between the stories triggers a question: Why did Belli tell the two conflicting stories in two books written twelve years apart when the clever attorney had to have known that someone might question why he did so? Did he simply forget what he had written previously, or is it likely that Belli simply made up the stories, albeit loosely based on facts, so as to confuse anyone searching for the truth as to how he became Ruby's attorney and why?

Through the years, Belli was right; there were those like authors Robert Blakey and Richard Billings who became puzzled by his representation of Ruby, but conflicting accounts appeared causing confusion across the board. Regardless, inspection of these accounts lends some illumination as to what may have occurred and whether each is somewhat truthful, an exaggeration, or even downright false. Once the explanations are considered, then common sense logic provides clarity toward the most plausible explanation for revealing those who contacted Belli and hired/persuaded/ordered him to represent Ruby.

Belli's assertion that Earl Ruby recruited him in a courtroom after a murder trial appeared suspect to those who were suspicious of Earl's motives for hiring Belli. Chief among them was actually Earl himself. He told the Warren Commission he had never heard of Belli until journalist Billy Woodfield told him about the lawyer. This occurred after Earl, quoted in several sources, said he had telephoned Reprise Records executive Michael Shore at the behest of Jack Ruby. Earl's doing so provided a connection between Oswald's killer and Shore. Earl's exact words regarding the conversation with Shore were: "Well, I mentioned that Jack had said people were interested in a story on Jack and Jack had said to contact him [Shore], [and] ask his advice. And so he [Shore] says, 'Gee, isn't that a coincidence,' he says, 'because I've got somebody sitting right here in my office that would be the perfect man to do a story on Jack if one is going to be done.' And he says, 'his name is Billy Woodfield. . . .' So he says, 'I think you ought to come out here,' the conversation got to that, 'so we can talk it over.' So I flew out there a day or two later."

Earl reported Shore and Woodfield met him at the Los Angeles airport. "The first thing they say, 'have you got a lawyer yet?' I says, No. . . . I tell them what is going on [several lawyers were being considered], so I am not sure yet. So they start talking about Melvin Belli. I have never heard of him. . . . And they say, 'By coincidence he is in town. He is in L.A.'"

Earl and Jack Ruby's sister, Eva, backed up his account according to a reference in Frank Sinatra's FBI file. It read, "On 4/14/64, Mrs. Eva Grant, sister of Ruby, testified before the US Attorney in Dallas, concerning the selection of attorneys to defend [Jack] Ruby." Her recollection: "She stated that her brother Earl Ruby made a trip to the West Coast to see Mike Shore, who knew Sinatra there, and 'they' figured they would know somebody and that was how Melvin Belli came into the picture as a defense lawyer for Ruby."

Earl Ruby's version was revealing, but one man swore he knew exactly what had occurred: Seymour Ellison, Belli's law partner. Understanding who he was, and his connections to the underworld that Belli frequented, provides the context for his comments about how Belli became Ruby's attorney.

Belli's former partner was as much enamored with the Mafia as Belli. Ellison told this author of his friendship with a man he identified as "Pussy R.," former driver for Chicago mobster Dutch Schultz, requesting that Pussy's last name not be revealed. During Ellison's college days at Colgate University his roommate was Mitch, Pussy's son.

According to Ellison, Pussy was quite influential in mob circles. When Ellison and his first wife honeymooned at a fancy Cuban resort in 1955, Ellison mentioned at Pussy's suggestion, that he was "Pussy's nephew." which triggered a "comped stay" and a lavish dinner with none other than Meyer Lansky. "Later, two of most gorgeous women I had ever seen joined me and my wife at the big table. And then in walked Meyer Lansky. I couldn't believe it."

Ironically, Ellison would later, through his association with Melvin Belli, represent the Desert Inn and its owner, front man Wilbur Clark. "I was their lawyer to collect gambling debts," Ellison remembered, "This really heightened my profile with the underworld since I would call the gambler and tell him he owed the Desert Inn money. He would say, 'My lawyer says I don't have to pay because you can't enforce a gambling debt.' I would reply, 'Tell your lawyer it's not a gambling debt but a promissory note with the Desert Inn and that it is enforceable. Believe me when I tell you I never failed to collect the money owed."

If meeting Meyer Lansky was a shocker, representing Mickey Cohen was even more so, according to Ellison, "[It was 1961] and Cohen was in Alcatraz at the time and Mel asked me to help him. Apparently Mickey had buried a lot of money somewhere that the government wanted and that Cohen did not want some Italian rival to have. He struck some sort of a deal that he would lead agents to the money if they would release him from Alcatraz for awhile so he could spend some amorous time with his sexy girlfriend. To get him out, they needed a lawyer to file a writ of habeas corpus. I was to be that lawyer."

Ellison, then a partner in the Belli law office, said the whole matter unfolded in a clandestine manner. Ellison said he was ordered to appear in front of the Hunt's Donut Shop on Chestnut Street in San Francisco at six thirty in the evening. When he did, a dark sedan picked him up and whisked him to the pier near the Alcatraz launch site. "We stand there a minute and then through the fog, I see the lighter (small boat used to transport convicts) appear," Ellison told this author, "A limo stood by with this beautiful woman in the back seat as the shackled Cohen appeared. 'Where's my lawyer,' he said, and as two beefy marshals stood by, I said my name and the fact that I was Mitch R.'s roommate at Colgate. Cohen said, 'Great, I was at his bar mitzvah. How's Pussy?' I said he had died, and that was that as Cohen was led to the limo. It left, the marshals left, and I was left standing until a dark sedan picked me up. What a time this was, the great Mickey Cohen."

‡

While Seymour Ellison's representation of Cohen confirms the fact that Belli and his firm were involved with the gangster two years *before* the

Dallas assassinations and counting, of greater interest is the story Ellison told about how Belli became Jack Ruby's attorney.

During several interviews prior to his death in 2009, Ellison said he became involved by merely answering the telephone on November 25, 1963. "Mel was in Vegas a lot in those days," Ellison said, "He knew Wilbur Clark and others associated with the Mafia. The day after Oswald was shot, a telephone call came in to our San Francisco office from Vegas inquiring about Mel representing Ruby. Mel was trying a small-time case in Riverside [south of L.A.] and so I took the message and left it on his desk that he needed to call this guy back."

Belli was nonplussed, Ellison told this author, when he talked to him on the telephone about the Ruby matter, "He told me, 'Hey, Sy, I'm really into this case. Can you handle it? Tell them I'll get back to them tomorrow.'"

Ellison swore he carried out his orders and was told that Belli had to call by ten o'clock in the morning the following day. Three hours before the deadline, Ellison recalled Belli telephoned him. "Mel said, 'Did you call me last night and say something about the Oswald case?'" Ellison recalled, "And I said yes, that I understood from the Vegas people that Jack Ruby's brother Earl wanted to talk to him. Mel finally figured it all out and called Vegas and then talked to Earl and the two made a deal. I always was amazed because Mel almost missed out on the case of his life due to the piece of shit, worthless case he was trying."

Is this story credible? Is it even plausible that Belli, the arrogant lawyer with an ego the size of Texas, would react to becoming involved in the "Trial of the Century" in such a lackadaisical manner? Common sense requires dismissing Ellison's recollections especially since lapse of time, he told this author, caused the former Belli law partner to forget the identity of the Las Vegas caller who insisted on contacting Belli about the Jack Ruby case. "It was not Earl Ruby," Ellison said in the interview, "And not a lawyer. It was someone connected with what I called the 'gaming industry.'"

Years earlier, Ellison had told somewhat conflicting stories. In 1981, Ellison was more certain about the source of the call about the Ruby case.

He told author Robert Blakey that he had received it from "a Las Vegas attorney who said, 'Sy, one of our guys just bumped off the son of a bitch that gunned down the President. We can't move in to handle it, but there's a million bucks net for Mel if he'll take the case.'"

The identity of the caller, Ellison swore, was included in a memorandum in the Ruby files that Belli returned from the trial. "There were five or six boxes stuffed with them," Ellison told this author, "I remember that a memo also had a reference to Oswald, Ruby, Frank Ragano, and Trafficante, but I don't recall exactly what it said." Pressed for details on several occasions, Ellison could not recall any.

Belli, Tonahill, and Ellison's conflicting stories about how Belli was first contacted, and then hired as Jack Ruby's attorney, point to the confusion surrounding this important aspect of the Ruby case, one critical to understanding who masterminded the Dallas assassinations, and who may have controlled Belli's actions during the Ruby case. A separate account is provided by John G. Christian, coauthor along with former FBI agent Bill Turner of *The Assassination of Robert F. Kennedy*. During an interview with this author, Christian, based on extensive research, explained that Belli took the case "because the mob brought him in to keep Ruby quiet," a statement intimating that Belli may have had no choice in the matter. The offer to represent Ruby, Christian suggested, "was one million dollars, NQA [no questions asked]." Asked to elaborate, Christian said, "Listen, Mel would say anything for money, do anything for money. He had very little integrity."

Continuing, Christian reported that "Belli agreed to take the case before he ever boarded a plane [for Dallas]." At the San Francisco airport, Christian said Belli had a press conference where he told reporters, "I have been asked to represent Jack Rubinstein."

Christian told this author that Belli then left for Texas. "He had quite an entourage with him," Christian recalled, "Fourteen people or so. They rented ten or eleven rooms at a hotel." But then, Christian said, "someone called Ellison and told him the deal was off, that Belli was out as Ruby's lawyer because another attorney had gotten Ruby's ear. But then Mel came up with the psychomotor epilepsy defense and he became Ruby's lawyer."

Regarding how Belli became Ruby's lawyer, author G. Robert Blakey informed this author that he was told the story matching the one where Earl Ruby visited a murder trial Belli was handling and then snagged Belli for Jack Ruby's defense. Earl, Blakey said, disagreed with this version, telling Blakey that Belli was his fourth choice behind Percy Foreman, Jake Erlich, and Charles Bellows, each an experienced criminal defense lawyer unlike Belli. Earl's proclamation certainly conflicted with what Belli wrote in *Dallas Justice*: "It turned out I was Jack's own choice. He had lived in San Francisco for a time, and he knew of my experience with medical cases."[14]

Further, Blakey recalled, Earl said he spoke to Michael Shore, a friend in Los Angeles, who referred him to Billy Woodfield as a writer for Jack Ruby's life story. This scenario was confirmed by author Curt Gentry. He noted that Belli's story about Earl Ruby having slipped into a courtroom to watch Belli at the murder trial was false, writing, "Earl says he did not go to California to scout one of Belli's trials."

William Read "Billy" Woodfield, who died in 2001, was an Emmy-nominated writer and producer residing in Los Angeles. His scriptwriting credits included the television programs *Columbo* and *Mission Impossible*, but it was first photographs of Elizabeth Taylor and Jayne Mansfield, and then of Marilyn Monroe on the set of the film *Something's Got To Give*, captured without her wearing a bathing suit and climbing out of a swimming pool, that brought Woodfield fame.

The photographer's link to Frank Sinatra occurred when Woodfield designed record albums and magazine covers for Reprise Records, Sinatra's Hollywood-based company. A series of his photographs of Sinatra appeared in the book *Sinatra: The Artist and the Man*.

Woodfield, according to Earl Ruby's disclosures to Blakey, called Belli after Woodfield spoke to Shore. Belli allegedly called back and left a return message for Woodfield that said, "Get me that case—I want it so badly

---

14 Research by this author has uncovered no evidence in any investigation or publication indicating that Jack Ruby ever lived in San Francisco, or that he had any knowledge of Belli's "medical cases," casting doubt on Belli's assertions in *Dallas Justice*.

I can taste it." This confirmed the version of the story Woodfield's wife Lily told this author at her home in Los Angeles. After telling this author "Billy knew Belli before the Ruby case," she said Billy told her *"I want a lawyer I can control* [emphasis added]*"* whereupon he called Belli and left the message, "Do you want the case?" with Belli responding, "I want it so much I can taste it." Her husband, Lily said, also had told her at a party on the Friday night before Ruby shot Oswald, "He [Oswald] won't live to see the trial." Billy had mentioned how "connected" Michael Shore was, an obvious reference to his association with the Mafia.

Complicating these various stories is the revelation by author John H. Davis suggesting a Jack Ruby/Shore/Mickey Cohen connection. He wrote, ". . . after a mysterious trip to Las Vegas, [Jack Ruby] made five [telephone] calls that were most definitely suspicious. Three of these calls, made on October 25, 26, and 31 [1963], were to California recording executive Michael Shore, who was a friend of West Coast mobster Mickey Cohen. . . . " That Ruby had apparently spoken to Shore, who had definite links, according to Davis, to Cohen, three times within a month before the assassinations conjures up speculation about that connection, but no evidence as to the motive or substance of the calls has ever surfaced. Earl Ruby, as noted above, said brother Jack asked him to call Shore, at least confirming the fact that the two men knew each other.

Adding to the mystery is author Seth Kantor and his book *Who Was Jack Ruby?* He wrote: "Belli was 'approved' as Ruby's attorney. [Earl] already had checked out Belli through a contact in Chicago, [most likely Irwin Weiner] and had heard all-right things about the lawyer who had good underworld references. Jack Ruby was assured from mob figures that 'Belli was alright.'"

Examining the veracity of any of the explanations for Belli's becoming Ruby's attorney requires recalling one important fact: any statements that Jack Ruby did not know of Belli before his brother Earl contacted Shore, Weiner or others isn't credible, since Jack Ruby was aware of Belli through the attorney's representation of Candy Barr during the Dallas narcotics case prior to the Oswald murder. Whether Jack Ruby told Earl of this fact is unknown, but when Jack first heard that Belli was in the mix from whatever source, he must have rejoiced, since he knew of Belli's mob connections, especially with Cohen. This meant that Belli was "mob approved," a fact substantiated by Belli associate John O'Conner's statement to this author: "Mel was tight with Mickey Cohen and talked about him all the time. He certainly was one with connections [to the underworld] and my understanding was that Mel was approved as 'okay' by the mob."

Whether Belli and Jack Ruby ever spoke about the Candy Barr case and Cohen is unknown, but neither ever mentioned the connection to any journalist or author. Belli left it out of both his books, instead apparently concocting two stories that didn't mesh. Why Ruby was secretive about the nondisclosure is subject to speculation, but common sense logic infers he did not want anyone to know of Belli's underworld connections since that might trigger inspection of Ruby's own links to the mob.

While attempting to sort out the truth, one must recall mob-connected Chicago bailbondsman Irwin Weiner's statement to the HSCA that Earl knew of Belli and that "Earl wanted to hire him." This meant either Earl knew of Belli or Jack had told Earl about him. Either way, this presents a direct conflict with Earl's statement that he did not know who Belli was until told about him by Mike Shore in Los Angeles.

If anyone could have uncovered the Belli/Cohen connection, and reported at least the potential that Cohen and his gangster friends might be involved in the Ruby case, it was four members of the media who were close by during the hiring of Ruby's attorney: lead writer Bob Huffaker, an investigative reporter who broadcast on CBS and won an award for a courtroom interview with Ruby;[15] Bill Mercer; George Phenix; and Wes Wise. Their 2007 book, *When the News Went Live: Dallas 1963*, chronicled the evolution of Ruby obtaining counsel based on first-impression recollections at the time.

The reporters admitted knowledge of the bevy of competent criminal defense attorneys available to handle the "Trial of the Century," among

---

15 At the time of the Oswald assassination, Bob Huffaker worked for KRLD-TV in Dallas. His words, "He's been shot. He's been shot," screamed within a few feet of Oswald, alerted the world to Ruby's diabolical actions.

whom were the following: homegrown Dallas lawyer Tom Howard; Texas-based Percy Foreman, a true master of courtroom tactics whose most famous client would be Martin Luther King's alleged assassin James Earl Ray; San Francisco attorney Jake Ehrlich, whose flamboyant life in the courtroom provided the model for the *Perry Mason* television series based on his slogan, "never plead guilty," and Charles Bellows of Chicago, renowned for his courtroom theatrics. Each practiced criminal law as their specialty, something Belli only did on a sporadic basis, if that, since he was much more focused on big-ticket personal injury cases where damages stretched into the millions.

According to Bob Huffaker, "A few local lawyers showed up to bail Jack Ruby out, but Tom Howard was the only one left to represent him when the charge evolved into murder." Describing Howard, Huffaker called him "a veteran criminal defense attorney" and "a friend of Ruby's family." According to the book, he had been called by Ruby's business partner Ralph Paul, and "despite his low-budget operation from a storefront office with neither secretary nor law library," Howard was responsible for defending clients in more than twenty-five capital murder cases. No death penalty verdicts had resulted. In Huffaker's opinion, "[Howard] was very good at his job. And he looked like Harry Truman, even to his hat."

Huffaker said Howard was preparing a defense strategy focused on "murder without malice" carrying penalties of no more than five years. "But," Huffaker said, "Ruby's family thought that the case deserved a better-known attorney. Even though Charles Tessmer of Dallas and Percy Foreman of Houston, two high-profile defense attorneys, were available, Ruby's family brought in a far-fetched specialist to tort [personal injury] law" when a "California friend steered them to the flamboyant, self-promoting San Francisco plaintiff's lawyer, Melvin Belli . . . ."

From the moment Belli began repeatedly reminding Huffaker that his name was pronounced "Bell-eye," the reporter was skeptical of his motives: "Belli, the self-proclaimed 'King of Torts' loved the spotlight and prided himself in representing Hollywood's beautiful people, but clients had trouble getting between him and the nearest camera." Regarding Belli's motives, Huffaker believed ". . . he came to Dallas apparently determined that defending the vigilante avenger would make him a Clarence Darrow in the nation's eyes." This included portraying Ruby as mentally unstable, something offensive to Ruby, who, according to Huffaker, "fancied himself a hero . . . he was deflated when the King of Torts hired specialists to sully his righteousness with hints of mental problems."

With all due respect to Huffaker and his colleagues, no mention of Mickey Cohen, or for that matter, Candy Barr, appears in their book. Though there were suspicions causing a curiosity as to how and why Belli became Ruby's attorney, any thoughts to that end hit a dead end because they, like others who were eyewitnesses to history, had not recalled the Barr/Cohen/Belli connection a few short years earlier despite the *Dallas Morning News* articles and their media experience. This meant they missed the fact that Belli was connected to one of the most notorious gangsters of his time, one with connections to Carlos Marcello and other underworld figures.

The confusion surrounding Belli becoming Ruby's attorney softens when one realizes an important undisputed fact: out of all the qualified candidates in the country to defend Oswald's killer, including many of the most respected men in the criminal defense profession, a specialist in tort (personal injury) law with no experience in high-profile criminal trials became Ruby's lawyer. This illogical development, in hindsight, astonishing to say the least, certainly raises red flags, but it also points once again toward a more common sense explanation, the likelihood that Belli was simply contacted, through any of the intermediaries including Ellison, Shore, or the Las Vegas "gaming industry" by Belli's client and friend Mickey Cohen who was connected to Carlos Marcello and others that needed a lawyer they "could control," as Billy Woodfield put it, to defend Ruby. The latter inference is certainly plausible when it is recalled that the very first person Cohen visited after his victory party upon release from prison was Marcello where payment of $3,000 took place with another $25,000 paid to Cohen by Frank Sinatra.

If this occurred—that Belli was recruited by Mickey Cohen—with whom Belli was in contact throughout his prison sentence, either through the intermediaries or by Cohen himself, just after Oswald was arrested or immediately after Ruby killed Oswald, then it is no wonder that Jack Ruby was thrilled when the "mob approved" Belli, a man he knew was Mickey Cohen's personal attorney, agreed to be his lawyer. Little did Ruby know he had been set up for the kill since, as illogical as it appeared to the media and the public in general that Belli had entered the case, the defense strategy Belli employed was even more illogical, causing more warning signs to appear on the scene when the Ruby trial was over.

‡

Before assessing Melvin Belli's trial strategy, a very important quote from Ruby's attorney, one never disclosed before, must be considered. J. Kelly Farris, a close friend of the San Francisco attorney, told this author that during a restaurant discussion the two had shortly after Belli was told Lee Harvey Oswald was dead, Belli said, "Shit, there goes my client," an apparent reference to his representing Oswald, and then, "I guess I'll have to take Ruby's [case].'"

At face value, Belli's comments are alarming, leading to all sorts of questions, but when considered in light of what Judge Joe Brown wrote in the book, *Dallas and the Jack Ruby Trial*, Farris's recollections ring true. Referring to Belli's examination of Detective L. C. Graves, the officer who helped wrestle Ruby to the ground and take his pistol after Ruby shot Oswald, Brown is quoted as saying, "Continually during the questioning of this witness, Belli confused Ruby with Oswald. He asked the witness if [detective] Leavelle was handcuffed to Ruby [instead of Oswald]; asked the witness if he knew there was an armored car waiting for Ruby, rather than Oswald . . . but not once did Belli comment on or apologize for confusing the two men, one his client, and the other, the victim killed by his client. It was almost as if Belli thought he was conducting a defense for Lee Harvey Oswald for the shooting of President Kennedy."

Judge Brown's observation along with Farris's statement raises this question: Was Belli simply boasting to Farris? Or had Belli accidentally provided a most plausible reason, the true reason for his entering the Ruby case: he had already been contacted by the Mafia regarding representation of Oswald, or anyone else arrested for the JFK assassination? This would have meant that Belli was on "standby," ready to pounce on the Oswald defense after the dust cleared in Dallas. But then Oswald was killed, and now Belli would defend Ruby, according to what he told Farris, a plausible explanation for the remarks.

‡

Since the Ruby trial occurred within a few months of the JFK assassination, the focus was still on Oswald's being the assassin, the lone assassin according to all of the law enforcement agencies involved including the FBI. The public and the media certainly wondered why Jack Ruby had killed Oswald, but most believed he simply acted out of anger when he assassinated the most hated man in the world. When the trial was over, and the *Warren Commission Report* had been issued, most of the public and the media's thoughts were confirmed: Oswald was the lone assassin and Ruby simply killed him and should be put to death. Through the years, the focus of anyone attempting to question these beliefs focused on why JFK was killed, while ignoring the Ruby case. This meant dismissing any inspection of Belli's defense of Ruby since a jury had dismissed it as inconsequential. This line of thinking prohibited any thought of considering whether a focus on why, for instance, Robert F. Kennedy *wasn't* killed instead of why JFK *was*, a scenario that will, as we will learn, lead directly to Joseph Kennedy's doorstep as the one most responsible for the president's assassination.

If Belli's defense strategy had been scrutinized at any time before, during, or after the Ruby trial in light of his connections to the Mafia, the reaction might have triggered an *aha* moment since common sense dictates the strong likelihood that restrictions on the type of defense Belli could present were part of any deal by those who may have recruited/ordered Belli to aid with a cover-up. These restrictions would logically have included keeping Ruby silent about any orders he may have received to eliminate Oswald while making it appear that Ruby wasn't credible if he indeed had to testify and begin naming names as to who might have been involved with him in the killing.

If this occurred, then it is logical to presume that the clever Belli considered how he could defend Ruby within the bounds of the restrictions while still appearing to represent his client in a competent manner with an outside, against all odds chance of gaining an acquittal based on the chosen defense. The latter would have been Belli's ego talking, but he may have convinced himself the not-guilty-by-reason-of-insanity verdict was actually possible.

Always interested in the medical arena due to his expertise in personal injury cases, the wily veteran of the courtroom, after much consideration, must have determined that one defense fit all: the defense of insanity. Yes, this was perfect, Belli must have decided, since he could portray his client as mentally unstable so that even if Ruby did testify or opened his mouth after the trial was over, nobody would believe him. At the same time, it would look to the world as if the ingenious Belli had fulfilled his duty to Ruby by concocting an innovative defense. The one chosen was psychomotor epilepsy, unknown to everyone who first heard of the trial tactic.

When considered logically, this legal strategy made perfect sense. Belli may have been flawed in many ways, but no one questioned that he was a great courtroom tactician in a civil courtroom. To reporters close to the Ruby case, he was defending his client in an admirable manner; to his Mafia friends, those most likely to have hired/ordered him into representing Ruby, he was making it nearly impossible for Ruby to expose anyone who may have ordered him to kill Oswald. According to Belli's shaky moral values, he did what he thought was right. He knew that Ruby, who had later told Supreme Court Chief Justice Earl Warren, "I have been used for a purpose," was telling the truth; he had been used and then thrown to the wolves like a sacrificial lamb. Now Belli could try to save him from the death penalty while keeping his mouth shut and casting dispersions about his mental makeup. If this occurred, then the defense employed was not "anemic" as Vincent Bugliosi surmised, but in fact, brilliant despite Belli's inexperience with high-profile criminal cases.

To Belli's way of thinking, his job was to provide Ruby with the finest defense available within the restrictions imposed upon him by those who had assigned/ordered his representation of Ruby. To this end, and with the arrogance-driven thought that he could actually win the case, he gathered an all-star cast of psychiatrists, used every bit of knowledge and professionalism during Ruby's trial, and presented what everyone agreed was a stirring final argument. But he was bootstrapped into going for broke due to choosing the insanity defense since he had to make Ruby look like he was crazy *when no one else in the real world thought he was*. In retrospect, based on what happened, it was the only defense available, just as Ruby had been the only one the mob could trust to kill Oswald due to Ruby's fringe Mafia connections, his shaky financial standing, and the friendships he had with Dallas police, providing access to the basement where he could kill Oswald. If so, then Belli was the perfect lawyer to defend the perfect killer, the attorney with close ties to Mickey Cohen and his Mafia friends, the one whose office represented the mob-infested Las Vegas Desert Inn with Seymour Ellison. It was perfect all around until Belli could not convince the jury that Ruby was insane.

But this didn't matter to those controlling Belli because to the world Ruby *was* insane, or at least mentally unbalanced, due to Belli's insistence that anything his client said about the Oswald killing was dubious at best. This included statements Ruby made about "being used for a purpose" to Chief Justice Earl Warren, disregarded at the time and since.

Perhaps without realizing it, Belli also played into J. Edgar Hoover's hands since Hoover could argue that he and the FBI were powerless to have prevented either JFK's killing or Oswald's since a "nut"—Oswald—had killed the president and a "lunatic"—Ruby—had assassinated Oswald. This saved face for Hoover, one reason he was so adamant about closing the door on any conspiracy theories immediately after the Dallas killings. No wonder that when Ruby took a lie detector test at his request, Hoover put an end to any conclusions as to whether he was telling the truth or lying by pronouncing, as noted, "In view of the serious question raised by Ruby's mental condition, no significance should be placed on the polygraph examination and it should be considered non-conclusive as the charts cannot be relied upon." Game, set, and match regarding Ruby's credibility, just as Belli had hoped.

No wonder the savvy Belli, as noted in the pages that follow, never discussed the Ruby case with anyone. He knew he had gambled with Ruby's life, he had sold out his client, albeit with the best of intentions: the misguided belief that he could save Ruby by convincing the jury he was crazy. This would have led to Ruby's release after a few years at most if Oswald's killer was pronounced sane by a medical governing body. By then, anything he said, Belli knew, would be discounted because of his unstable mental state. But, despite Belli's effort, the strategy, condemned by the jurors, did not work since the jurors never considered Belli's illogical defense plausible.

Ironically, while writing *Reclaiming History*, author Vincent Bugliosi had landed on an important point about why Belli was hired to represent Ruby, but he did not realize it. In his book, Bugliosi chastised those who disagreed with his "Oswald Alone" theory. After calling any conspiracy theories "utterly vapid and bankrupt," the former prosecutor mentioned those who believed that the mob ordered Ruby to kill Oswald while asking the question "Who was supposed to silence Jack Ruby?" Bugliosi then made light of the choice of Ruby by the mob to silence Oswald by arguing that no mobster would choose a man to silence Oswald who was known to be loose with his tongue, temper-prone, and mentally unbalanced. He then called both Oswald and Ruby "goofy," and the possibility that Ruby was ordered to silence Oswald "laughable" before suggesting that the mob could just as well have visited Disneyland and recruited "Mickey Mouse and Donald Duck" into the fray.

In his book, Bugliosi also included a joke about the potential for the mob to have ordered Ruby to kill Oswald by presenting a lengthy mock conversation between some fictitious mafioso and Ruby. The mafiosi assures Ruby that after some time had passed, "the guys will spring you."

What Bugliosi never realized was that "springing" Ruby was likely a part of any deal with Ruby to assassinate Oswald since, presto, within days after the killing, Belli appeared like magic. This occurred after Ruby's first telephone call from the jail had been placed to Joe Campisi, a call confirmed by the mobster to the FBI during a December 1963 interview. The *HSCA Report* had also noted that Campisi and his wife were the first Ruby visitors. He, as noted, may have very well told Ruby help was on the way in the person of a lawyer with mob ties who would "spring" him in a matter of months. Author Larry Hancock believed it didn't make any difference what Campisi said, writing, "Campisi need not have said anything to Ruby . . . his visit simply endorsed the syndicate 'code'; if [Ruby] kept his mouth shut, he and his family would be supported; if he broke the rules, he knew the consequences."[16] Unwittingly, Bugliosi had proposed a scenario fitting perfectly with what may have very well occurred based on the facts, especially those involving Belli's unexplained participation in the case.

One must wonder whether Bugliosi would have reconsidered his remarks if he had added "The Belli Factor" to the equation regarding who might have been ordered to "silence Ruby." Based on a common sense scenario, with Cohen having likely pulled Belli into the assassination mix through his representation of Ruby, amid instructions to keep him silent, and to further extinguish any possibility that he might be believed if he did talk by portraying him as crazy, Belli was indeed the one lawyer in the world to handle the "silencing" of Jack Ruby. This made perfect sense when one considers that men as smart as those masterminding/orchestrating the assassinations would have certainly had an exit strategy in place concerning both Oswald, if he was apprehended, and then Ruby, after he was enlisted to kill Oswald.

---

16 That Jack Ruby had more than a passing interest in the underworld is bolstered by, as previously mentioned, the undisputed physical evidence that a copy of a *New York Sunday Mirror* article about Joseph Valachi, the gangster who ratted on his fellow mafiosi before the McClellan Committee, and coined the phrase, "Cosa Nostra," was discovered in the trunk of Ruby's car after Oswald's assassination.

BOOK IV

CHAPTER THIRTEEN

Belli's Strange Defense of Ruby

Clarifying by whom, and why, Melvin Belli, mob-connected to the nth degree, became Jack Ruby's attorney permits extended interest in the most mind-boggling facet of his representation: the defense strategy formulated at trial. If it can be shown that Belli took a dive, threw the case like a fighter who throws a ten-rounder, this could help identify those who controlled his actions during the Ruby trial leading to the truth about the Dallas assassinations including Joe Kennedy's complicity in the death of JFK.

If Belli, the man of secrets, was truly acting on his own representing Ruby, then there is one argument to be made for the strategy he employed: that the attorney truly believed the psychomotor epilepsy defense was the best defense possible. If he was acting on orders from others, then inspection of the defense utilized must be considered with a nod toward why those pulling the strings were so concerned with what Ruby might divulge either by testifying or through post-trial comments. This would impact selection of a lawyer for him so as to prevent Ruby from testifying while implying to the rest of the world that he was crazy.

Without exception, no authors, so-called assassination experts, or investigative commissions concerned with the truth about the JFK and Oswald assassinations ever probed this area of interest except in passing. If they had done so, what would they have learned?

According to author Seth Kantor, when Melvin Belli and Earl Ruby flew to Dallas, Earl believed a meeting between Oswald's killer and the famed lawyer was necessary to see if the two were of similar mind about how to defend Jack. Belli, writing in *Dallas Justice*, disagreed with this conclusion, telling Earl they already had a deal, that Belli would decide on the proper defense. To emphasize the point, Belli told a swarm of reporters upon landing in Dallas that he was "in charge" of the Ruby case. The conflict in the two stories, Earl Ruby's and Belli's, is yet another question mark about Belli's participation in the Ruby case.

Understanding Jack Ruby's mindset at the time is important to considering why he would have permitted Belli to be "in charge." As noted, due to the publicity surrounding the Candy Barr case, Ruby must have known of Belli's connection to Mickey Cohen. In turn, Ruby knew Cohen was a gangster; one with a national reputation, one he idolized (recall Blakey and Billing's book comment that "[Ruby] . . . often appeared to be acting out a 'junior version of Mickey Cohen."). If this was true, and since Ruby, who would have given anything to *be* Mickey Cohen, knew Belli and Cohen were connected, it is no wonder that Ruby permitted Belli to run the show, to select the defense he believed could be successful, since he had no reason to question his judgment. Such a conclusion is backed up by Seth Kantor's disclosure: "Jack Ruby was assured from mob figures that Belli was alright."

Ruby thus trusted Belli to assist him without questioning ulterior motives. Recall that Belli said no plea bargain was possible, a statement Ruby prosecutor Bill Alexander disputed. In fact, Alexander told this author, "Belli never approached us about settling the case prior to trial. He never made an offer, no effort there. It was the opinion, and I was not alone on this, that the case needed to be tried so the public would know what the facts were. But if Ruby had wanted to plead guilty, there could have been the possibility of probation or short-term imprisonment because we did not want to see him convicted." Asked whether the prosecution ever made an offer, Alexander said, "I don't think so." Asked whether there was any mention of a plea bargain during trial, Alexander said, "No discussion at all. Belli was so sure he was going to win that it never came up."

Belli's refusal to even attempt to plea bargain Ruby's case is cause to wonder whether he was told by those directing his trial efforts that this was not an alternative. But that is pure speculation. Many lawyers never suggest settling a case, but with the death penalty a potential, one may question why Belli would not at least have made inquiry about keeping his client from being electrocuted. This line of thinking is bolstered by the knowledge that Ruby had not killed an ordinary person, but instead the hated man who had allegedly assassinated a beloved president. Alexander's statement that he, and apparently other prosecutors, did not want to see Ruby convicted and sentenced to death echoes many sentiments at the time. Regardless, Belli turned his back on any deal to spare Ruby the chance he could die if convicted. This attitude continued, as Belli never argued against Ruby being given the death penalty during his final argument.

If a plea bargain had been agreed upon, Ruby would have, in all likelihood, as lawyer Tom Howard proposed, spent a few years in prison, if that, before being released. But Ruby, whose mental state would never have been in question under that scenario, would have been able to shout to the world any information he had about the details of the Oswald killing. This certainly was not what anyone masterminding/orchestrating the assassinations had in mind, with the better alternative being a trial by jury where Ruby was alleged to be insane, one where there was never any risk of his tattling on anyone who had ordered him to kill Oswald since Belli's directive, his control of the case, made this impossible.

However, since, according to Belli, no plea bargain was available, two options existed: a not guilty verdict (impossible based on millions of eyewitness to the crime) or the insanity defense (possible, but unlikely in the view of everyone but Belli). In all likelihood, Ruby did not know that Belli never intended for him to testify, believing this was an open question.

To those around Ruby at the jail, it appeared he was stable, that, in fact, he had cooled down to where he made perfect sense when he talked to those permitted to visit him. This despite observations such as the one offered by Carousel stripper Janet "Jada" Conforto. She told the *El Paso Herald Post* in January 1964, "Ruby was totally unpredictable . . . completely emotional. One minute he is nice, and the next minute he goes berserk."

Such disclosures caused problems for those who believed Ruby was an instrument of death ordered by the mob, or anyone else, to kill Oswald. Warren Commission members had been the first to express this concern. They, and others through the years, believed Ruby must have acted on his own since there was no logic to the supposition that anyone could trust an uncontrollable, unreliable loudmouth like Ruby to silence Oswald. But author G. Robert Blakey had the answer for them: "The mob needed someone connected, but not connected. Someone who needed their support, and someone with access to the police department. Jack Ruby was the perfect one." Author Seth Kantor agreed: "The most logical person in [Dallas] to be brought in to perform the hit [on Oswald] was Ruby, a violent man who carried concealed weapons routinely, a police informant who could gain access to the police station without question and who provided police with regular favors."

Seth Kantor's remark, that the "mob needed someone connected, but not connected," was as appropriate concerning Belli as it was toward Ruby. Those who had masterminded JFK's demise were now masterminding how to rid themselves of Oswald's killer. Belli was indeed "connected, but not connected," the perfect choice to be Ruby's attorney as evidenced by the fact that no one ever linked Belli to the Mafia as they would have if another attorney, one directly linked to the heavyweight gangsters of the day, gangsters such as Trafficante, Marcello, or Sam Giancana, had taken the case. Yes, Belli was linked with Mickey Cohen, but no one bothered to probe that relationship then or in the years that passed.

What a team the two made; both had been chosen for their respective duties: Ruby to silence Oswald, and then Belli to silence Ruby. But Ruby did not know he was going to be silenced. With Belli's help, Ruby must have believed no jury in the world would convict him of murder, and if they did, the insanity defense meant minimal time spent in a mental institution before release. By no stretch of the imagination could Ruby have believed he would be convicted and sentenced to death. In all likelihood, that potential never crossed his mind since he had arguably the most famous attorney in the world, one with great credentials, one "mob-approved," one who represented his favorite mobster Mickey Cohen, in his corner. This comfort zone, and it disappearing at trial, may have led to Ruby's extemporaneous speech before appearing at the Warren Commission in June 1964. Emphasizing the words printed in bold indicate that Ruby may have been sending a signal to those who questioned his killing of Oswald and what had occurred at trial.

> The world will **never know the true facts** of what occurred. **My motives.** I'm the **only person** in the background that **knows the truth** pertaining to everything relating to my **circumstances. The people** who have had **so much to gain** and had such an **ulterior motive** to **put me in this position** I'm in **will never let the true facts** come above board to the world.

If Ruby did have a worry after shooting Oswald, it had to be the prospect that Oswald might *not* have been silenced, that he wasn't dead. Ruby must have agonized over this potential, one that meant he had not done his job as directed. How do we know? The answer was provided by Dallas police department detective Don Ray Archer, the policeman charged with placing Ruby in Oswald's jail cell immediately following Oswald's killing. He was the same Archer who later testified at Ruby's trial that Ruby had uttered the words, "You killed my President, you rat" shortly after the shooting. Archer also told the jury, "I said, 'I think you killed him [Jack],' And [Ruby] replied, 'I intended to shoot him three times.'"

In 1988, Archer agreed to an interview for the Nigel Turner-produced British documentary, *Viewpoint 88: The Men Who Killed Kennedy*. Facing the camera in a suit and tie with a receding hairline, oversized glasses, a square jaw, large ears, and a direct speaking style, Archer said:

[Ruby's] behavior to begin with was very hyper. He was
sweating profusely. I could see his heart beating . . . He
asked me for one of my cigarettes. I gave him a cigarette.
Finally, after about two hours had elapsed, the head of the
Secret Service came up and I conferred with him and he
told me that Oswald had died. This should have shocked
[Ruby] because it would mean the death penalty. I returned
and said, 'Jack, it looks like it's going to be the electric chair
for you.' Instead of being shocked, he became calm, he quit
sweating, his heart slowed down. I asked him if he wanted a
cigarette and he advised me that he didn't smoke. I was just
astonished at this complete difference of behavior from
what I had expected. *I would say his life had depended on
him getting Oswald* [emphasis added].

The impact of Archer's impression cannot be underestimated. But no
one to date who has researched the assassinations appears to understand
its significance, that this eyewitness to Ruby's state of mind had exposed
a huge clue to the almost certain likelihood, based on his reaction to
Archer's having informed him that Oswald was dead, that Ruby was actually *relieved* that Oswald was dead instead of the other way around. Instead
of screaming, "Oh, no, I am going to get the death penalty," or something
similar, he "became calm, he quit sweating, his heart slowed down." Since
he had told Archer, "I intended to shoot [Oswald] three times," it was no
surprise that Ruby wondered whether he had succeeded in killing Oswald
as ordered since Ruby had been able to only squeeze the trigger once.

Since Ruby was known to be the nervous, fidgety, hyper type, the kind
of behavior Archer describes in the jail cell is most revealing, spontaneous
as it was. Why else would he act this way unless he knew his greatest fear
was not possible legal punishment for his actions but possible repercussions if he failed to complete his mission to kill Oswald from those who
had ordered him to do so? Certainly, Ruby knew those behind the death of
JFK posed much more of a threat than the legal system, one he was quite
familiar with through his Dallas dealings with police and prosecutors like

Wade and Alexander. At the worst, Ruby must have felt that a slap on the wrist, a few years in prison at the most, might be the maximum punishment possible. But if he had screwed up and not done his job, payback was the penalty. But now because Archer told him Oswald was dead, he could relax since he had done his job and silenced Oswald once and for all.

Although he didn't know it, Ruby should not have relaxed, since those responsible for masterminding the assassinations turned their attention on how to deal with Ruby *even though he had done his job*. Due to his scatterbrained nature, quick temper, and loud mouth, Ruby had to have been considered a loose cannon by those who ordered him to kill Oswald.

Now, Belli would represent the loose cannon. Adding insight to Belli's perspective of the Ruby case was chauffeur and close friend Milton Hunt, who accompanied his boss to Dallas. He told this author Belli said, "*The Ruby case is fixed* [emphasis added]. I'm just going through the motions. It's simply being staged for the sake of publicity. There's an inside thing, and no way to win. It's a whitewash." Whether Belli meant the "inside thing" referred to Mafia controls placed on him, Hunt was uncertain, but Belli's use of the words "whitewash," meaning cover-up, and "no way to win," is alarming, an admission that Jack Ruby never had a chance based on the restrictions placed on his attorney by those pulling the strings.

These comments were reminiscent of the ones Belli uttered moments before the verdict. Recall his turning to Ruby after scanning the faces of tight-lipped jurors, and whispering, "It's bad. Take it easy. We expected this all along . . ." another indication that while Belli may have been confident of victory, he knew the chances of Ruby being acquitted based on insanity were slim to none. For Jack Ruby, that was the worst news possible. For Belli's controllers, it didn't matter since, one, Belli had panned Ruby as mentally unstable, and, two, he had never testified.

Even Jack Ruby gave up. Early in the trial, brother Earl said Jack told him, according to Seth Kantor, "Don't spend any more money on lawyers. They're gonna give me the chair. Just go on home and forget about me."

Based on this statement, perhaps Ruby finally realized he was the doomed, the one who was left to take the fall. Belli, his white knight, his paladin, had not succeeded. Instead, Ruby had been portrayed as crazy, and, if the jury did not believe he was, then the electric chair was the only option. Ruby must have been confused and dismayed but unable to change the course of events since Belli was in charge. When he told his brother, "They're gonna give me the chair," he could very well have realized that he had been duped, that Belli wasn't the saving grace he had been promised. Ruby knew he had, and he finally realized that those who had used him were using Belli to make sure Ruby was seen as mentally unbalanced so no one would believe anything he had to say. He was indeed the doomed assassin, one sentenced to die.

‡

As Jack Ruby waited day after day in his jail cell to attend his trial, he must have wondered, as others did at the time and ever since, why Belli chose the psychomotor epilepsy insanity defense to defend him. Absolutely no one associated with the case agreed with that strategy, including the Ruby family. Seymour Ellison told this author of his having warned Belli that the defense was a loser. Law firm partner Bob Lieff told a similar story.

Later, reporter Bob Huffaker joined the chorus of those wary of Belli's defense writing, "Before Belli arrived, Tom Howard had been pursuing the smartest strategy: get Ruby off with five years on murder without malice." This would occur, Huffaker suggested "by proving that the act had been impulsive, a sudden outburst of anger from an otherwise sane person." The reporter called Howard's strategy "a solid case." But, Huffaker surmised, "Belli insisted on being the star." When the Ruby family, during early days of the trial, was "appalled at Belli's flagrant courtroom behavior and his preening before the press," they "infuriated" Belli by suggesting he contact defense attorney Charles Tessmer. Who was he? At the time, Tessmer was a premier Dallas defense lawyer, a red-haired wonder boy dubbed later by the *Dallas Observer*, "a master magician both at trial and on appeal." During his career, he would represent more than one hundred and seventy-five people facing the death penalty, and never lose a single client to the executioner. The *Dallas Observer* called him, "The Don of Dallas criminal defense lawyers." Bottom line: Tessmer was a real criminal

Melvin Belli—King of the Courtroom. Belli's true motives for utilizing a psychomotor epilepsy insanity defense for Jack Ruby have never been scrutinized until now.   Credit: Nancy Belli.

defense lawyer, a courtroom heavyweight, who unlike Belli, a personal injury lawyer who dabbled from time to time in criminal cases, knew Texas criminal law like the back of his hand.

What was Belli's reaction when the Ruby family suggested that an experienced defense lawyer join the team? Reporter Huffaker wrote, "When Belli got wind of the overture to include Tessmer on the defense team, he refused to allow such a thing, and angrily confronted Ruby during jury selection." According to Huffaker, Ruby agreed to make his family "back off." He thus never realized that his mob-infested attorney was intent on pushing aside any other lawyer who might meddle in his strategy by questioning the absurd insanity defense. The "star" had made up his mind to defend Ruby his way and certainly without any intrusion from a real criminal defense lawyer like the experienced Tessmer, who wasn't taking orders from anyone.

Belli's co-counsel, Joe Tonahill, told this author, "Belli fell in love with the psychomotor epilepsy defense, and I couldn't get him off of it. He loved legal-medical theories, hell, he knew more about medicine than most doctors I knew. He thought a sophisticated jury would buy his defense, but we didn't have that kind of jury."

Tonahill said his intended legal tactics differed from Belli's. "I wanted to pursue the patriotic insanity defense," he said, "and argue that he was doing the Kennedy family and the world a favor. I also wanted to put Jack on the witness stand since I thought he could handle it. But Mel was afraid he'd blow up."

Thomas Howard, the Dallas lawyer who was briefly a member of the Belli defense team after being passed over as lead counsel, had his own suggestions for Belli regarding a defense for Oswald's killer. "I would have pleaded Ruby guilty to murder without malice," he told the *Dallas Morning News*, "which in Texas is worth five years in prison at the most." He believed the murder "had a pattern to it similar to just another nigger murder case—the kind of passionate thing that is expected to happen in black neighborhoods on Saturday night." Belli rejected this advice as well. Judge Joe Brown commented on what he thought Howard's defense strategy would have been had he been Ruby's lawyer: "If Howard had tried the case, I think he would have put Ruby on the witness stand. Belli has said he didn't do this because Ruby begged him not to, and [Belli] was convinced that Ruby would break down completely if he had to testify in court." Then the judge added an important point: "This, if it had happened, could have done more to convince a jury of Ruby's [mental] problems than the scientific testimony."

The prosecution, from Henry Wade to Bill Alexander, was baffled by Belli's conduct with Wade telling *Time* magazine, "It was as weak a case of psychiatric defense as I've seen. I would have tried to go for leniency." Alexander, asked to comment to reporters within days of the trial, first described the reaction to the famed lawyer entering the case. "We were sure scared when we heard that Melvin Belli was coming," he said. "I'd been hearing about him since I was in law school. Then he came into town like God on a sunbeam, spouting words all over the place. He's a real talkin' piece of furniture. I tell you, we had an inferiority complex around a high-class-talkin' gentleman like that."

Regarding Belli's defense of Ruby, Alexander then added, "Nobody was more surprised than we were when he started plumbering the case. He made things so easy for us, we thought it was a trap. We kept wondering when he would drop the psychomotor stuff and spring his real case on us. But he never did."

Summing up, Alexander, said, "Belli gave it to us by going for broke— all or nothing. He forced the jury, if it thought Jack had even a little bit of guilt, to give him the chair. He told them it was acquittal or nothing. You can't give the jury that kind of dare."

In a later interview, this one with author Gerald Posner, Alexander expanded on his comments. He said, "Belli took a good five-year murder-without-malice-case, and made it into a death penalty for his client. He came down here thinking he was going to teach us 'hicks' in Texas a lesson. He probably thought we had never heard the word psychiatrist before. Well, he put on this God-awful defense, and day by day Jack melted—he just looked worse and worse. . . . It was humiliating for Ruby. I actually felt sorry for him."

In wide-ranging interviews with this author, Alexander discussed multiple topics regarding Belli, Ruby, and the Ruby trial. Differing on some matters from previous interviews, Alexander, still practicing law in Dallas in his early nineties, was as sharp-tongued as he had been in his prime, when he was one of the most feared prosecutors in the country. Asked about his impressions of Belli, Alexander said he "was a damn good lawyer, in his field: personal injury, medical cases. He just felt he was going to roll into Dallas and overwhelm us. But he couldn't." Judge Joe Brown agreed, writing in *Dallas and the Jack Ruby Trial,* "I believe Belli reached Dallas thinking that he was going to swoop into the Court, dazzle the jury, and depart town a triumphant hero with a scrapbook of press clippings. He was going to utter the two magic words, 'psychomotor epilepsy,' he chose to use as Ruby's defense, and the legal ties binding Jack Ruby would snap. He was going to show us as quaint country hicks."

Ruby's chief trial prosecutor Bill Alexander's most telling revelations occurred when he discussed with this author the punishment alternatives for Jack Ruby. He believed that Belli backed the prosecution into a corner, one that hurt Ruby's chances to walk out of the courtroom a free man. Asked about the D.A.'s office's intentions in the Ruby case, Alexander told this author of the atmosphere present after Belli entered the fray. "It had to be first degree murder and the death penalty," Alexander said. "Lee Harvey Oswald killed the president and Jack Ruby killed Oswald. But Belli made the decision for us by daring us, daring the jury, to give Jack the death penalty."

Sounding somewhat disappointed even though several decades had passed since the Ruby trial, Alexander said, "What Jack Ruby did was take the best murder case in history [against Oswald] away from us. And he gave us the worst murder case in history. Hell, who can be mad at the guy who shot the guy who shot the president of the United States?"

Alexander, who finally left the district attorney's staff in 1968, laid out a scenario that he believed would have made much more sense: "After the prosecution finishes their case, the defense lawyer says 'we call Jack Ruby to the stand.' The questioning then goes like this—'Mr. Ruby, you heard the testimony from the prosecution witnesses. Is it truthful?' Answer, 'yes.' 'Mr. Ruby, then the evidence is true?' Answer, 'yes.' 'Mr. Ruby, is this the pistol that you used to kill Lee Harvey Oswald?' Answer, 'yes.' 'Mr. Ruby, did you own this pistol?' Answer, 'yes.' 'Mr. Ruby, so you killed Lee

Harvey Oswald?' Answer, 'yes.' 'Mr. Ruby, why did you do that?' Answer, 'Because he killed my president.' 'What penalty do you believe is right for what you did, Mr. Ruby?' Answer, 'I don't know, whatever the jury feels is right.' Defense lawyer—'defense rests.' DA—'pass on the witness.' What are you going to ask a man who admitted the crime?"

Alexander first refused to speculate on what the outcome might have been if the above strategy had been employed, but probed for an answer, said, "Suspended sentence. Who knows? Jack might have walked right out of the courtroom because he killed the man who killed our president."

‡

Apparently Jack Ruby lost faith in Belli as the trial progressed as well. According to newspaper accounts, at one point when his lawyer appeared weary, over-caffeinated, and on the verge of collapse to the point of telling the judge, "I am just too tired to respond to that one, Judge," journalists surmised that Ruby saw too much of himself in the fallen legal giant. Responding to one Belli outburst, Ruby turned to Joe Tonahill and said, "Why is he doing that, Joe?"

Forgotten through the years was the fact that Jack Ruby discussed Belli's representation in an exchange with Chief Justice Earl Warren during the Warren Commission investigation [pertinent points in bold]:

Chief Justice Warren.
Go ahead. All right, Mr. Ruby, tell us your story.

Mr. Ruby.
. . . **Mr. Belli evidently did not go into my case thoroughly, circumstantially. If he had gone into it, he wouldn't have tried to vindicate me on an insanity plea to relieve me of all responsibility, because circumstantially everything looks so bad for me. It can happen—it happens to many people who happen to be at the wrong place at the right time. Had Mr. Belli spent more time**

with me, he would have realized not to try to get me out completely free; at the time we are talking, technically, how attorneys operate.

Chief Justice Warren.
I understand.

Mr. Ruby.
Different things came up, flashed back into my mind, that it dirtied my background, that **Mr. Belli and I decided—oh yes, when I went to say that I wanted to get on the stand and tell the truth [about] what happened that morning, he said, "Jack, when they get you on the stand, you are actually speaking of a premeditated crime that you involved yourself in." But I didn't care, because I wanted to tell the truth. He said, "When the prosecution gets you on the stand, they will cut you to ribbons."** *So naturally, I had to retract, and he fought his way to try to vindicate me out of this particular crime.*

By the time Ruby made these statements, he must have realized, in all likelihood, that Belli had led him down the path to the electric chair. Instead of being the saving grace, Belli had, by all appearances, forsaken his client in the interest of those who had assigned/ordered him to defend Ruby at trial. Alexander and others had known it before he did, but Ruby must have realized he was the fall guy and would pay with his life. Not only had he been found guilty, but most everyone, except the jury, believed he was crazy. And he wanted to tell them he was not, as evidenced by his statement to Chief Justice Warren: "*I wanted to get on the stand and tell the truth [about] what happened that morning.*"

One who continued to believe Ruby was sane, as chronicled in Elmer Gertz's book, was prosecutor Alexander. He actually *defended* Ruby in a hearing held during the appeal process. It followed a federal court hearing in 1965 where Ruby had exclaimed, "I never had any defense . . . I never had any defense."

The case was finally removed from Judge Joe Brown's consideration of any appeal after it was exposed that he was writing a book about the Ruby case. To promote the upcoming publication, the judge had appeared on the Mort Sahl television program where he discussed Ruby's trial at length. Having already shocked onlookers when he said that he thought Lee Harvey Oswald had not intended to shoot President Kennedy, but Texas Governor John Connally, but had missed him and hit JFK when he got "in the line of fire," Brown said he had "talked to the jury" and they had told him "that Belli offered them no alternative but either an acquittal or an extreme penalty." Brown then scolded Belli for never fitting the facts to the possibility of "murder without malice, a homicide committed under extreme passion created by passion or horror, or resentment or horror that renders a mind incapable of cool reflection." This verdict would have resulted in a maximum prison term of five years.

Once a new judge had been appointed to hear the initial appeal, the process moved forward with both sides agreeing to a Ruby sanity hearing. This finally occurred in March 1966 with the state, through prosecutor Alexander, presenting evidence that Ruby was indeed sane.

Called to testify, according to court records, were jailers and the prison doctors. Evidence presented included testimony that Ruby was a "pretty good gin rummy player" who "cheated occasionally," that Ruby "loved to read" and "knew quite a bit about current events," that "he has a very fine mind" and "exceptionally good memory," and that Ruby "worked cross-word puzzles." Alexander added to Ruby's portrait at the time by telling this author, "Ruby was always a little squirrelly, but he was sane."

When Ruby was permitted to speak at the hearing, he said, "I never tried to camouflage my true mental capacity . . . I don't know who conspired to do that [spread the story that he was insane]." Prosecutor Alexander summed up the State's position, "Jack Ruby is in a better position than his lawyers because he takes a realistic view of things."

At the end of the hearing, Ruby was adjudged sane. Such a conclusion causes additional concern about Belli's attempts to prove that Ruby was insane. If he did so, as appears logical, to discredit anything Ruby said about killing Oswald and to keep him silent at trial, then Belli committed a terrible injustice by making it appear that his client was crazy. Doing so, according to *every* lawyer associated with the case including his co-counsel and all of the trial observers, had resulted in the death penalty for Ruby when Belli could have very easily, as Alexander, Judge Brown, and others suggested, chosen a defense that permitted a verdict resulting in five years or fewer in prison.

If the attorneys surrounding the case were surprised at Belli's courtroom strategy and his presentation, the Ruby jury felt the same way. Foreman Wayne Causey, who had kept a diary during the trial, noted, as mentioned before, "The biggest shock of the trial came about 9:15 AM March 11, when Mr. Belli rose to his feet and told the court, 'the defense rests,'" Causey then wrote, "I personally feel that Mr. Belli and his team selected a nearly impossible defense for Ruby. . . . In my layman's opinion, any good lawyer could have gotten Ruby off with something less than a death sentence if he had thrown Ruby on the mercy of the court and pleaded plain old 'temporary insanity' brought on by emotional stress over the loss of [Ruby's] beloved president."

Ironically, one letter to Judge Brown Causey included in his book contained an interesting notion: "As for Melvin Belli . . . I just can't realize how in the world he ever got to be an outstanding lawyer. Looks as if he was bribed and is only putting in an act, he precisely chose the least defensible angle for a fruitful defense." Juror Douglas J. Sowell, quoted in the book, said, "Yeah, [Belli] was too flashy. We didn't need that. I mean, he was like a popcorn salesman at a fair or something. He didn't give me the impression that he was a lawyer. He didn't conduct himself like a lawyer, even during the trial. . . . Belli hurt his case."

Analyzing the trial, Northwestern Law School Professor Jon R. Waltz was especially critical, noting, "The American legal system foundered badly at the trial level in Jack Ruby's case. A national news magazine referred to it later as a 'legal disaster.'" Waltz then quoted another law professor, Lawrence Friedman, who wrote in the *Wisconsin Law Journal* that the

Ruby trial was "an American tragedy" while stating that, in his view, the trial judge and Belli, among others, "stood indicted of incompetence or worse." Waltz then concluded, "There was no wedding of law and science at the trial of Jack Ruby . . . [there was a] stench [to the] Ruby trial."

Despite the "stench," no one at the time or since bothered to investigate why the trial was "an American tragedy." Why? Because Melvin Belli, the man with the secret, the man retained/ordered to represent Ruby, had hoodwinked, sucked everyone—his client, his co-counsel, the prosecution, the judge, Ruby's family, the media, and yes, later on, every investigative body and every author writing about the twin assassinations—into believing that he was something he was not: a trial lawyer acting with the best interest of his client. Belli had worn a mask; he was deceptive. He was the errand boy, the missive to make certain Ruby went down for the count so as to protect those who masterminded/orchestrated the Dallas killings.

This becomes clear when one considers Belli's brilliant ruse: that the jury really wasn't his ultimate audience. Oh yes, if he could convince them Ruby was insane so much the better, but Belli, from the moment he was hired/ordered to represent Oswald's killer, was speaking certainly to the court of public opinion but more to those who might investigate the Dallas assassinations since they would be the ones threatening to uncover any conspiracy to kill JFK. Using the media to his best interest through newspaper and magazine articles and his outbursts about Ruby being crazy, Belli created a portrait of Ruby as mentally deranged through the psychiatric reports, ones reported in the media before the trial and during it. Belli may not have been able to convince twelve jurors Ruby was crazy, perhaps because, as some noted, the jury did not care for Belli himself and his trial tactics, but to most looking on, including reporters and those who would ultimately either sit on investigative bodies or write about the assassinations, the San Francisco barrister succeeded, with his client the clear loser, due to Belli having cleverly planted the seed from day one that Ruby was mentally incompetent, since crazy men don't get second chances at believability. Nobody cared anymore what Ruby had to say, not then, not since. Melvin Belli, the illogical lawyer with the illogical trial strategy, had done his job protecting those who masterminded the assassinations.

CHAPTER FOURTEEN

Belli's Curious Silence

On the wayward trail that will lead to the one man, more than any other, ultimately responsible for John Kennedy's death, Joseph P. Kennedy, it is important to consider what Melvin Belli said after the Jack Ruby trial and what he did not say.

When Ruby suddenly died of lung cancer in 1967, Belli did not appear to be surprised. Carol Anna Lind, his office manager at the time, told this author that after learning of the death, Belli said, "Something's not right. Maybe *they* injected Ruby with cancer cells." Others, including Seymour Ellison, who told this author Belli said the same thing "many times," all wondered what Ruby's lawyer knew that no one else did. Who was "they," and was it true that Ruby had been murdered? The very fact that Belli believed it possible that "they" had shut Ruby up for good by injecting him with cancer cells—farfetched, of course—is revealing.

Earl Ruby, according to various news reports, was certain that Texas officials, and those who ordered them to do it, simply let his brother die. "He told them all about the pain he had," Earl said, "But they thought he was a crazy man and kept giving him Pepto Bismol. I was there the day he died. A blood clot just went through his heart and killed him."

Two years earlier, in 1965, Belli telephoned Dr. Martin Schorr, a San Diego-based forensic scientist, who was later to become involved in the

Sirhan Sirhan/Robert Kennedy murder, after case regarding medical opinions regarding Jack Ruby. The telephone call to Schorr from Belli coincided with the death of the famed columnist Dorothy Kilgallen, called by conspiracy theorist and author Mark Lane, "the only serious journalist in America who was concerned with who killed John Kennedy and getting all the facts about the assassination."

Kilgallen had covered the Ruby trial during which a friendship with Belli was born. They dined frequently and Belli apparently confided in her and columnist Bob Considine. According to Lee Israel's biography of her, Kilgallen became suspicious during the trial of whether the federal government was being forthright concerning disclosure of important documents regarding the JFK and Oswald assassinations. To that end, she wrote a biting column that included facts from a ten-page letter Joe Tonahill had written to J. Edgar Hoover requesting the documents. Hoover declined the request. Kilgallen wrote, "It appears that Washington knows or suspects something about Lee Harvey Oswald that it does not want Dallas and the rest of the world to know." She added, "Why is Oswald being kept in the shadows, as dim a figure as they can make him . . . ?"

For reasons unknown, Kilgallen's column impressed Jack Ruby, who asked to meet her. To the irritation of the multiple reporters wanting to interview Oswald's killer, Judge Brown approved the meeting. Kilgallen and Ruby shook hands and chatted at the counsel table. She then wrote, according to Israel's book, "I went out into the almost empty lunch-time corridor wondering what I really believed about this man."

Kilgallen, a slight woman with deep brown hair and a pixy-like demeanor, was permitted to interview Ruby once more during the trial. In her biography, author Israel suggested, "This may not have been the first [private] meeting between the New York columnist and the accused murderer of Lee Harvey Oswald. [Joe] Tonahill received the impression that they seemed to know each other, that they related in a way that bespoke previous acquaintanceship." Author Israel also reported that Kilgallen "had a message to give to Ruby from a 'mutual friend' of hers and Ruby's." No identification of this friend was ever revealed.

The eight-minute discussion between Kilgallen and Ruby occurred in a small office adjacent to the courtroom. The columnist never wrote of the interview, instead telling associates that whatever information garnered would become part of a dossier she was preparing on the JFK and Oswald assassinations. A chapter on Ruby was also designated for a book Kilgallen was writing for Random House, *Murder One,* which was to contain startling new information about the assassinations.

In the fall of 1964, Kilgallen angered the government by securing a copy of Jack Ruby's testimony before the Warren Commission. *Life* magazine published it, triggering an investigation by the bureau regarding how Kilgallen possessed the secret document. During the ensuing months, she published articles denouncing the investigation of the JFK and Oswald assassinations. To several friends, according to Israel's book, she said, "This has to be a conspiracy."

During 1965, Kilgallen continued to complete her book chapter on Ruby. In October, while preparing for the TV show *What's My Line?* on which she was a panelist, the columnist, according to author Israel, told her make-up woman, Carmen Gebbia, she was "all excited." When the friend asked, "Is it Kennedy?" Kilgallen replied, "Yes, and it's very cloak and daggerish."

Kilgallen informed Gebbia that she was about to go to New Orleans to "meet someone who is going to give me information about the case." She told Gebbia, "If it's the last thing I do, I'm going to break this case." Regarding her opinions about the Warren Commission, Kilgallen told Mort Farber, an attorney and music talent agent, "it's laughable . . . I'm going to break the real story and have the biggest scoop of the century." She also told friend Shirley Martin, "This has to be a conspiracy."

Before Kilgallen left for New Orleans, she was discovered dead in her New York apartment on November 8, 1965; the cause of death, first listed as a heart attack, was revised to "acute ethanol and barbiturate intoxication . . . circumstances undetermined." In layman's terms, Kilgallen died of too much alcohol and too many pills. For many of those who knew her, the results were inconclusive. The true cause of death remains a mystery to this day.

Within hours after learning of the death, Melvin Belli telephoned Martin Schorr in San Diego. The attorney's exact words, Schorr told this author, were, "They've killed her [Kilgallen]; they'll go after Ruby now." Again, the identity of the "they" in "they've" and "they'll" was not disclosed. Is it possible that the "they" Belli referenced with Kilgallen's death was the same "they" he noted when Ruby died, and even perhaps the "they" RFK related to Justice Department spokesman Ed Guthman when he said, "There's so much bitterness, I thought they would get one of us . . . "

That Kilgallen was headed for New Orleans to "meet someone who is going to give me information about the case," and then died before doing so under somewhat mysterious circumstances, must be evaluated regarding that city being the home of Mafia don Carlos Marcello. The reporter could have gone to many cities, but New Orleans was her destination. With this in mind, her words, "If it's the last thing I do, I'm going to break this case," and "This has to be a conspiracy," take on new meaning in light of Marcello's hatred for the Kennedys—especially Bobby—and the likelihood, if Frank Ragano is to be believed, that Marcello and Trafficante had masterminded the twin Dallas assassinations. If Belli was correct when he said "They've killed her," then common sense dictates that Marcello could very well have been part of the "they" Belli referenced.

‡

While Melvin Belli was front and center during the Ruby case and screamed about the verdict, he quickly withdrew from public interest when attention turned to the *Warren Commission Report*. And when this investigative body applauded the "Oswald Alone" theory, it was game over regarding the need to further investigate the sad events in Dallas. Belli was never called as a witness; thus "The Belli Factor" was not a part of the eventual "no conspiracy" conclusions reached.

Belli's curious behavior contributed to lack of public interest with forging ahead with any further investigations on his part. The man who was known for his loquacious behavior was curiously silent regarding his participation in the Ruby case except for the conflicting accounts in two of his books. Associate Kent Russell told this author, "I pumped him about it because I sensed something was wrong with his representation. But he wouldn't give any thought or consideration to a conspiracy. He just kept saying how bad Dallas was." After some reflection, Russell added, "He just totally shut the door about Ruby. He didn't want to go there. I never quite understood that."

Close friend J. Kelly Farris recalled that Belli didn't talk about how he entered the case, instead concentrating on "problems he had with Ruby at trial" and with the judge whom he labeled a "cracker-asshole." Paul Monzione, a protégé of Belli's and arguably his closest associate during the later years of his life, also was rebuffed: "[Jack Ruby] was one subject he simply would not discuss. I said, hey Mel, you're the insider here, what really happened, but he wouldn't go there. He didn't want to touch that at all. And when it came to conspiracy theories, he wouldn't have any of that. He simply wouldn't discuss it."

What former FBI agent turned author Bill Turner recalled most about Belli was that he did not discuss the Ruby case. "I didn't bring it up and he didn't either," Turner said, "even in the presence of someone like Jim Garrison." This coincided with Nancy Ragano's recollection of the day when she and Frank had met Belli and Garrison in New Orleans: "Frank sensed that Belli was closer to Jack Ruby than attorney/client, and he couldn't figure out how close and he suspected that Belli was more involved with the mob than Frank knew. When we were out with Garrison, it seemed odd to Frank that Ruby was never mentioned by Belli in talking with Garrison about the various people they mentioned. Frank's intuition told him that there was more to Mel and Ruby than he could figure out and in turn Mel's connection to the mob. I think Santo didn't want Frank to know how close Mel was with the mob."

Office receptionist Maggie Quinn, who earned Belli's confidence, told this author, "It [after the Ruby trial] was about the only time he kept his mouth shut. He'd just say 'I can't talk about it.' I think he knew more than he ever let on." Secretary/receptionist Sharron Long concurred, telling this author, "He would talk about anything, but he stayed away from the Ruby case. That was most unusual."[17] Unusual, yes, but predictable since Belli was fully aware of the underworld's allegiance to omertà, the code of silence.

Belli's silence regarding another matter also adds to the mystery. Frank Ragano's *Mob Lawyer* suggested through Santo Trafficante's words of warning to Ragano including "Che, whatever you do you, don't ask Belli about Jack Ruby. It's none of your business," that Trafficante was not only familiar with Belli, but with his representation of Ruby. Surprisingly, Belli never took steps to refute Ragano's innuendos indicating that there was more to Belli's representation of Ruby than had been disclosed. In fact, Belli's inaction was telling since under normal circumstances where any sort of disparaging remark had been made about him, he would have marched to the courthouse to file a multi-million-dollar lawsuit for defamation of character. But Belli never did so, never commented on the book. According to Nancy Ragano, Belli never even contacted Ragano with such a threat.

Another part of the mystery concerns money. Various accounts including those from Belli, his associate Seymour Ellison, Billy Woodfield, and even Earl Ruby conflict regarding how much money Belli actually ever received. He acknowledged accepting $11,000 from Earl Ruby, although there is no indication where this money came from and a subsequent check bounced. This was confirmed by Seymour Ellison's disclosure to this author, "The first check was good, but the second wasn't. Then a third to cover the second bounced as well. I had to beg and borrow at the Pacific National bank to keep the firm going since Lou Lurie, our man at the bank, didn't care for Ruby. Finally, Mel had to meet Lou and convince him to fund us before the money was advanced."

If the firm was on the brink and that little money was earned from the Ruby case, one must return to the comments made by author John Christian to this author regarding Belli's presence in Dallas: "He had quite an entourage with him: fourteen people or so. They rented 10-11 rooms at

---

17 It may be recalled that, according to HSCA counsel G. Robert Blakey, the HSCA was stonewalled by Belli as well. He told this author, "Belli was interviewed but that went nowhere."

a hotel." This expense, which must have been extensive in addition to airfare and meals before, during, and after the trial, must also be considered in tandem with other costs, the fees and expenses incurred by the bevy of prominent psychiatrists.

Who paid these fees and expenses? Joyce Revilla, working for Belli in the San Francisco office, recalled that she assumed Mr. Belli fronted the money, but Ellison's comment that the firm was on the verge of going under questions this assessment. Attempts to reach Dr. Roy Schafer, the only one of the medical experts alive as of 2011, were unsuccessful causing only speculation that those who had retained/ordered Belli to defend Ruby may have footed the bill behind the scenes.

Evidence of such payment, or indications of who may have been the ones who retained/ordered Belli to represent Ruby could have been contained in the Ruby files Belli had collected during the trial. They had been deposited into boxes in Belli's office basement. Former Belli associate John O'Connor, who examined the boxes, told this author he wished he had copied portions since he was unable to recall the full extent of their content: "The [Ruby] files that I reviewed during my long nights in Belli's basement library were replete with the 'hair-trigger patriot' profile that the other lawyers thought a layup to get Ruby a reduced charge/five-year sentence."

Maggie Quinn, a Belli office receptionist who recalled receiving telephone calls for Belli from Mickey Cohen and ruthless mobster Meyer Lansky, and hearing the names of Carlos Marcello and Santo Trafficante discussed while she worked at the Belli offices, also saw the files. "We were told to leave them alone," she told this author, "I did because I was afraid of them."

‡

Rebecca Tonahill, Belli's co-counsel Joe Tonahill's daughter, offered fresh evidence regarding the motives behind Belli's representation of Jack Ruby. Speaking with this author, Rebecca revealed that she was seventeen years old during the trial of Oswald's killer.

"Father spent thirty-five years lying to us," Rebecca stated. "He was involved with bad people. He lied until his last breath," she said.

Asked to elaborate, Rebecca began by revealing that her father had been a co-counsel during Belli's representation of Candy Barr a few years before the assassinations. Rebecca confirmed that her father knew of mob involvement in the case, telling this author,

"Mom was frightened when he did that [represented Barr]. Mobsters and all. She didn't want him to take that case. But he wanted the notoriety. There wasn't any lawyer advertising back then and he thought the case would help him. He wanted the type of clients that Belli had. I remember my seventh grade teacher showing me a picture of the stripper. I was embarrassed, but Dad defended her with Belli." Asked whether Candy Barr could provide insight into the Ruby case, Rebecca said, "She knows more than anyone alive. She's afraid for what she knows."

Rebecca's disclosure that her father knew of the "mobsters and all" aspect of the Barr case prove Tonahill must have had knowledge of Belli's links to organized crime. One has to wonder whether he questioned Belli's account regarding how he became Ruby's lawyer, but, like everyone else hoodwinked by the famous barrister into looking in all directions except his, Tonahill was fooled. Or because of his fascination with Belli, simply didn't care.

Concerning the money used to assist Ruby's defense, Rebecca said her father and mother argued over it. "Dad would call and ask for money for this and that," she said. "And they would argue. Mom would say, 'What is this for?' and Dad would tell her it was for an expert or something like that." If true, this explains where at least a part of the money came from for the airfare, hotel, meal expenses, and to pay the medical experts' fees and expenses.

Asked if she would be surprised to learn that Belli and, through him, Tonahill were brought into the Ruby case by members of the underworld with a stake in the JFK and Oswald deaths, Rebecca said, "Absolutely not. Dad didn't want to get involved at first. He was afraid. But he went ahead. And this is not just me guessing about all this. Others have too. And Dad could keep a secret like nobody else. He sat on a lot of secrets. And he wanted to be like Belli."

Rebecca Tonahill's revelation that her father, a huge man, a bulldog of a man, was "afraid" is most revealing. Who was he afraid of? Certainly not Ruby. Not the prosecutors, or the judge? Was he afraid of Belli? Doesn't seem likely. More plausible is that he was afraid of the "mobsters and all" Rebecca referred to. His being afraid also raises the question of whether Belli might have been afraid too, especially to speak the truth about his involvement in the Ruby case. Certainly he knew the penalty for those proven disloyal to the Mafia.

Based on Rebecca's fresh revelations regarding her belief that the mob was involved in the Ruby case, one must ask what may have caused Belli to never think twice about accepting the representation. Did the mob have some information to hold over his head? Did the mob know of misdeeds by Belli, the man whom author John Christian said "had very little integrity." Certainly, Belli's business practices left something to be desired. Certainly, his private life was filled with splotches of scandal. Certainly, his representation of controversial clients such as Mickey Cohen and Candy Barr caused reason for him to bend the law if required. Perhaps Belli had secrets, and if so, perhaps the Mafia knew of these secrets and informed him that unless he represented Ruby, they would be secrets no more.

One possible explanation exists in a little-known entry in an obscure CIA file. The source is *Legacy of Secrecy* by Lamar Waldron and Thom Hartmann. In the book, the authors expanded on the knowledge that Belli visited Mexico City after the Ruby trial echoing Belli's own account in his autobiography, *My Life On Trial*. There, he called Victor Velasquez, "The great Mexican jurist." Waldron and Hartmann, using CIA file 104—10435-10001 as the source, depict Velasquez as a drug smuggler. In the CIA memo (F8593), dated April 1, 1964, Belli's one night visit with Velasquez is reported with the notation that the Mexican attorney's "reputation among local lawyers is shabby. While he [is] an effective defense lawyer with excellent batting average, [he is] said to be completely without ethics."

Another CIA file Waldron and Hartmann mention is undated but a companion memo bears the date, June 5, 1958. Several notations are included, but one focusing on Belli reads, *"Belli was reportedly involved in illicit drug traffic* [emphasis added] with Morris ELOWITZ in 1958. Elowitz was a suspected contact of [mobster] Lucky Luciano." In the same memo, a reference is made to Jack Ruby having met with Colonel L. Robert Castorr "to plan a Cuban smuggling operation." No further information is provided about Elowitz in the memos, and this author's inspection of the CIA file and other research sources produced no background material regarding him.

While questions may surround the Belli visit with Velasquez, there is no evidence this author has uncovered to indicate that the San Francisco barrister was "involved in drug trafficking" based on FBI files, extensive research, or interviews with those closest to the attorney. If true, this would provide one explanation for why Belli may have been assigned/ordered to represent Ruby and to keep him silent based on the threat by underworld figures to expose Belli's illegal conduct.

Regardless, there appear to exist substantial reasons as to why Belli may have felt compelled to represent Ruby, especially since Belli was a mob wannabe. If he feared repercussions from the Mafia based on their threat to expose him for any number of wrongdoings, ones that Joe Tonahill's wife recognized as being realistic, Belli did not reveal them to anyone. Never one to admit weakness, Belli's character flaws dictate that he would have kept any such fear to himself, afraid to let the world know that the great man could be controlled by underworld figures. True to this credo, he went to his grave without ever revealing the inside story of his most famous client, Jack Ruby.

Based on Belli having succeeded in portraying Ruby as mentally deranged so as make it impossible for anyone searching for the truth to believe anything he said, attention must now turn to the identities of those most likely to have masterminded/orchestrated the twin assassinations including the cover-up aided by Belli's efforts. When this occurs, when the common sense element of motive enters the equation, there exists a clear link to the one man who hated the Kennedys the most, the one man who had the strongest motive to kill JFK, *and those who caused the hate to occur.*

BOOK V

CHAPTER FIFTEEN

Motive, Motive, Motive

From the beginning of time, the saying "hate begets hate" has signi-fied an action/reaction scenario where the motive of revenge becomes paramount. Nowhere is this more significant than during a fresh look at the twin assassinations with the focus on why RFK *was not* killed instead of why *JFK was*. This permits certain plausible conclusions to be drawn leading to a clear view of why those who hated the Kennedys, specifically RFK, hated them enough to eliminate JFK. When this happens, the path to Joseph Kennedy as the one most responsible for JFK's death becomes clear.

Dealing with this element of motive based on revenge first requires dismissing a long-held myth about the assassinations, one pointing toward the fact that Lee Harvey Oswald acted alone. With all due respect to Gerald Posner, Vincent Bugliosi, and others such as Bill O'Reilly (*Killing Kennedy*) and even Stephen King (his *11/22/63* novel targeted Oswald as the lone JFK killer), who continue to advocate this theory, there is simply too much evidence to the contrary, much of it featured in this book. Hopefully, these men and others will agree, albeit reluctantly, when they add "The Belli Factor" and other fresh information presented here to the equation.

To be certain, "Oswald Alone" theorists must face the realization that additional evidence on several fronts during the past several years slaps their reasoning in the face. Various experts have noted the impossibility of Oswald having fired his weapon three times during the time sequence permitted (6 1/2 seconds) and the likelihood that more shots were fired and from other locations than the book depository, including the infamous "grassy knoll." In addition, in *JFK: The Case for Conspiracy* produced by Robert J. Groden, the finest medical documentary on the subject, several Parkland Hospital doctors provided eyewitness testimony clearly indicating that an *entrance* bullet to the president's throat culminated in a massive *exit* wound to the *right* side of the back of his head, ripping his skull apart. The angle of that bullet indicated that it could not possibly have come from the book depository but instead, in all likelihood, from behind a retaining wall on the grassy knoll. This means that others besides Oswald, if he did indeed fire at the president, were present, undermining those who advocate the "Oswald Alone" theory.

Conjecture about these aspects of the assassinations will continue into the ages, but when it comes to the importance of motive, there should be little to disagree about when the myth is considered. Why? Because throughout the exhaustive study of the assassinations, authors, self-proclaimed assassination experts, and investigative commissions have had one thing in common: difficulty in explaining motive, the Achilles' heel regarding any and all theories, save one.

The illogical attempt to establish motive on Lee Harvey Oswald's part borders on the ridiculous. The *House Select Committee on Assassinations Report* was only able to do so in general terms. Agreeing with the Warren Commission's perspective, the report listed possible motives as "Oswald's overriding hostility to his environment, his seeking a role in history as a great man, his commitment to Marxism, and his capacity to act decisively without regard to the consequences when such action would further his aims of the moment." These generalizations caused the HSCA to conclude that the Commission "offered a reasonable explanation of [Oswald's] motives to kill the president." The report later added, "It seems reasonable to conclude that the best single explanation for the assassination was [Oswald's] conception of political action, rooted in his twisted ideological view of himself and the world around him." This is the best the Select Committee, and before them in hindsight, the flawed Warren Commission, could do.

To be certain, Vincent Bugliosi, one of the chief advocates for the "Oswald Alone" theory, addressed the issue in his 2007 book *Reclaiming History*. But like every other author or investigative body attempting to avoid any conspiracy theories, he struggled with this matter. Bugliosi pointed out that Oswald was violent, angry, "a first class nut" who despised JFK and the society he represented before suggesting that there was "something test-tube" about Oswald, "something mechanical."

Bugliosi went on to assess the psychological profile of someone who might kill a president deciding that Oswald fit the profile perfectly. He mentioned that Oswald had the mental makeup and the motive to kill JFK before summarizing his belief that Oswald's actions were "consistent with his personality."

That's it. Nothing concrete, just an important loose end to be certain. Nothing about Oswald hating JFK, nothing evidenced by nasty letters to the president, speeches denouncing him, or even one witness who could verify Oswald's tirades where he threatened to kill Kennedy. If Oswald truly was "not someone who had the normal components of mankind," as Bugliosi lamented, then how in the world did this man single-handedly plan the attack on Kennedy with such precision? The answer: he could not have, a belief shared by more than 80 percent of the American people according to a 2012 Gallup Poll.

Despite this viewpoint, and evidence flying in the face of the "Oswald Alone" theory, those such as Gerald Posner and Vincent Bugliosi continue to perpetuate the very type of myth John Kennedy noted in a June 1962 Yale University Commencement address: "The great enemy of truth is very often not the lie – deliberate, contrived, and dishonest – but the myth – persistent, persuasive, and unrealistic. Belief in myths allows the comfort of opinion without the discomfort of thought." JFK could not have known that his words would wax quite prophetic when describing later viewpoints about his death, but they certainly do, with many of these myths "persistent, persuasive, and unrealistic."

Concluding as he did that there was sufficient motive for Oswald to kill JFK, and do so alone, Bugliosi ignored the learned opinion of others including David Scheim, member of the Board of Advisors of the Assassination Archives and Research Center who noted in *Contract on America* that "there was no apparent motive for Oswald" to kill Kennedy. Bugliosi and other "Oswald Alone" theorists will also not in all likelihood believe Ruby prosecutor Bill Alexander, who cooperated with Bugliosi on *Reclaiming History*. Alexander, an eyewitness to history who had firsthand access to mounds of assassinations evidence, told this author, "I never bought Oswald's motive. It just did not make sense."

‡

The names of every person who hated Robert F. Kennedy would extend several volumes. Bill Alexander summed up this point best when he told this author: "I was surprised that JFK got killed because I knew Bobby Kennedy was going to get killed. He was . . . a Kennedy who had been canonized, but I got a lot of telephone calls telling me how rotten Bobby was. As many people as he had screwed, ones like local law enforcement that he stepped all over, or with people he hadn't kept his word with, underworld people like [Carlos] Marcello, politicians and so forth; he just had too many enemies, many more than his brother."

Why did Alexander believe what he did, an opinion expressed by a primary source, an eyewitness to history, one who had his nose to the ground in 1963, one who was fully aware of the rumors and the facts regarding what was occurring in and around Dallas before JFK was assassinated? This was due to a gritty prosecutor paying attention to what was common knowledge: that Bobby had mortal enemies, ones who had killed before and would kill again, especially if their freedom or livelihood were put in jeopardy.

Among those with the strongest feelings toward RFK was Melvin Belli's pal Mickey Cohen. This ill-will dated back to the Cohen/RFK confrontation at the McClellan Hearings and because Cohen believed Bobby had fingered him for income tax evasion. Author John H. Davis described the Mickey Cohen/RFK relationship: "Kennedy [RFK] had singled out Cohen for intensive investigation and eventual prosecution." Author Tere Tereba chronicled RFK "leaping toward Cohen" in anger after a testy hearings exchange after Bobby had "aggressively pressed and prodded the West Coast gang boss, grilling him about muscling in on LA and Orange County labor rackets." Common sense indicates that Belli had to be aware of Cohen's hatred for RFK.

Besides Cohen, three RFK enemies stand out from the rest. Robert Kennedy not only intended to prevent these three from enjoying the power they relished and the multi-million-dollar incomes they earned through various illegal ventures, but he intended to send them to prison for the rest of their lives, or, in one man's case, deport him. Who were these men who hated RFK? One was the man Bill Alexander mentioned, Carlos Marcello, the bloodthirsty New Orleans Mafia don. The others are easily identified when motive is considered—Teamsters union president James Hoffa, and Tampa, Florida don Santo Trafficante. Inspecting *why* each had sufficient reason to harbor ill-will towards RFK provides the backdrop for understanding why the motive existed, why desperate men were forced into desperate action in late 1963: because they had no other choice.

To defeat these men and render them powerless, RFK's weapon was the Justice Department's Organized Crime and Racketeering Section, including what became known as the infamous "Hoffa Squad," a misnomer since it was intended not only to stop Hoffa but members of organized crime as well. To enhance its potential, Bobby, after he became attorney general, increased the force from 17 attorneys to 63, more than a 300 percent increase. Between 1960 and 1963, according to multiple sources, the number of days government attorneys spent in the field increased from 660 to more than 6,000, the number of days these attorneys spent before grand jury from 100 to more than 1,300, and the number of days these attorneys spent in court from 61 to more than 1,000. This increased workload, ordered by RFK, yielded a 500 percent increase in the number of defendants indicted (121 to 615) and a 400 percent increase in the number of convictions, from 73 to 288. While some applauded RFK's efforts to prosecute known criminals, author Gil

Reavill quoted one justice department official as saying, "Kennedy's zeal to break up the syndicates was reminiscent of a sixteenth-century Jesuit on the hunt for heresy."

Since James Hoffa was singled out by mob lawyer Frank Ragano as the one who told him to direct Trafficante and Marcello to eliminate JFK, examining Hoffa's bitter feelings towards RFK provides a starting point to ascertain who had the strongest motive to render RFK powerless.

To recognize the full extent of Hoffa's emotion, it's important to recall what Ragano wrote in his autobiography: "Hoffa hated the Kennedys as much as the two mobsters [Trafficante and Marcello] did. In the first months of 1963, Jimmy was consumed by the prospect of looming indictments and his animosity to the Kennedys. A day rarely went by without him unleashing his customary obscenities at 'Booby,' his unflattering sobriquet for the attorney general."

To emphasize Hoffa's ill-feelings toward RFK, Ragano detailed an incident where Hoffa actually attacked the attorney general, an indication of his true hatred for JFK's brother. This occurred when the two met in Washington DC so Ragano could inspect records to be used at a Hoffa trial. According to Ragano, RFK kept Hoffa waiting while walking his dog. Bitter words were exchanged when RFK finally arrived including RFK, according to Ragano, telling Hoffa, "I'm in charge, not you." Ragano said Hoffa lunged at Kennedy and started choking him. "You son of a bitch," he screamed, "I'll break your f____ing neck. I'll kill you." Ragano said he pried Hoffa's beefy fingers from RFK's throat. Frank's wife Nancy confirmed the incident, telling this author that Frank was "visibly shaken" by the encounter before adding, "[Frank] thought Hoffa was going to kill Kennedy." Nancy also noted that her husband believed Hoffa "had begun to lose it [since] Bobby Kennedy was getting to him." She affirmed what her husband Frank wrote in *Mob Lawyer*, "I viewed Robert Kennedy exactly as Jimmy did: an intractable, vicious foe who used illegal tactics and had to be resisted to the bitter end."

One central figure in JFK's life was John Seigenthaler, a presidential confidante and former administrative assistant to RFK. When asked by this author whether James Hoffa could have ordered the killing of JFK,

Seigenthaler said, "My first thoughts [after the killing] were blank, but then when they mentioned Oswald and Russia, I thought of that. But not of Hoffa, he didn't have the capacity to want it done. And I have been skeptical of any and all conspiracy theories across the board."

After being apprised of "The Belli Factor," Seigenthaler reconsidered his position. "Well, the hatred, the hostility from Bobby was certainly there. I cannot deny the depth of it that Hoffa had for Bob and vice versa. Maybe Hoffa was capable. Certainly his involvement with the mob was deep rooted. And he was extremely paranoid. Maybe I should have been thinking of Hoffa [after JFK's death]." Summing up, Seigenthaler said, "I did not feel RFK 'lived and died' with Jimmy Hoffa. He was not obsessive about it. *But Jimmy was obsessive toward RFK.* [emphasis added]"

Similar thoughts caused close JFK confidante and future Attorney General Nicholas Katzenbach to observe, "There is no question that Bobby hated Jimmy Hoffa and everything he stood for . . . . " He added, "In candor, I think a number of us felt uncomfortable with Bobby's fixation on putting Hoffa in jail."

Dueling reasons for the hatred between Hoffa and RFK varied, according to the books they wrote. In *Enemy Within*, published in 1960, Bobby compared Hoffa and "his chief lieutenants" to gangsters: "They have the look of [Al] Capone's men. They are sleek, often bilious and fat, or lean and cold and hard. They have the smooth faces and cruel eyes of gangsters; they wear the same rich clothes, the diamond ring, the jeweled watch, the strong, sickly-sweet-smelling perfume." Describing Hoffa's control of the union, RFK added, "As Hoffa runs it, [the Teamsters] is a conspiracy of evil."

During the 1963 McClellan hearings, columnist Russell Baker told author David Heymann, "It seemed like they [Hoffa and RFK] were two scorpions in a bottle. They just detested each other." Author David E. Koskoff wrote, "It was at the McClellan hearing that Ahab and the whale, Robert Kennedy and James Hoffa, first met." Quoting Professor Monroe H. Freedman in a *Georgetown Law Review* article, Koskoff added, "From the day that James Hoffa told Robert Kennedy that he was nothing but a rich man's kid who never had to earn a nickel in his life, Hoffa was a marked man." Koskoff then wrote, "Bobby became obsessed with Hoffa. There would be no forgetting."

In 1975, Hoffa struck back at his enemy in the autobiography *Hoffa: The Real Story*. In chapter one, the union leader wrote, "I made two disastrous mistakes in my life. The first was coming to grips with Robert F. Kennedy to the point where we became involved in what can only be called a blood feud." In a later chapter titled, "The Spoiled Brat," Hoffa called RFK "power mad and publicity crazy." These words from a Teamster boss that author Evan Thomas quoted as saying, "I do to others what they do to me." In his book, Hoffa continued to ridicule Bobby, calling him "the runt of the litter." He wrote, "Okay, so I didn't like him. Like him? Hell, *I hated the bastard* [emphasis added]. He was a parasite who had to work for the government because he wouldn't have known how to make an honest living. He used a knife for a crutch and if it hadn't been for his family he wouldn't have made somebody a good law clerk."

Even Vincent Bugliosi admitted Hoffa's hatred for RFK in *Reclaiming History*. He noted that any suggestion that Hoffa would plan to kill JFK was clearly "a fabrication of Frank Ragano's" but agreed that Hoffa, while never actually ordering any killing, had mentioned the potential of having RFK, "his chief nemesis," eliminated.

Bugliosi pointing out that Hoffa discussed the potential to kill RFK, not JFK, (nowhere in *Reclaiming History* is there the mention of such threatening language by Oswald or anyone else toward JFK) is relevant as is the comment that RFK was Hoffa's "chief nemesis." This admission could have easily shifted the famous prosecutor's attention to focusing on why RFK *was not* killed instead of why JFK *was*, but it never did since doing so was certainly not in line with the "Oswald Alone" theory Bugliosi advocated.

CHAPTER SIXTEEN

Enemies Galore

Regarding Santo Trafficante's hatred for RFK based on Bobby's being responsible for a tax evasion indictment of the Tampa don, no less an authority than historian Arthur Schlesinger wrote: "Like all members of his trade, Trafficante regarded Robert F. Kennedy as Public Enemy Number One. No attorney general in history had pursued the syndicates so relentlessly." Schlesinger added, "There was every indication . . . that the worst was yet to come. Trafficante . . . was a friend of Jimmy Hoffa's. A year before, he had discussed the President with a Cuban acquaintance. 'Have you seen,' the gangster said, 'how *his brother* [emphasis added] is hitting Hoffa, a man who is a worker, who is not a millionaire? . . . Mark my words, this man is in trouble, and he will get what is coming to him . . . [RFK] is going to be hit.'"

Bill Bonnano, son of mobster Joe Bonnano, wrote of Trafficante's "feelings of betrayal and loss following the Bay of Pigs invasion" when Trafficante "saw all his Cuban interests go down the drain," and "Bobby Kennedy's subsequent targeting of southern Florida [where Trafficante resided] for Justice Department action against drug trafficking."

But if Trafficante hated RFK, his reasons for doing so paled in comparison to those of Carlos Marcello, whose strong motive was regarding Robert Kennedy as the foremost threat to his empire and his very freedom. This threat extended to Marcello's livelihood which was continually jeopardized by RFK's relentless crusade to either deport or imprison him.

Most important, at no time did this threat exist more clearly than within the few months leading up to John Kennedy's assassination. As evidenced by Marcello's precarious legal status, he became desperate and easily the most dangerous man alive when it came to Robert Kennedy's survival.

To understand Marcello's mindset, it should be recalled that one of RFK's strongest intentions shortly after becoming attorney general was to bring down Marcello. Why? One reason was the government's certainty that the Guatemalan passport that Tunisian-born Marcello had used to remain in the United States was forged. To that end, author G. Robert Blakey wrote that the passport was the result of a $100,000 bribe paid to Antonio Valladares, the law partner of Guatemala's prime minister.

Within a few months of the Kennedys taking office in January 1961, Bobby masterminded the deportation of the unsuspecting don by Border Patrol plane from New Orleans to Latin America where he was unceremoniously dumped in Guatemala City. A *New York Times* article dated April 4, 1961, quoted Marcello's lawyers as calling the deportation, "cruel and uncivilized." A day later, a *Times* reporter wrote, "The American Civil Liberties Union denounced today as 'totalitarian tactics' the methods used to deport Carlos Marcello."

One may only imagine the humiliation Marcello experienced especially when he was deposited without luggage and with little cash into Guatemala's capital city. In an April 10, 1961, interview with noted newspaper columnist Drew Pearson titled "Guatemalan Carlos Marcello," the deported don complained of being "kidnapped," while telling Pearson he was turned over "to a mysterious official, later known to be Colonel Antonio Batres, 2nd in command of the Guatemalan Air Force."

Fortunately for Marcello, his brothers rescued him with cash and clothes, but after he took residence in a hotel suite, President Miguel Ydígoras Fuentes expelled him from the country. With nowhere to go, Marcello and his lawyer, as author Blakey noted, "were unceremoniously flown to an out-of-the-way village in the jungle of El Salvador." Stranded, the two men, dressed in expensive clothes, were apprehended by Salvadorian soldiers and imprisoned for five days. A seventeen-mile trek through the hot, insect-infested jungle during which Marcello fainted three times led them to a village where they convinced natives to help them. The two exhausted men (Marcello had fallen and broken two ribs) finally arrived at a small coastal town. Contacts in the United States snatched the pair and they were flown to Miami in a Dominican Air Force jet where Marcello entered the country illegally. Author John H. Davis believed that it was I. Irving Davidson, a top lobbyist with connections to Marcello, James Hoffa, and even Lyndon Johnson's political adviser Bobby Baker, who had arranged Marcello's flight. Davis wrote, "So close had Davidson been to Marcello at the time of Carlos' deportation in 1961 that Davidson turned out to be the only person in Washington D.C. who had Carlos' telephone number in Guatemala after Bobby Kennedy dumped him there."

While it is easy to brush over what occurred to Marcello, one must consider the extent of anguish he experienced believing he had been treated with disrespect through conduct reserved for a common criminal. Based on this scenario, common sense dictates that the venom within his soul had reached a crescendo. To say he hated RFK is in all likelihood an understatement. He must have despised the man while swearing revenge at the earliest possible moment.

Author John H. Davis reported that Marcello's attorneys later proved that Bobby and his Justice Department envoys had "broken the law by violating a Supreme Court ruling that Marcello be given seventy-two-hours notice before deportation could be carried out." Such conduct caused Davis to write: "The hatred of Bobby Kennedy [by Marcello] would know no bounds."

Marcello's attitude toward the attorney general was noted in the *HSCA Report* where Ed Reid, the former editor of the *Las Vegas Sun*, was quoted. He said Marcello told those gathered at a clandestine meeting in Louisiana, "Don't worry about that little Bobby son of a bitch. He's going to be taken care of." Reid then added, "[Marcello] knew that to rid himself of Robert Kennedy, he would first have to remove the President. Any killer of the Attorney General would be hunted down by his brother; the death

of the President would seal the fate of the Attorney General." Author
Blakey offered a similar account through quoting Marcello as saying to
an informant, "The President was the dog, the Attorney General Kennedy
was its tail. If you cut off the tail, the dog will keep biting; but if you chop
off the head, the dog will die, tail and all."

This sort of scenario (JFK as the head, RFK as the tail) was confirmed
by James Hoffa's Teamsters official Frank "The Irishman" Sheeran. He
was quoted by author Charles Brandt as saying, "Bobby Kennedy . . .
knew more about the inner game of organized crime than any 'outsider'
in the country. Bobby certainly knew that, in the absence of a mob war,
bosses did not ever eliminate another boss' underboss. It would bring a
major retaliation." Sheeran added, "To effect a desired change in policy,
mob bosses have traditionally eliminated . . . bosses, not underbosses.
On an international scale it is called regime change. To the Italian
bosses it is merely a matter of following the old Sicilian maxim that to
kill a dog you don't cut off its tail, you cut off its head." This, Brandt
wrote, had caused RFK to tell former White House aide and bestselling author Richard Goodwin two years after the *Warren Commission
Report*, "I never thought it was the Cubans [who killed JFK]. If anyone
was involved, it was organized crime. But there is nothing I can do
about it. Not now.'

If Frank Ragano is telling the truth that he passed on James Hoffa's
directive of July 23, 1963, that JFK had to be eliminated, it landed in
Marcello's lap during a time when hitting back at Bobby was foremost
on his mind. Mickey Cohen, Santo Trafficante, and James Hoffa may
have hated RFK, but this hatred in all likelihood paled in comparison to
Marcello's degree of rage towards the attorney general. This was because
Bobby had launched a three-pronged attack against Marcello designed
to get rid of him once and for all. The attack included: (1) an April 1961
IRS filing of a $835,396 tax lien against Marcello and his wife Jacqueline,
(2) an indictment for illegal entry by Marcello in the US filed June 8,
1961, six days after his attorneys announced that the mobster was back in
the country, and, (3) an indictment for conspiracy to defraud the US in
connection with his false Guatemalan birth certificate.

According to an October 31, 1961, story in the *Lake Charles American Press*, the federal grand jury indictment was announced by a gleeful Robert Kennedy in Washington DC. He told reporters, according to the story, "Marcello was charged with conspiracy to get a false birth certificate in Guatemala and later perjured himself by swearing he had nothing to do with the certificate." The story depicted Marcello as a "51-year-old swarthy boss of a rackets empire centered in Jefferson Parish [New Orleans]" while noting that the government had been attempting to deport the don since 1952, claiming Marcello was actually born in Tunis, a territory of Italy, instead of Guatemala. Marcello's lawyer Jack Wasserman was quoted as alleging that the indictment was "part of the persecution of the Justice Department," a certain reference to RFK proving that in Marcello's mind,

Carlos Marcello, Santo Trafficante, Frank Ragano, and other Mafia figures at New York City's La Stella Restaurant—1966. Historian Arthur Schlesinger wrote: "Like all members of his trade, Trafficante regarded Robert F. Kennedy as Public Enemy Number One." Author Nick Pileggi (**Wise Guy,** *later made into the film* **Goodfellas**) *said of Marcello: "Tough. Impossible to seduce and the kind of Sicilian mafiosi you didn't want to turn into an enemy." Credit: Getty Images.*

Bobby had crossed the line from being a prosecutor to being one who was persecuting him, a far more personal attack.

Most important to realize is that Marcello's back was to the wall; he knew RFK would never quit pursuing him until the don fell from power. Marcello was not about to let Bobby Kennedy win their private war, one that escalated toward a climax after RFK had successfully thrown Marcello out of the country to win the first round only to learn that the Mafia don won the second round by sneaking back into the country illegally. A final round would determine the winner with both of the egotistical men bent on showing the other who had more power. The war had become personal, not business; Marcello vs. RFK, *mano a mano*, a fight to the finish.

Little known legal maneuvers virtually ignored at the time and since point to reasons why Marcello knew his days were numbered, that he had no way out of his legal troubles. After several appeals of adverse immigration rulings failed and then desperate to avoid his deportation, Marcello's lawyers gave it one last shot in late 1962. The complaint alleged "the Government had utilized a false birth certificate [allegation] to procure [Marcello's] entry into Guatemala, that the deportation was accomplished in violation of the three days notice, that Marcello was denied the assistance of counsel and that the statutory provision for deportation was unconstitutional." A district court dismissed the complaint and a federal appeal was unsuccessful. This meant that Marcello had apparently exhausted every legal avenue open to him regarding deportation while he still faced a November 1963 federal court trial on conspiracy charges in New Orleans. This was a case Robert Kennedy personally monitored from his Washington DC offices as evidenced by his having called, as author John H. Davis pointed out, the Marcello prosecutor on the eve of the trial to wish him luck. RFK must have felt he had Marcello on the ropes ready for a knockout blow, one that would cause him to be down for the count, ridding Bobby of a dreaded enemy.

What did Marcello, connected, as noted, to Ruby lawyer Melvin Belli through their mutual friend Mickey Cohen, have at stake if RFK continued his pursuit with intent to deport the Mafia don, or imprison him, and thus break his empire? Former HSCA counsel G. Robert Blakey and

Carlos Marcello leaving a New Orleans federal court building after a 1961 Deportation Hearing.
After Bobby Kennedy directed the Mafia don's deportation to the jungles of Guatemala, Marcello
became a desperate man in a continuing war with the president's brother.   Credit: Corbis Images.

his coauthor Richard Billings wrote, "By 1963, the mobster was grossing many millions annually, $500 million from illegal gambling, $100 million from illegal activities in over 1,500 syndicate-connected bars, $8 million from professional burglaries and holdups, $6 million from prostitution, and $400 million from diverse . . . 'investments.'" When he wanted to relax, Marcello could enjoy the benefits of the 22-million-dollar, 6,500 acre estate, Churchill Farms, he owned near New Orleans.

As the calendar turned to 1963, Marcello must have faced the truth—the attorney general of the United States, arguably the second most powerful man in the country (Some called him a "co-president;" author Evan

Thomas used the phrase "all-purpose consigliere."), had the mafiosi square in his gun sights and was determined to win at all costs. How to alter that disposition must have been a continual point of discussion by Marcello and his brethren by moving forward on at least two fronts: creating a plan to eliminate JFK so Bobby would become powerless with the result being no deportation, and pushing ahead in the courtroom to beat the conspiracy charges. Regarding the former, revenge was also a motive since by having the president killed, Marcello would rob RFK of what he treasured most in his life—brother John. Finally, Marcello could pay Bobby back in spades.

Ironically, Marcello's no-brainer, no-alternative decision had an added benefit since killing the president to render Bobby powerless had been requested by James Hoffa through Frank Ragano's directive. Marcello wanted JFK dead for his own reasons, but doing Hoffa a favor by having the president assassinated very likely would pay future dividends.

RFK may have been temporarily blunted in his attempt to deport Marcello, but the attorney general was confident of a favorable jury verdict in the New Orleans federal trial. Prosecutors in that case had an eyewitness, Carl Irving Noll, who swore that "he had an arrangement with Marcello to obtain a false birth certificate." The defense countered with allegations from a witness, the only one it called, that Noll was a "con man" not to be believed.

Marcello's trial had begun on November 1, 1963, in a New Orleans federal court when Carlos and brother Joe faced a jury charged with "conspiracy to defraud the United States government by obtaining a false Guatemalan birth certificate" and "conspiracy to obstruct the United States Government in the exercise of its right to deport Carlos Marcello." Author John H. Davis wrote, "The Marcello family was up in arms over the charges, which they knew had originated with Bobby Kennedy and which they believed were totally unfair. What galled the family was their conviction that Bobby Kennedy had illegally deported Carlos in the first place." Davis added that the family believed "a vindictive Bobby Kennedy was trying to get back at Carlos for having had the guts to defy the deportation order and reenter the country." This set up, Davis stated, "a duel to the finish with Attorney General Kennedy."

The timing of the trial, just three weeks before President Kennedy was due in Dallas, was important, since, during the trial, Marcello visited nearby Churchill Farms. Among those Marcello met with, according to author Davis, was David Ferrie, Lee Harvey Oswald's friend from the days when he lived in New Orleans during the summer and early fall of 1963. Ferrie acknowledged meeting with Marcello on consecutive weekends as the trial proceeded. Author Davis suspected Marcello was planning the Dallas assassination.

Thursday, November 21, 1963, became a day when two events occurred within eight hours driving distance that, for many, had no apparent connection. However, when later considered in light of "The Belli Factor" and the focus on why RFK *was not* killed and JFK *was*, one inevitably ponders the effect of one event on the other. In New Orleans, defense attorneys for the Marcello brothers rested their case, and in Texas, President Kennedy landed in San Antonio to begin his political tour of the state. Amazingly enough, a verdict in the Marcello case, after closing arguments were completed, was expected a day later when JFK visited Dallas.

On the fateful day of Friday, November 22nd, as Carlos Marcello awaited a jury's decision in the New Orleans courtroom, the clock struck 1:00 p.m., the very time the president of United States was pronounced dead in Dallas. One half hour later, just as the Marcello jury was about to commence deliberations (David Ferrie was in the courtroom at the time according to author Davis), a bailiff handed Judge Herbert W. Christenberry a note. He winced, bowed his head, and then announced to the court that JFK had been shot and was dead. One and one half hours later, the jury returned an acquittal verdict for the Marcello brothers.

Coincidently, on the very day the president was assassinated, Marcello was freed of the deportation fraud charges. This caused author Davis to write, " . . . November 22, 1963, had to have been the most triumphant day of Marcello's life."

Without question, Carlos Marcello had won his fierce battle with RFK. The Mafia don had bet on a friendly verdict in the deportation case in New Orleans, a city he controlled, and won (prosecutors alleged a juror had been bribed). Even if he had lost the case, Marcello, with RFK no longer in the picture, must have believed he could win on appeal with friendly judges in his pocket.

Based on compelling evidence dealing with motive, Marcello had also bet on a successful termination of the life of John F. Kennedy in nearby Dallas, a city where Marcello had vast resources through his Mafia brethren. The mechanics of the operation must have begun once the New Orleans don received quite a gift—knowledge that John Kennedy would visit Dallas in November. According to the HSCA records, a newspaper item dated April 23, 1963, indicated JFK might visit Texas cities that summer or fall. The information's source was Vice President Lyndon Johnson.

The list of cities certainly would have included Dallas. No city in America could have been more welcome news to Marcello. Killing Kennedy in New Orleans would have been too close to home, but the Mafia don also controlled the underworld in Dallas, five hundred twenty miles to the west. Proof of Marcello's domination abounded. Marcello's lawyer Frank Ragano wrote, "Santo [Trafficante] mentioned that Marcello's power extended to Texas, where he had placed an underboss Joe Civello, to run rackets out of Dallas. I recalled from newspaper stories that Civello, in fact, had represented Marcello at the Apalachin convention in 1957." Author Mark North confirmed through *New Orleans Times-Picayune* clippings that Robert Kennedy certainly was aware of the Marcello/Civello connection writing, " . . . AG Robert Kennedy, in a Chicago speech, branded Marcello and Civello a 'malignant threat' to society."[18]

---

18 The "Apalachin convention" Ragano mentioned was a confab of criminals, gangsters from across the country who gathered in Upstate New York in 1957 to settle various "family" matters. Among those in attendance (twenty-four crime families were represented) were the crème de la crème of the underworld: Vito Genovese, Carlo Gambino, Joe Bonnano, Sam Giancana, and Santo Trafficante. Author Gil Reavill wrote that Carlos Marcello was represented by Joe Civello. Reavill wrote, "Texas-born dope dealer Joe Civello, himself recently ascended to the top leadership post in the old Piranio crime family of Dallas [was there]. Given mob geography, which held that Dallas existed as a suburb of New Orleans, Civello acted as boss Carlos Marcello's blade runner, underboss, and summit representative." Reavill also noted the attendance of Marcello's brother Joe, writing, "Not a mob boss but a relative of one, Joe Marcello journeyed up from New Orleans as an envoy of his brother Carlos Marcello, the 'Mafia Kingfish' . . . who generally ran the rackets in the Big Easy."

Joe Civello, and his underling Joe Campisi, are very important to understanding the most plausible means by which Carlos Marcello set up the mechanics for JFK's assassination. Not only did these two gangsters know Dallas streets backwards and forwards to pinpoint a logical spot for the assassination, but, as author John H. Davis pointed out, Civello was on friendly terms with the Dallas police force. In fact, Davis wrote that Civello "was observed having dinner with a Dallas police officer by the name of Patrick T. Dean . . . " Davis added, "Six years later, it was Sergeant Dean who was in charge of basement security when an associate of Joe Civello's, Jack Ruby, entered the basement of Dallas Police Headquarters and murdered Lee Harvey Oswald in front of over seventy armed police officers."

Since Marcello must have known in April 1963 that JFK might be headed toward Texas in the summer or fall, he and his cohorts had adequate time to plan an assassination. In September, the White House confirmed to the media that a trip to Dallas was to be made in November, permitting Marcello time to work with his local connections on possible logistics two months before the visit. Now only the exact details of where the motorcade would travel was an unknown, but it is not a stretch to believe that through Joe Civello's police contacts the exact route may have been passed on before November 18th, four days before the president's arrival, when the route was made public.

For the New Orleans don, the timing was perfect. In addition, since it was common knowledge that the president had reservations about keeping Lyndon Johnson on the 1964 ticket, time was of the essence. Who knew whom JFK might replace LBJ with; perhaps even his brother Bobby?

When they learned that JFK's motorcade would pass through Dealey Plaza, where access to the president's limousine was available from all sides with no quick access for a getaway, Marcello and his underlings, Civello and Campisi, among others, must have smiled since the motorcade route was ripe for the assassination. It was as if the perfect storm was approaching, one that would eliminate JFK, land LBJ in the Oval Office, and render Bobby powerless all in the wink of an eye.

That Carlos Marcello's dastardly, but predictable, act of assassination had been carried out made perfect sense. John Kennedy simply walked into a death trap at Dealey Plaza where a flurry of gunshots changed the course of history. But then one potential problem immediately confronted Marcello since Lee Harvey Oswald, arguably the "nut" involved in the plan, was apprehended. Fortunately, a ready solution was available before Oswald could begin naming names since Jack Ruby, connected to Civello, was ordered to eliminate Oswald. This was carried out since Ruby's allegiance to the underworld was well-known even to Robert Kennedy. Author C. David Heymann wrote: "[Bobby] knew that Jack Ruby was a Dallas racketeer connected to the national Mafia."

This is where "The Belli Factor" makes such a difference deciding who masterminded JFK's death. Before, suspicions certainly existed pointing fingers in the direction of Hoffa, Marcello, Trafficante, and others including Chicago mobster Sam Giancana as logical suspects in the killings. But when "The Belli Factor" is thrown into the mix, the common sense understanding that amidst fears Ruby might expose Marcello and others in the plot to kill President Kennedy, Belli, as ordered, came riding to the rescue with his illogical psychomotor epilepsy defense. This tactical move not only guaranteed the perception that Ruby was crazy, but guaranteed his silence as well since Belli ran the show. When J. Edgar Hoover and Dallas Police Chief Jess Curry announced that Oswald had acted alone, and the media acquiesced with little or no argument, any investigation was thwarted before it began. Months later, the Warren Commission played its part with the "Oswald Alone" theory and it was case closed with Marcello and company the winner in a romp. Bill Bonnano, son of Joe, offered confirmation of what occurred, writing that a "captain in our family," Smitty D'Angelo, spoke with Santo Trafficante shortly after the Dallas shootings. According to Bonnano, D'Angelo told him, "Trafficante wasted no time in telling Smitty all he needed to know. His Family was involved, along with Carlos Marcello's and Sam Giancana's. Jimmy Hoffa was involved, but was not responsible for much."

Since the president was now dead, and the loose ends of Oswald, dead, and Ruby on trial with a mob-connected lawyer tied up in a neat package since Belli called the shots, Marcello bet that RFK's power would diminish or simply vanish with his brother no longer in the Oval Office. Time would show that the Mafia don was right. Marcello and Trafficante, and their brethren, escaped RFK's wrath forever. This was ensured because Marcello now had a less antagonistic figure in the White House: President Lyndon Johnson. The moment LBJ was sworn in on Air Force One, RFK was reduced to simply being an attorney general without a brother as president. Author David Heymann wrote, " . . . [Bobby] was [now] *only* attorney general, not the roving presidential alter ego who commanded the obedience of the secretaries of state and defense and the CIA director . . . he was one department head among many, deprived of his special mission as his brother's dogged defender and merciless enforcer."

One clear indication of loss of power, Heymann noted, was evident: "Not long after November 22, [J. Edgar Hoover] disconnected the telephone line which ran from his office to that of the attorney general." This coincided with comments made by author Jack Newfield. He wrote, "The assassination punctured the center of Robert Kennedy's universe. . . . It took away, in one instant of insanity, all of the power they struggled together for ten years to achieve, and gave it to another, whom they both mistrusted."

Bottom line: Carlos Marcello was never deported. Based on court records, it appears the government finally lost interest or simply gave up trying to deport the don.

Without question, RFK's power had been stripped from him because LBJ, despite public appearances to the contrary, had no love lost for Bobby Kennedy. Resentment between the two men had festered for years. Specifics abound, but author Jeff Shesol perhaps sums up the ill feeling best. He wrote, "Lyndon Johnson and Robert Kennedy loathed each other. 'This man,' Kennedy said of Johnson, 'is mean, bitter, vicious—an animal in many ways.' Johnson considered Kennedy a 'grandstanding little runt.' Their mutual contempt was so acute, their bitterness so intense and abiding, they could scarcely speak in each other's presence." In *LBJ*, a PBS documentary aired in 2006, John Connally said of the rivalry, "LBJ and Bobby hated each other," and Bobby Baker, Johnson's political adviser, added, "mutual dislike between LBJ and RFK was second to none in the world."[19]

---

19 After being at war with the Kennedy's over the 1960 presidential nomination, and finally accepting a bitter defeat, he agreed to be the vice-presidential nominee to the surprise of

Author Jeff Shesol elaborated on the contempt the men had for each other, pointing out, as others did, that Johnson was belittled by RFK at every turn. One may only imagine how Johnson sizzled when he read headlines, Shesol pointed out, such as "Robert Kennedy: Number Two Man in Washington," the "Assistant President," prompting others, the author suggested, to ask, "Whatever happened to Lyndon Johnson?"

Joe Kennedy certainly knew the score regarding Johnson's view of RFK especially when Joe learned that LBJ had called Bobby "Sonny" on the Senate floor among other unflattering names. According to author Woods, Joe told future House Speaker Tip O'Neill, "You can trample all over him [JFK], and the next day, he's there for you with open arms. But Bobby's my boy. When Bobby hates you, you stay hated." On another occasion reported by author Richard J. Whalen, Joe said, "Bobby resembles me much more than any of the other children . . . He hates the same way I do." Celebrated novelist Gore Vidal, who proclaimed that James Hoffa "had long been Moby Dick to Bobby's Captain Ahab," confirmed RFK's propensity to hate, writing, "I have read that the two people Bobby most hated (a rare distinction because he hated so many people) was the head of the Teamsters [Hoffa] and me."

Bobby's hatred had abounded toward Hoffa and Trafficante, but especially with Marcello. But as a new day dawned on November 23, 1963, Marcello could celebrate: JFK was dead, Bobby was powerless without his brother to back him up and his days as attorney general were numbered, and Lyndon Johnson was president. During the nine months he remained attorney general, RFK distanced himself from the Warren Commission;

---

both JFK and RFK, who believed Johnson would refuse the offer. When he accepted, peace was necessary but never fully achieved. One significant reason, according to author Randall B. Woods in his 2006 book *LBJ, Architect of American Ambition*: Bobby never forgave LBJ for an incident at his Texas ranch in midsummer 1960. This occurred during a visit by RFK when LBJ suggested a deer hunt. He outfitted all of the other hunters with deer rifles but gave RFK a ten-gauge shotgun. When Bobby pulled the trigger, Woods reported, "Recoil knocked him down, cutting his eye." Helping the thirty-four-year-old Bobby to his feet, LBJ remarked, "Son, you've got to learn how to handle a gun like that." Bobby sizzled over the embarrassment causing Woods to surmise, "By the closing days of the campaign, LBJ and his staff had come to view Bobby Kennedy more as an enemy than a friend."

disbanded what was known as the "Hoffa Squad;" traveled to Indonesia, West Germany, and Poland; considered becoming LBJ's running mate (Johnson squashed that idea); and then finally resigned to run for the senate from New York. Marcello, Trafficante, and the other Mafia king-pins were now in the rear view mirror, no longer a priority for an attorney general who had clearly lost his passion to battle the underworld bosses. This undermines what Vincent Bugliosi called "the anemic argument [that the mob killed JFK so Bobby would leave them alone] since organized crime would have no assurance that Robert Kennedy would not continue to be attorney general under LBJ, which in fact he did for almost a year . . . " Yes, Bobby remained AG, but he was never a threat to the underworld again, just as those who killed his brother had predicted. Even when he later became a United States senator from New York, there was no compunction to hound Marcello, Hoffa, or any underworld figures.

Regarding Lyndon Johnson, Hoffa and the mafiosi believed they had greased both sides of the wheel by donating money to Johnson, JFK, and Richard Nixon as the 1960 presidential election neared. According to John H. Davis, Johnson had Marcello ties dating back to his days as a Texas senator. Davis wrote, "Of all the Texas politicians Marcello . . . supported, the most powerful was Senator Lyndon Johnson. It has been estimated that the Marcello . . . group funneled at least $50,000 a year of the Marcellos' gambling profits along to Lyndon Johnson, and in return, Johnson helped kill in committee all legislation that could have harmed Marcello [and his associates]." Author Davis believed these bribes were the reason Marcello had a free hand in Dallas and provide the impetus for understanding why Marcello and his Mafia brethren were confident LBJ would derail any train, in case RFK continued his assault on impeding their ability to continue operation of multi-million-dollar illegal operations. RFK did not, but Johnson, according to Davis, was an insurance policy in case he had done so. More importantly, LBJ helped the cause by appointing the infamous Warren Commission, whose inept investigation provided a dead end to any substantial probe of Mafia involvement in the assassinations.

Targeting the crafty Marcello as the one man with more motive to mastermind and orchestrate the assassinations is enhanced through comments uttered by Bobby's confidante Frank Mankiewicz. He told this author, "I've never bought the Warren Commission [Report] and I've always thought Carlos Marcello was in the picture somewhere." Mankiewicz's conclusion about Marcello was corroborated by the *HSCA Report*. It stated, "The committee found that Marcello had the motive, means, and opportunity to have President John F. Kennedy assassinated though it was unable to establish direct evidence of Marcello's complicity." Certainly, without doubt, Marcello was "in the picture somewhere," especially when "The Belli Factor" linking the mob to Ruby's defense is mixed in.

While all of these comments are relevant, it is the words of Frank Ragano, an eyewitness to the hatred Hoffa, Marcello, and Trafficante had for RFK, that are most compelling. Bugliosi, and Gerald Posner before him, discredit Ragano's version of the facts, but who is more believable, Ragano, an eyewitness to history, or Bugliosi, whose book only devoted portions of *eight pages* out of sixteen hundred to any mention of Hoffa despite Hoffa and RFK having been bitter enemies according to an unlimited number of reliable sources.

Concerning Marcello and Trafficante, or the Mafia at large, Bugliosi actually made light of any motive on their part without exploring strong facts pointing in the other direction or conveniently leaving out information dispelling his "Oswald Alone" theories. Not one mention of Marcello's battle to the finish with RFK is mentioned in the former prosecutor's book regarding Marcello's federal conspiracy trial; not one note regarding the desperation Marcello experienced as the clock ticked toward his being expelled from the US as November 1963 appeared on the horizon. With a hint of arrogance to the writing, he decided, " . . . for the Mafia to murder Kennedy, they'd have to be crazy," and later in the book, " . . . the thought that Trafficante, Marcello, or any of the mob leaders would plot to murder the president of the United States is too ridiculous to even mention." These assertions completely disregard the element of motive, but, like others before him, this is what occurs when one focuses solely on why JFK was killed instead of why Bobby was not and attempts to rationalize his inability to provide substantial reasons as to why Oswald acted alone.

Backing up Frank Ragano's assertions are wife Nancy's recollections to this author of the champagne dinner in Florida where husband Frank and Trafficante celebrated on the evening of JFK's assassination with the latter telling Ragano, "Isn't that something, they killed the son-of-a-bitch. The son-of-a-bitch is dead. This is like lifting a load of stones off my shoulders. Now they'll get off my back, off Carlos' back, and off Maretuzzo's [Hoffa's] back." This bolsters the fact that Trafficante acknowledged that JFK's death would benefit Marcello, Hoffa, and him, an assertion that proved true when RFK's Justice Department rackets squad was disbanded. Proof exists through the opinion of William Hundley, the chief of the Organized Crime Section of the Criminal Division of the Department of Justice under RFK. Author Charles Brandt wrote that Hundley said, "The minute that bullet hit Jack Kennedy's head, it was all over. Right then. The organized crime program just stopped." Author Robert Sam Anson wrote, "Organized Crime had considerable cause for relief, for with [John] Kennedy's murder . . . the statistics added up to a quiet, largely unnoticed surrender in the war Robert Kennedy had declared [on the Mafia.] It had cost only one casualty: the life of his brother."

This seals the verdict regarding who benefited most from JFK's death: the two mobsters and Hoffa, but especially Marcello since his chief nemesis, the man who wanted to deport or imprison him, was now powerless. Since the mobsters, especially Marcello with contacts in nearby Dallas, certainly had the means to kill the president through recruitment of as many foot soldiers as required to carry out the assassination (in all likelihood recruited from those loyal to Marcello, Trafficante, Hoffa, and others who ultimately benefited from JFK's death and by extension, RFK's fall from power), and the opportunity, a given since JFK was the proverbial "sitting duck" when he was paraded through Dealey Plaza. All four of the homicide detective's best friends—motive, means, opportunity, and benefit from the crime—exist through any sort of common sense examination of the assassinations. When "The Belli Factor" is added to the equation, the likelihood that the mob used Belli to silence Ruby, the nails in the coffin are complete. The scenario Ragano described where he served as the conduit between Hoffa and Marcello/Trafficante by telling the latter that

Hoffa wanted JFK dead, makes sense. This set of facts, it will be recalled, triggered HSCA counsel G. Robert Blakey's belief that Ragano's story was "the most plausible and logical explanation" of the assassinations. Such an assertion was backed up by both Selwyn Raab and Nicholas Pileggi, each a respected journalist, each of whom checked out Ragano's story and believed it credible, as did author David Kaiser and others of note.

Supplementing Ragano's overall assertions, and the account provided by mobster Bill Bonnano are two confessions, one each from Trafficante and Marcello, which bolster the argument. The former's confession was provided by Ragano in *Mob Lawyer*. His relationship with Trafficante, Ragano wrote, fluctuated between a professional one and personal, with strong feelings positive and negative a staple. But on March 1987, the mob lawyer swore that Trafficante, his health waning due to poor heart and kidney condition, suddenly called asking to meet after having been out of touch for some time. Describing the aged mobster when he visited his modest Tampa home, Ragano wrote, "Dressed in gray pajamas and a matching terry-cloth robe, he wobbled in a flat-footed gait rather than walked. He had aged radically. His cheeks were hollow, his skin wrinkled like parchment . . . There was no longer any mystery about this emergency meeting. Santo was dying."

Huddling in Trafficante's living room, Ragano said the mobster began unloading several disclosures regarding his Mafia days. Then, Ragano reported, "Santo said 'we need to take a ride.'" With Trafficante still wearing pajamas and a bathrobe, the two, Ragano wrote, settled into Ragano's gray Mercedes-Benz for a drive around Trafficante's neighborhood. "Suddenly," Ragano noted, "his talk turned to the Kennedys." Ragano wrote that the mobster then continued by saying, ". . . Bobby made life miserable for me and my friends. Who would have thought that someday [JFK] would be president and name his goddamn brother attorney general? Goddam Bobby. I think Carlos f____ up in getting rid of Giovanni—maybe it should have been Bobby."

Ragano, attempting to decipher what Trafficante meant, concluded, perhaps too boldly, "to my astonishment, abruptly and without warning, [Santo] was confessing that he and Carlos Marcello had conspired to kill the president. 'Giovanni' was John in Italian. I considered pulling over to a side street and parking so we could discuss this fully, but I drove on as he repeated the admission."

If Ragano had been too quick to include Trafficante in the mix with Marcello concerning the death of the president since the Tampa mobster had only noted, "I think Carlos f_____ up getting rid of Giovanni," what Trafficante said next confirmed Ragano's suspicions. The mob lawyer wrote, "These electrifying words, 'Carlos é futtutu. Non duvevamu ammazzari a Giovanni [John]. Duvevamu ammazzari a Bobby.' ["Carlos f_____ed up. We shouldn't have killed Giovanni. We should have killed Bobby."] struck [me] with the force of a sledgehammer." Later, considering the impact of what he had heard in connection with his having passed on James Hoffa's order that JFK be killed to the twin mobsters, Ragano wrote, "In my loyalty to the three men [Hoffa, Trafficante and Marcello as their lawyer], I have ignored basic logic and obvious hints: each of them had participated actively or behind the scenes in the assassination [of JFK]. . . . Most probably, Carlos and Santo plotted against the president for their own selfish reasons. . . ."

The mob lawyer explained Trafficante's inclination to confirm the hit by concluding that he had "a Machiavellian reason for confessing the crime of the century—a Costa Nostra conspiracy to assassinate John Fitzgerald Kennedy." This was possible, Ragano stated, since "the admission did not violate his private code of morality—his oath of omertà—since he was talking to me, not to a law-enforcement agent." Another reason Trafficante confessed, Ragano decided, "was his perverse pride that he and his mob partners had eliminated a president, outwitted the government's top law-enforcement agencies, and escaped punishment." Ragano's son Chris saw it another way, telling the History Channel, "Trafficante used my father as a confessing priest." Nick Pileggi, who had sorted through Ragano's assertions before writing the foreword to *Mob Lawyer* and found them to be credible, told this author he recalled Ragano telling him the exact same story regarding Trafficante's car confession.

Trafficante acknowledging that "Carlos" was part of the "we" Trafficante noted substantiates each being involved in JFK's assassination while causing suspicion that perhaps Trafficante wanted to have RFK murdered instead of JFK. But it was Marcello who prevailed, who decided that killing JFK would cause Bobby to become powerless while avoiding JFK pursuing the assailants with all of the government's power.

The second confession, this one relating to Marcello, was detailed by authors Lamar Waldron and Thom Hartmann. Arguing that new information from FBI files proved connections between Marcello, Oswald, and Ruby, the authors, who boasted that their book was "the result of 20 years of research – with help from some of the best investigators of today and from the past," turned to evidence supplied by a "trusted FBI informant" to indicate conclusively the Mafia don's masterminding of the JFK and Oswald assassinations. This was accomplished through transmissions from a "special transistor radio the informant kept in the small Texarkana, Texas prison cell he eventually shared with Marcello" in 1985. Mined from declassified FBI files at the National Archives in 2006, "hundreds of hours" of tapes revealed Marcello's mindset about his empire. Details emerge regarding his having earned millions of tax-free dollars from illegal New Orleans operations and how the don was "partners with a man that ran the Mafia in Florida, [named] Trafficante." But, Waldron and Hartmann pointed out, the files reflected a statement from the informant to the effect that "by far the most important thing that I reported to the FBI was Marcello's hatred for the Kennedys."

After providing the links between Oswald and Marcello (he had been introduced to Oswald "by a man named Ferris [Ferrie] who was Marcello's pilot . . . he said he thought Oswald [was] crazy"), and Marcello and Ruby (Marcello set him up in the bar business in Dallas and "Ruby would come to Churchill Farm [owned by Marcello] to report to Marcello"), the authors then unloaded the blockbuster informant statement to the effect that Marcello said, "Yeah, I had the little son of a bitch killed, and I would do it again; he was a thorn in my side. I wish I could have done it myself," with "little son of a bitch" a reference to JFK. That Marcello did not mention RFK is predictable since the two men were discussing the president's assassination.

To their credit, Waldron and Hartmann succeeded in substantiating the credibility of the unnamed informant's proclamation by producing well-documented foundations for other disclosures. Later in the book, the authors provided additional details as to how the informant met Marcello, the means by which a "bug" was installed in the cell he shared with the don, and the admission of guilt regarding the JFK assassination, one that apparently occurred in a prison courtyard on December 15, 1985, two days before the informant left the prison. In total, Waldron and Hartmann decided, "the informant's statement [had] a high degree of creditability" especially in tandem with the informant's disclosure that before leaving, Marcello called him aside and said, "My son, if your enemies get in your way, you bury them in the ground, the grass grows over them, and you go about your business," a statement the informant understood to be a threat of death if he disclosed any of what the don had told him.

Whether Marcello's "confession" is valid is subject to conjecture, but the quote "My son, if your enemies get in your way, you bury them in the ground, the grass grows over them and you go about your business," has a ring of truth to it. To that end, JFK was buried, and without him sitting in the Oval Office, Marcello and his mafiosi brethren went about their business without any interference of any kind from Robert F. Kennedy. When the dust had settled, the mobsters had won the battle, won the war. In effect, the clever Marcello and his cohorts had outsmarted the Ivy League boys with a devious plan that would stand the test of time without being exposed.

To those who question the viability, the plausibility of the scenario presented here regarding how the assassinations of JFK and Oswald played out, one argument would be that the events noted are simply coincidence, that when pieced together they make little sense since attempting to prove what occurred fifty years ago is a futile effort. They might say that it *just happened* that Marcello was the most desperate of anyone who hated Bobby Kennedy; that it *just happened* that Marcello ruled the underworld in Dallas where JFK was headed in late 1963; that one of those he controlled, Joe Civello, *just happened* to have police connections valuable to anyone planning an assassination of the president; that it *just happened* that one of those possible "foot soldiers" Marcello was aware of was Lee Harvey Oswald as noted above; and that it *just happened* that when Oswald was apprehended, Marcello could rely on Civello to contact, out of all those who could have been chosen, Jack Ruby, a mid-level bookmaker and Mafia roustabout who was also friendly with Dallas police. And it *just happened* that Ruby, through these police contacts, ones familiar to Civello, could wander into the Dallas Police Department basement and kill Oswald; and it *just happened* that when Ruby was arrested, riding to the rescue out of the hundreds of attorneys, many famous and every one a criminal defense expert, came Melvin Belli, mainly a civil lawyer and the chief attorney for one of the country's most notorious gangsters, Mickey Cohen; who *just happened* to be connected to Marcello. What are the odds of this occurring?

Of all of what might be called happenstances by those who doubt the theory presented in this book, it is Belli's appearance in the Ruby case that boggles the mind especially when it might be contended that it *just happened* that Belli, instead of throwing Ruby to the mercy of the court or plea bargaining the case, chose the ludicrous psychomotor epilepsy insanity defense, one designed to portray Ruby as crazy and keep him silent, the perfect closure to Marcello's clever plan. Using common sense, are these simply happenstances, coincidences, or, more likely, a plausible approach to what occurred in Dallas in November 1963?

The key is Melvin Belli, connected to Marcello through Cohen for the first time in any investigation or publication. Belli, the mobster wannabe who "loved the mob and they loved him," the man who "was intoxicated with the Mafia," the man who "loved the power, the money, the irreverence [the Mafia] had for authority just like he did," the man with "little integrity who would do anything for money," the man who was "approved by the mob," the man who told chauffeur and close friend Milton Hunt, "*The Ruby case is fixed* [emphasis added]. I'm just going through the motions. It's simply being staged for the sake of publicity. There's an inside thing, and no way to win. It's a whitewash," and the man who, despite being a loudmouth who talked about anything and everything, refused to discuss the Ruby case with anyone, friend or legal colleague, through the years after the Ruby trial was over.

Yes, Melvin Belli was the true mystery man of the assassinations, the forgotten man, the one man Carlos Marcello needed to make certain that responsibility for the Dallas killings would never reach his doorstep. Like Belli, he had hoodwinked the world and headed conspiracy theorists in all the wrong directions.

CHAPTER SEVENTEEN

Bobby's Remorse

B olstering the common sense, logical proposition pointing toward Carlos Marcello as the chief architect of both President John Kennedy and Lee Harvey Oswald's assassinations is the fact that two men had to have known the dangerous New Orleans don was front and center when motive was introduced into the equation. No others—not Cuban dissidents, CIA operatives, paramilitary officials disappointed with JFK's decisions about Vietnam, or even those associated with Vice President Lyndon Johnson, all of whom have been targeted for possible responsibility over the years—hated the Kennedys, specifically RFK, as Marcello did.

The first to know who killed his brother was none other than Robert Kennedy. He may have been characterized as having many faults, but being stupid was not one of them.

Where's the proof? The beginning point, as noted in this book's prologue, is the undisputed statement RFK made shortly after he was notified by FBI director J. Edgar Hoover that JFK was dead. Bobby, his words barely audible, told friend, former Pulitzer Prize-winning journalist, and then Justice Department spokesman Ed Guthman: "There's so much bitterness I thought *they* [emphasis added] would get one of us, but Jack, after all he had been through, [I] never worried about it . . . I never thought it would happen. I thought it would be me . . . there's been so much bitterness and hatred . . . " In a subsequent interview with David Talbot, Talbot said Guthman told Talbot he was certain RFK used the word "they," not "he."

John McCone, CIA director in 1961, said in an oral history for the John Lowery Simpson Oral History series, "[RFK] wanted to know what we knew about it and whether it had been a Cuban or perhaps Russian hit. He even asked me if the CIA could have done it. I mentioned the mob but RFK didn't want to know about it. I suspect he thought it was the mob. He said, '*They* [emphasis added]—whoever '*they*' were—should have killed me. I'm the one they wanted.' He blamed himself because of all the enemies he had made along the way and also because he advised his brother to go to Dallas."

Aware of the hatred Marcello and his cohorts Hoffa and Trafficante had for RFK, who, logically speaking, could Bobby have been referring to when he said, "they" in reference to "bitterness" and "hatred" other than these three men and others of the same ilk? He had crusaded against Hoffa, determined to topple him from power, hounded Trafficante to the extent of the government hitting him with a huge tax lien, and embarrassed and humiliated Marcello by having him temporarily deported. Recall that Bobby had used the same "they" word to describe men like Marcello and Trafficante when he insulted them in his book, *The Enemy Within*, writing, "*They* have the look of [Al] Capone's men. *They* are sleek, often bilious and fat, or lean and cold and hard. *They* have the smooth faces and cruel eyes of gangsters; *they* wear the same rich clothes, the diamond ring, the jeweled watch, the strong, sickly-sweet-smelling perfume." Just imagine the reaction Marcello, Trafficante, and other mobsters must have had when they read these harsh words, and others JFK threw at them over the years. RFK had turned them into enemies of the first degree, ones plotting revenge as fall 1963 approached.

Predictably, when *they* could take it no more, they struck with a thunderbolt. Violence was the result, death the conclusion, the death of a Dallas police officer, the death of a president, the death of Oswald. Through his actions, Bobby had put not only himself in jeopardy, but more importantly, he put his brother John in jeopardy, since RFK, for whatever reason, did not realize that pounding ahead with personal relent-lessness toward these enemies could result in their having no alternatives but to strike back. Bobby should have known better, but he ignored the obvious until it was too late to save his brother.

If additional proof is required, former *Newsweek* managing editor and author Evan Thomas, provides it. In his biography of Bobby, Thomas focused on RFK's suspicions as to who had killed his brother. Thomas wrote, "[RFK] could not free himself of the worry that his brother had been killed by a mobster whose real enemy was himself . . . he continued to worry about the mob and one mobster in particular."

Thomas then characterized Carlos Marcello by writing, ". . . the don of New Orleans had a fierce grievance against RFK," while pointing out why Marcello had the "fierce grievance" toward the attorney general due to the embarrassing deportation of the mafiosi to Latin America. Thomas stated, "[Marcello] believed that the attorney general had been out to persecute him. [Marcello] had reputably vowed to get even."

Author Thomas then reported a startling revelation by Robert Kennedy: "One night during the summer of '67, RFK, in a rare moment of disclo-sure, told advisor and speechwriter Richard Goodwin that he thought his brother had been killed by 'the guy from New Orleans,' meaning Marcello."

While RFK's admission that he worried about "one particular mobster" being responsible for JFK's death is certainly relevant, the most revealing words Thomas wrote were, to repeat, "[RFK] could not free himself of the worry that his brother had been killed by a mobster whose real enemy was himself." No stretch of the imagination requires the realization that Bobby knew it was *his* enemies, *not* the president's, who had killed JFK. Such a proclamation is bolstered through the words of JFK presidential confidant Ken O'Donnell when asked about Bobby's suspicions regarding the assassination, "I mentioned the Syndicate—the Mob—as a possibility. I'm certain he thought the Mob had been involved. He suspected Carlos Marcello, the New Orleans capo to whom Jack Ruby had ties. . . . All he kept saying was 'They should've killed me,' without indicating who *they* were."

Bobby's admissions, never once mentioned by "Oswald Alone" authors Gerald Posner and Vincent Bugliosi, gains strength when one considers what RFK would have done if brother John had *not* been assassinated in Dallas, but only wounded. Is there any doubt that Bobby would have used every investigatory and legal weapon at the Justice Department's disposal to apprehend who was responsible? No, because at that point in time, RFK was still an attorney general with power, not the one who was rendered virtually powerless when JFK was killed.

With John Kennedy still in the Oval Office, Bobby would have gone to the ends of the earth to discover who was behind his brother's shooting, and to that end, where would he have looked? Isn't it logical to assume that Bobby would have sorted out the "usual suspects" based on motive? But once Bobby had scanned this list, doesn't common sense dictate that he very well could have turned his attention away from who might want the president dead for personal motives to those who wanted *him* dead so that Bobby would lose face and be stripped of his power? If he did, then square in his sights had to be Hoffa and Marcello since RFK knew they hated him more than anyone else in the world. Armed with this knowledge, it makes perfect sense that Bobby would have pursued both men. That this would have been the scenario is confirmed by RFK's disclosures to Richard Goodwin as documented by Evan Thomas and those of former CIA director John McCone, among others.

RFK's reaction to the death of his beloved brother is most revealing. Logically, Bobby's trip into depression had as much to do with personal guilt as it did with the loss of his brother/best friend. Former *New York Times Magazine* editor-in-chief and author Edward Klein wrote, "Bobby—who could never shake the suspicion that his enemies had retaliated against him by killing his brother—began reading ancient Greek tragedies for consolation." This was understandable according to the words author David Heymann wrote: "Bobby's despair was in no small measure a result of survivor's guilt. JFK had been warned of a climate of hatred in Dallas. . . . Moreover, it was RFK who suggested that the president ride through the streets of Dallas in a car without using the specially outfitted bulletproof top. 'It will give you more contact with the crowd,' he had said." Heymann then observed, "Bobby's advice to visit Dallas, however, weighed less heavily on him than did his conduct over the whole of his brother's term in office, for he had been the driving force in the Kennedy administration's most aggressive operations. He had pushed the government to hound the mob, to chase down Hoffa, to destroy Castro. . . . He knew that Jack Ruby was a Dallas racketeer connected to the national Mafia."

What a burden Bobby had to bear, to live the rest of his life with the knowledge that his enemies had killed his dear brother. Since RFK was a smart, logical, common sense man, he had to realize when he carefully considered who had killed JFK, when he sat awake in the middle of the night and pondered what had happened with a gut-wrenching feeling in his soul as tears filled his eyes, that somewhere Marcello was celebrating his total victory. While RFK suffered the loss of the man he treasured most in the world, Marcello, like Trafficante and Ragano, and Hoffa, was toasting the end of Bobby Kennedy and his wrath of persecution. How this knowledge must have gnawed at RFK; he must have felt like a fool since the handwriting had been on the wall; messing with powerful men, men of danger, men who had killed and would kill again, was like trying to tame a rattlesnake in the desert with the bite worse than anything he could have imagined. In effect, he was . . . the one who was going to rid America of the gangsters, and of the corrupt Hoffa, but he had lost, lost everything due to the death of his beloved brother. Perhaps one Bible verse that may have haunted him was from Genesis 4:10: "The voice of thy brother's blood crieth unto me from the ground."

RFK's sorrow was apparent to anyone who knew him. Author Randall B. Woods wrote, "The assassination did more than take away a beloved brother, it destroyed Bobby's purpose in life." The author then quoted Ethel Kennedy: "You couldn't get to him. His whole life was wrapped up in the President . . . [Bobby] was just another part of his brother—sort of an added arm."

Author Woods observed that after JFK's death, "[Bobby] wandered around in a daze, turning the justice department over to Undersecretary Nicholas Katzenbach." Woods wrote that RFK's college friend David Hackett told him, "It was as though someone had turned off the switch."

Such statements caused Woods to surmise, "Bobby began to display all of the signs of clinical depression: sleeplessness, moodiness, detachment, despair, and melancholy. He would take long nighttime rides in freezing weather in his convertible with the top down." He then added, "What made his slough of despondence particularly deep was that he feared he might have been indirectly responsible for his brother's death. As counsel to the McClellen Committee, he had directly pursued the Mafia with relentless energy, and had continued that crusade as attorney general."

Arthur Schlesinger wrote that "Robert Kennedy was a desperately wounded man" after JFK's assassination. John Seigenthaler, RFK's close associate, according to Schlesinger, observed, "I just had the feeling that it was physically painful, almost as if he were on the rack or that he had a toothache or that he had a heart attack. I mean it was pain and it showed itself as being pain. . . . It was very obvious to me, almost when he got up to walk, that it hurt to walk." In February 1964, William Manchester met with RFK, observing in *Controversy*, his collected essays, "Much of the time he seemed to be in a trance, his face a study in grief." Close friend Frank Mankiewicz saw it another way, telling author Seymour Hersh, "I must say I have never been as appalled at the sight of a human being since seeing a concentration camp as a nineteen-year-old. He was so wasted, like he disappeared into his shirt . . . [he] was haunted and thin wristed . . . he seemed out of it."

These comments were symbolic of those relating to RFK's inability to seek the true killers of his brother due to what the *House Select Committee on Assassinations Report* concluded about Justice Department inactions following the assassinations. Without doubt the Committee was on the right track by pointing fingers at possible suspects such as Hoffa and Marcello. But it required the final pieces of the puzzle that knowledge of "The Belli Factor," and other information, could have provided. This is apparent when one considers a critical quote from the report: "The committee believes on the basis of the evidence available to it, that President John F. Kennedy was probably assassinated as a result of a conspiracy. The committee is unable to identify the other gunman or the extent of the conspiracy." The report then stated: "The investigation [by

the Justice Department] into the possibility of conspiracy in the assassination was inadequate."

These Committee assertions were followed by the bold statement: *"The
Department of Justice failed to exercise initiative in supervising and directing the investigation by the Federal Bureau of Investigation of the assassination.* [Emphasis added]." To detail this failure, the report included the
accusation that "the Federal Bureau of Investigation failed to investigate
adequately the possibility of a conspiracy to assassinate the president."

According to the report, the Committee decided to much more actively
probe its accusations than the Justice Department, headed by RFK, had
done in its job in overseeing or actively participating in the assassinations
investigation. Most revealing is this Committee statement: "In the aftermath of the assassination of President Kennedy, the Justice Department
participated in various discussions with the White House and FBI officials,
and it had a major part in the formation of the Warren Commission. *The
committee found, however, that the department largely abdicated what should
have been important responsibilities in the continuing investigation* [emphasis
added]." It then added that *"officials at Justice did not exercise any significant
role in shaping, monitoring, or evaluating the FBI's investigation, despite the
bureau's organization status with the Department* [Emphasis added]." Even
more troubling, the report stated that "the committee discovered little
indication that Justice Department officials moved to mount a sophisticated criminal investigation of the assassination, *including its conspiracy
implications, an investigation that could have relied on the enormous resources
of the Department – its specialized investigative sections and attorneys, as
well as the power and capabilities of a federal grand jury, and the granting of
immunity* [emphasis added]."

All this was possible, the committee concluded, since officials had
decided that federal jurisdiction *did* exist over the assassination, blunting a
reason some RFK backers employed as an excuse for his inaction and that
of the Justice Department. To give Bobby some slack for his failure to do
his job based on the grief he was experiencing, the report acknowledged
that his mental state "significantly affected the Government's handling of
the investigation." But the report then chastised RFK for not taking "a

strong position" with FBI director J. Edgar Hoover "on the course of the investigation."

Criticizing RFK's minions at Justice, the report stated that while officials "were instrumental in creating the Warren Commission" the "Department exercised little authority in the investigation that followed . . . ." Summing up, the committee stated, "It was regrettable that the Department of Justice was taken out of the investigation, for whatever reason. It was unfortunate that it played so small a role in insuring a most thorough investigation of President Kennedy's assassination. *The promise of what the Department might have realized in fact was great, particularly in the use of such evidence-gathering tools as a grand jury and grants of immunity* [emphasis added]."

Author Seymour Hersh commented on RFK's behavior following the assassinations: "Robert Kennedy did nothing to pursue the truth behind his brother's death in 1964. He would have done nothing even if he had won the Democratic nomination in 1968 and the presidency. The price of a full investigation was much too high: making public the truth about President Kennedy and the Kennedy family. It was this fear, certainly that kept Robert Kennedy from testifying before the Warren Commission."

Why did Bobby act this way; why didn't he utilize his power at the Justice Department to launch a full-scale investigation, a grand jury investigation of the assassinations? Hersh hints at the reason: the fear of "making public the truth about President Kennedy and the Kennedy family." But what were these truths? Speculation has focused on JFK's philandering ways with women; Bobby's questionable tactics regarding Hoffa, Trafficante, and Marcello; and the question of whether the Kennedys "stole" the 1960 election through any number of illegalities, especially in the states of Illinois and West Virginia.

More important is the realization that Bobby thwarted any attempt to permit the convening of the federal grand jury mentioned in the *HSCA Report* based on the premise that there was no federal law covering the murder of a president. He knew that, while this was true, a grand jury could be convened if there was any suspicion of a conspiracy occurring. As the *Warren Commission Report* noted, "*Had there been reason to believe that the assassination was the result of a conspiracy* [emphasis added], federal jurisdiction could have been asserted; it has long been a federal crime to conspire to injure any federal officer, on account of, or while he is engaged in, the lawful discharge of the duties of his office."

Under direct orders from RFK, Deputy Attorney General Nicholas Katzenbach was the first to block any potential that a conspiracy occurred. On November 24th, just two days after the assassination, he wrote, according to a Warren Commission document, a yellow pad memo to President Johnson's press secretary, Bill Moyers: "It is important that all of the facts surrounding President Kennedy's assassination be made public in a way that will satisfy people in the United States and abroad that all of the facts have been told and that a statement to this effect be made now. . . . The public must be satisfied that Oswald was the assassin; that he did not have confederates who are still at large, and the evidence was such that he would have been convicted at trial. Speculations about Oswald's motive ought to be cut off."

While Katzenbach was doing his part to kill any notion of conspiracy, Dallas Police Chief Jess Curry, who had told reporters, referring to Oswald, "We have the man who killed the president," and J. Edgar Hoover were accomplices. Even when Jack Ruby shot Oswald, this made no difference, author Curt Gentry surmised since, "In a telephone call with the White House aide Walter Jenkins immediately following Oswald's murder, Hoover stated, 'The thing I am most concerned about, and so is Mr. Katzenbach, is having something issued so we can convince the public that Oswald is the real assassin.' To this end, the FBI's Clyde Tolson sent two men to Dallas to review any findings so that "we can prepare a memorandum to the Attorney General [setting] out the evidence showing that Oswald is responsible for the shooting that killed the President."

Gentry's conclusion: "The agents couldn't fail to get the message: the director had decided that Oswald had acted alone, and any evidence to the contrary would not be welcome." This prompted, Gentry noted, the *HSCA Report* to state, "Hoover's personal predisposition that Oswald had been the lone assassin affected the course of the investigation, adding to the momentum to conclude the investigation after limited consideration of possible conspiratorial theories." No wonder Gentry expressed his opinion that "From the start, the FBI investigation . . . was seriously flawed. It was based on a faulty premise, the presumption that the director was never wrong." To that end, Hoover told the public in a November 25th press release, "Not one shred of evidence has been developed to link any other person in a conspiracy with Oswald to assassinate President Kennedy."

Aiding the effort was the direct order from Hoover to Jess Curry that every file, every bit of investigation by detectives was to be turned over to the FBI. Curry carried out the order and boxes of evidence were shipped to Washington DC. Hoover now controlled the investigations of the assassinations, ones embarrassing to Hoover since they had occurred on the director's watch. Now he wanted to close the door, to make certain that a "nut" like Oswald was the lone gunman since that indicated Hoover could not have prevented JFK's demise. In effect, Hoover was attempting to save face, to avoid blame, by stifling any consideration of a conspiracy since, as noted, if the "nut" Oswald was JFK's sole assassin and the "lunatic" Ruby killed him, then there was nothing Hoover could have done to prevent the twin tragedies.

This stonewalling prevented any investigative agency from probing all of the facts surrounding the JFK and Oswald assassinations. Whether such inquiries, especially by a federal grand jury, would have uncovered the elements of "The Belli Factor" connecting Ruby's lawyer to the mob, is pure speculation. But at least the potential exists that it would have, and if so, the course of history would have been altered since the trail could very well have led from Ruby to Belli to Cohen to Marcello and ultimately, based on motive, to the doorstep of Joseph P. Kennedy.

CHAPTER EIGHTEEN

Ultimate Responsibility

Without doubt, few families in history have been besieged with tragedy like the Kennedys.

These include the airplane crash that killed oldest son Joseph P. Kennedy
Jr. during World War II, the death of Kathleen Kennedy Cavendish in an
airplane crash in France in 1948, the sudden death of John and Jackie's
prematurely-born son Patrick Bouvier of hyaline membrane disease in early
1963, JFK's assassination later that year, and Bobby's death at the hands of
Sirhan Sirhan in 1968. Edward Kennedy's Chappaquiddick car accident
in 1969; Bobby's son David's death by drug overdose in 1984; William
Kennedy Smith's rape allegations two years later; Bobby's son Michael's
death through a skiing accident in Aspen in 1997; the untimely and shocking death of John F. Kennedy Jr., his wife Carolyn Bessette Kennedy, and
his sister-in-law Lauren Bessette in a airplane crash in 1999; and the alleged
suicide of Robert F. Kennedy Jr.'s wife Mary in 2012, add to the list.

While each of these deaths was devastating—especially Joe Jr.'s, since
Joe Sr. expected him to become president—it was JFK's demise that was
arguably the crowning blow, the worst of the worst, for it hit at the very
heart of the Kennedy family. For the most part, history would be kind to
the president after his death, with several biographers generally leaving his

image untarnished except for questions surrounding dirty tricks used to win the 1960 presidential election, the embarrassment of the failed Bay of Pigs Cuban invasion, and JFK's extensive womanizing, including sharing a girlfriend, Judith Campbell, with Mafia don Sam Giancana, which threatened the very foundation of the presidency. The latter was arguably JFK's deepest flaw. The mistresses involved, according to author Edward Klein, were two White House staffers; Jackie's press secretary, Pamela Turnure; socialite and artist Mary Pinchot Meyer; Marilyn Monroe; Judith Campbell, later Judith Campbell Exner; and, as exposed in 2012, White House intern Mimi Alford, who alleged to having sex with the president in Jackie's bedroom.

Without doubt, JFK's adulterous way compromised the presidency, leading some to conclude that he was morally and spiritually deficient, a man with what might be called a split character: one loyal to his wife and children and the other afflicted with a sexual addiction. His ethical standards also come into question since he apparently approved of RFK's questionable tactics as attorney general toward dangerous, desperate men who played for keeps, men who killed when enemies threatened their kingdoms. But did JFK deserve to die at age 46? Definitely not. Perhaps author J. Randy Taraborrelli summed up many people's feelings about JFK when he wrote, "He was a President who made Americans feel that anything was possible. His optimism and eloquence, his ability to communicate to all Americans the possibility of a better life, made him unique in every way as he challenged Americans to look beyond the selfishness of their daily lives and focus attention on their communities, their nation, their world." He added that Kennedy's inaugural address was "widely acclaimed as the most memorable and unifying symbol of the modern political age: 'Ask not what your country can do for you, ask what you can do for your country.'"

When those who disliked or even hated JFK are stacked against the list of men who hated Joe and Bobby, once again, comparisons indicate that JFK had far fewer people who truly had reason to have him assassinated. JFK, who must be commended for defusing the Cuban Missile Crisis and his efforts in the field of civil rights, among other accomplishments, was never vindictive like his father or brother. JFK was more forgiving, not out to get people, to hate those who opposed him, to destroy his enemies at all costs. Regarding Bobby, Papa Joe had admitted this, it may be recalled, when he boasted to future House Speaker Tip O'Neill, "You can trample all over him [JFK], and the next day, he's there for you with open arms. But Bobby's my boy. When Bobby hates you, you stay hated." These personality flaws in Joe and Bobby and not in JFK were the reason why those who hated Joe and Bobby did so with such vengeance and with revenge on their minds.

Regardless, when an atmosphere of hatred prevails, senseless acts of violence occur to those close to the ones actually causing the hate to prevail. In the end, JFK became a victim of his father's power-hungry arrogance, and then Bobby's obsession with destroying bloodthirsty, ruthless mobsters like Carlos Marcello whom RFK believed were the worst of the worst of American society.

When JFK died, the country and his family mourned, but it was Bobby left to deal with the brunt of the loss of the brother he dearly loved. Authors Gus Russo and Stephen Molton decided that "the fury that [RFK] had first aimed at God . . . now seemed to be [aimed] at himself." They pointed out that Bobby's Catholic beliefs, ones precious to him before JFK's death, took a back seat to other works including those by French author and philosopher Albert Camus, Greek philosophers, and classicist Edith Hamilton, all suggested by Jackie Kennedy. From Hamilton's *The Greek Way*, the authors noted, RFK selected a passage to remember: "The gods who hated beyond all else the arrogance of power, had passed judgment upon them." He also related, Russo and Molton wrote, to the words of Aeschylus: "All arrogance will reap a harvest rich in tears, God calls men to a heavy reckoning for overweening pride." Biographer Evan Thomas wrote, "[Robert] Kennedy discovered fate and hubris. He began to wonder if the Kennedy family had somehow overreached, dared too greatly." After mentioning the passage in Edith Hamilton's book above, and how RFK had underlined it, Thomas noted, "The Kennedys *were* the House of Atreus, noble and doomed, and RFK began to see himself as Agamemnon," the King of Mycenae whose family experienced evil through a dreadful curse.

‡

Since Robert Kennedy was the chief law enforcement official in the land, he truly believed that men such as Carlos Marcello, Santo Trafficante, Sam Giancana, James Hoffa, and other mafiosi deserved to be prosecuted to the full extent of the law. But RFK's personal obsession with prosecuting those he considered "scum" triggered a belief that he could skirt the very laws he was sworn to uphold.

This prosecutorial zeal, as author Richard D. Mahoney wrote, caused RFK to have an attitude where, "All [his] personality pointed to Bobby's chief failing: underestimating his enemies." In the case of Marcello, it was a grave error, since Marcello was described, as noted, by Nick Pileggi as "tough. Impossible to seduce and the kind of Sicilian mafioso you didn't want to turn into an enemy."

Certainly there were those who applauded RFK's crusade to rid America of dangerous men like Marcello, Trafficante, Giancana, and Hoffa, including those loyal to him in the attorney general's office, but Bobby's approval of questionable wiretaps during investigations of these men and others was another cause for concern. Author David E. Koskoff wrote that RFK "set the federal government on an out-of-hand 'bugging' jag that extended as far as the phones of the likes of Martin Luther King. . . . One government associate told Gore Vidal, 'It's not as if Bobby were against civil liberties . . . its just that he doesn't know what they are.'" This caused Koskoff to write that Bobby had a "stop-at-nothing approach to 'getting' mafiosi." These allegations were bolstered by author Jeff Shesol who noted that while "the public seemed to agree . . . that [RFK] by his own intelligence, initiative and courage established himself as a real 'comer' [in the AG's office] . . . to many others, Kennedy had revealed himself as a viscious, opportunistic zealot, eagerly trampling civil liberties to carry out personal vendettas."

Robert F. Kennedy—Dubbed "assistant president," Attorney General Robert Kennedy turned his wrath towards organized crime causing his chief weakness, as one author noted, "underestimating his enemies."   Credit: Corbis Images

Most important is that, regardless of whether RFK believed he was right in pursuing the Mafia and Hoffa using every investigative tool at his disposal, even if some of them were of questionable legal means, the perception by these men that he had crossed the line from prosecution to persecution. Based on eyewitness accounts as well as fresh information presented in this book, common sense logic points to those who masterminded JFK's assassination: the chief RFK haters, Marcello in collusion with Trafficante, while Hoffa cheered from the sidelines. They were the ones with the strongest motive, the ones who sought revenge of the highest degree. This raises a question: Could Bobby Kennedy alone have prevented the death of his brother John? On two counts, the answer is yes.

First, if RFK had heeded warnings in plain sight to ease up on Hoffa and the gangsters, or at least stopped making the matter personal instead of business, mean-spirited in their eyes, their motive to kill him or JFK might have disappeared. Second, if Teamsters official Frank "The Irishman" Sheeran was correct to the effect that Bobby knew the inner workings of the Mafia better than anyone outside the underworld. RFK was aware of an age-old ritual: in times of mob conflict the boss under fire eliminated the boss threatening him, not the underling, since retaliation was then the call of the day. By this logic RFK should have seen his brother's death coming since Bobby was indeed the underling. RFK should have realized that if he continued to chase the mob bosses there would be what Sheeran dubbed a "regime change," since, as author Charles Brandt quoted Sheeran, "To the Italian bosses it is merely a matter of following the old Sicilian maxim that to kill a dog you don't cut off its tail, you cut off its head."

Certainly, once JFK was dead, a "regime change" had taken place with the target JFK (the head) and not Bobby (the tail). That Bobby never considered this likelihood is evident through the words he uttered, as noted, to Justice Department spokesman Ed Guthman *after* JFK was assassinated to the effect that the bitterness Bobby knew existed caused him to believe that he might be harmed, but not his brother. This was a fatal mistake of judgment on RFK's part, one that led directly to JFK's assassination.

This supposition was enhanced during an interview Robert F. Kennedy Jr. provided to Charlie Rose, the PBS talk show host in January 2013. As part of a series of events at the Winspear Opera House in Dallas commemorating the fiftieth anniversary of JFK's death, RFK Jr. revealed several observations his father had about the assassinations. Among them were the revelations that Bobby believed the *Warren Commission Report* was "a shoddy piece of craftsmanship," and that "RFK spent a year trying to come to grips with his brother's death, reading the work of Greek philosophers, Catholic scholars, Henry David Thoreau, poets and others trying to figure out kind of the existential implications of why a just God would allow injustice to happen of the magnitude he was seeing."

Regarding the mechanics of JFK's assassination, RFK Jr. surmised that "the evidence at this point is very, very convincing that it was not a lone gunman [who shot JFK]" while avoiding any theories of his own. When Rose asked if he believed that RFK "felt some sense of guilt because he thought there might have been a link between his very aggressive efforts against organized crime," RFK said his father "had investigators do research into the assassination and found that phone records of Oswald and nightclub owner Jack Ruby, who had killed Oswald two days after the president's assassination, 'were like an inventory' of Mafia leaders the government had been investigating." RFK Jr. added that his father was "fairly convinced" that others were involved.

RFK's admissions to his son provide added impetus for throwing the blame in Bobby's direction, but if RFK is to be held responsible, another must be, and even more so, for he could also have prevented JFK's senseless death. Like RFK, he did not pull the trigger on the gun that killed the president, but he might as well have done so. Through the years, for whatever reason, as blame has been spread many times in a ludicrous manner toward illogical suspects, or none other than Oswald, this man has gotten a pass. No more.

Based on the fresh facts presented here including the desperation of the evil men mentioned above to extinguish RFK from their lives, "to get him off their backs," as James Hoffa put it, or to kill JFK to "get his brother, Robert Kennedy, off my back," one who had put "unprecedented heat on organized crime," as admitted by Vincent Bugliosi, the man to blame must be Joseph P. Kennedy Jr. Instead of wild-eyed theories that lead nowhere, Joe bears the ultimate responsibility.

Why? Because it was the patriarch of the Kennedy clan who made a fatal mistake, one without doubt triggering the chain reaction leading to three deaths in Dallas in November 1963. What was this mistake? The answer may be traced to an ill-fated decision Joe made, *one that changed the course of history*, one that he must have regretted for the rest of his life after his beloved son John was dead.

Since understanding this decision is so vital to realizing why JFK had to die, it is important to put it in context. Once JFK had been elected president, Kennedy family confidante John Seigenthaler, confirmed to this author that Joe was insistent on Bobby being attorney general. Seigenthaler said he was present during the two days in 1960 when JFK made his decision. "The president first floated the balloon about Bobby becoming the attorney general during a Florida golf match with Bill Lawrence of *The New York Times*," Seigenthaler recalled. "Bobby told me 'that's Dad,'" meaning Joe was insisting on the appointment and, behind the hint to Lawrence, that JFK was considering the appointment of RFK as attorney general.

"JFK was running the idea up the flagpole to see what kind of reaction he would get," Seigenthaler told this author, "and there was sharp criticism right away since Bobby was aligned with Joe McCarthy and had been on the McClellan Committee. But Joe was pushing the issue and so I drove Bobby around to various people so he could see what they thought. We went to the Mayflower [hotel] to see Harry Truman, and Bobby had coffee with him and came back dejected." Then, "we went to see [Supreme Court Justice] Bill Douglas, J. Edgar Hoover, then others including Senator William Fulbright. I used to accuse Bobby of having a 'cross face' when he was pissed off, and after all of these meetings that was how he looked since nearly all of them told him not to take the job as AG. In fact, Truman told him to get as far away as possible; he was really plain spoken and didn't like Bobby anyway."

That evening, Seigenthaler said he ate dinner with RFK and Ethel at their Hickory Hill home. "They talked about how RFK could teach, write, and travel and what a great career he had in front of him. Bobby wasn't going to take the job, and he said, 'this will kill dad,' a reference to disappointing Joe." But the next morning, during breakfast of bacon and eggs with JFK at his Georgetown flat, Seigenthaler said the incoming president responded to Bobby's initiating words, "now about my situation," by telling his younger brother, "There is no one around I really know. I need someone who will be interested in my interests and I need you." During the 70 minute monologue, Seigenthaler recalled, "JFK made his case, brief and concise by saying that Bobby was best qualified to handle organized crime and so forth. JFK then poured them both some coffee before Bobby said, 'well, I have some points to make.' But Jack had made up his mind and he said, 'let's just grab our balls and go.'"

For the PBS program, *American Experience*: "The Kennedys," JFK's personal counsel Clark Clifford confirmed the crux of Seigenthaler's recollections. Clifford said that after he mentioned the "historical importance of the Attorney General and the impact it had on a number of administrations," he told Joe Kennedy, "This [appointing Bobby] would be a serious mistake." Clifford recalled the elder Kennedy pausing and then replying, "You've presented it [your argument] very well. I want to leave you with just one thought. Bobby Kennedy *is* going to be Attorney General of the United States."

CHAPTER NINETEEN

The Poison Patriarch

Joe Kennedy's demand/order was no news to those who knew him as a strong advocate who got his way. As chronicled in several biographies, his past was packed with incidents where Joe played both sides of the law in order to amass a fortune and become one of the most elite power brokers in the world. This aspect of the elder Kennedy's personality comes through even in favorable accounts of his life. David Nasaw's 2012 book, *The Patriarch: The Remarkable Life and Turbulent Times of Joseph P. Kennedy*, was written at the request of Edward Kennedy and Jean Kennedy Smith. After admitting that Joe was alleged to be "an appeaser, an isolationist, an anti-Semite, a Nazi sympathizer, an unprincipled womanizer, a treacherous and vengeful scoundrel who made millions as a bootlegger and Wall Street swindler, then used those millions to steal elections for his son," Nasaw added, "that there is some truth to these allegations is indisputable," while noting that "they tell only part of a larger, grander, more complicated history."

"Complicated" may have been Nasaw's perception, but others did not hesitate to nail Joe Kennedy, who was dismissed as US Ambassador to Great Britain by President Franklin D. Roosevelt over his appeasing attitude toward Hitler and his isolationist position regarding the United States' involvement in World War II. Authors Peter Collier and David

Horowitz wrote, "Rumors of numerous extramarital affairs, illicit business dealings, and even ties to crime only added a piquant touch of mystery to his reputation and made [Joe] seem all the more romantic, Gatsbyesque." Collier and Horowitz then quoted a *Fortune* magazine article to make their point: "The legends of Joe Kennedy make him at once the hero of a Frank Merriwell captain-of-the-nines adventure, a Horatio Alger success story, an E. Phillips Oppenheim tale of intrigue, and a John Dos Passos dillusioning report on the search for the big money." The article continued, "The truth makes him a central character of picaresque novel of a sort not yet written . . . [Joe] was more than a ruthless opportunist," a characterization as relevant to RFK as to his father.

Author C. David Heymann noted that as early as the days when Joe was about to marry Rose, her father "sensed a moral defect in young Joe . . . initially opposed the marriage." Heymann noted that Joe, alleged to have been a bootlegger during prohibition in business with racketeers such as New York's Frank Costello, had "circumvented the law by importing thousands of cases of spirits under 'medicinal' licenses" before selling them "for millions more than he paid for them." Perhaps more importantly, Heymann wrote, "Even more diligently than he accumulated great wealth, [Joe] poured into his sons everything he learned and wished for himself."

This may be why author Seymour Hersh alleged that both Bobby and Ted Kennedy personally distributed bribes and other payoffs in West Virginia during the 1960 election. Like father, like sons. Joe had been fixing elections since his early days in Boston. Evelyn Lincoln, President Kennedy's secretary, admitted, Hersh wrote, "I know they bought the election," a comment backed up by Evan Thomas's allegations: "Votes were sold in West Virginia, and the Kennedys paid for them."[20]

---

20 During a 2000 interview on *Sixty Minutes* to promote her book, *My Father's Daughter*, Frank Sinatra's daughter Tina confirmed that, "[My father] got Chicago mob boss Sam Giancana to help John F. Kennedy win the presidency by asking him to talk to the Mafia about securing the labor union vote in the crucial West Virginia primary in 1960." An editorial on the Sinatra family website, established by daughter Nancy, read, "Please keep in mind when reading or hearing stories about JFK, FS, and Sam Giancana that it was Joseph Kennedy Sr. who approached Frank for help in contacting Sam Giancana because he knew Frank, like all others on the circuit, performed in nightclubs owned by mob bosses."

Hersh also pegged Joe as a partner with the notorious Frank Costello during Prohibition despite denials by the elder Kennedy: "Joe Kennedy played by his own rules in running his personal life and in amassing his personal fortune. He employed the same ruthlessness and secrecy with all—his wife, fellow businessmen, organized crime figures and political figures."

Joe Kennedy's business acumen during the Depression was both praised and ridiculed. Some believed his shrewdness permitted savvy investments, but others, such as author David E. Koskoff, believed Kennedy took advantage of insider trading, showing "a steely disregard for the consequences of his actions to anyone but himself. While insider trading was not outlawed until 1933, Koskoff concluded that "[the elder Kennedy] was about making money and that's what counted. Years later he would brag about this least praiseworthy period of his life." Author Ronald Kessler focused on a disturbing characteristic of the elder Kennedy: his anti-Semitism and lack of concern for the victims of Nazi oppression and what amounted to genocide. Among those who substantiated this claim was Morton Downey Jr., a Kennedy family friend. According to Kessler, Downey said, "Joe Kennedy's feeling toward Jews was that the only way he could be a success was that every day when he got up, he would focus on one deal involving a Jew, and he would win that deal. That was his whole driving spirit . . . Joe and his father would refer to Jews by a code word—'Canadian geese,' apparently because of a perception that Jews have long noses."

Joe the womanizer was the predecessor to JFK and RFK, the womanizers; like father, like sons, carbon copies of their father, each suffering from sexual addiction and intent on instant gratification without a care for the consequences. Among those whom Joe cheated with during his long marriage to Rose were, according to Kessler, Claire Boothe Luce, later a congresswoman from Connecticut and wife of *Time* magazine publisher Henry Luce; sexy fashion models supplied to Joe by famous designer Oleg Cassini; Kay Stammers, a British tennis star; and the woman Kessler called "Joe's Hollywood trophy," the glamorous starlet Gloria Swanson, "the reigning queen of the movies," Joe's girlfriend in the late 1920s. Marilyn Monroe became JFK's trophy mistress during his presidency, but it was Joe who had first enjoyed a clandestine sexual relationship with a Hollywood celebrity years earlier. In fact, as author Christopher Bigsby pointed out through a quote from Hollywood cameraman Leon Shamroy, "[Monroe] had a kind of fantastic beauty, like Gloria Swanson, when a movie star had to look beautiful."

Author David Nasaw, in writing about the elder Kennedy's infidelity, pointed out that Joe had affairs with women from all walks of life. Regarding the Swanson affair, Nasaw wrote, "Gloria Swanson offered him the vehicle he needed to climb to the top of his profession."

The author then documented the first time Swanson and Joe had sex (January 1928 shortly before Joe and Rose Kennedy's fifth child was born), their sexual trysts in Beverly Hills and the odd occurrence where Swanson, Rose, and her sister Margaret actually sailed together from Paris to New York. Nasaw added: "That [Joe] wandered from the marriage bed was inconsequential to him. Adultery was a sin, but one easily forgotten."

Based on these disclosures, the saying, "the apple doesn't fall far from the tree," is certainly appropriate when it comes to discussing Joe, John, and, yes, Robert Kennedy's love lives. Each was an adulterer of the first degree with John and Robert having had an excellent tutor in this regard. Ted Sorenson, arguably JFK's closest adviser, whose book soft-soaped Kennedy family flaws, wrote, "[JFK was] . . . unfailingly flirtatious with all young women, particularly pretty, single women. . . . Like his father before him, JFK did not resist these temptations when they became available."

While these characterizations shed light on the flawed man who "poured into his sons everything he learned and wished for himself," Joseph Kennedy's 738-page FBI file, acquired by this author under the Freedom of Information Act, provided more information about how Joe was clearly a clever man who played on both sides of the street. Little known is the fact that as early as 1937, he was under scrutiny by the bureau. Even less known is that Joe and future FBI Director J. Edgar Hoover became friends during a time when both interacted with the National Maritime Union.

When Hoover was appointed head of the bureau, this would lead to an obscure posting in Kennedy's FBI file indicating that in October, 1944 "[Joe Kennedy] was enlisted in this office [Boston] in the case entitled Bureau File #1—8039." The reference, based on further file notations, was to his becoming a "Special Service Contact." Nine years later, in a file memo, one commenting on Joe's qualifications to be appointed to the Commission on Governmental Reorganization, the notations included, "The Bureau's relations with Kennedy over the past years have been very cordial."

This apparently meant Joe could be helpful based on his position as "an outstanding financier and industrialist and [being] highly regarded in business, governmental and professional circles." An earlier memo called him "a Special Services Contact of the Boston Division for many years," one who was "valued." The November memo noted that Joe was "a close personal friend of the Director and the Bureau."

In 2010, when the Edward Kennedy FBI files were released, Joe Kennedy's high admiration for Hoover was apparent throughout. The file divulged that Joe, in 1955, had written to Hoover saying, according to the FBI director, "that he understood I was interested in becoming a candidate for the Presidency. He urged me to run for this position either on a Republican or Democratic ticket, guaranteeing me the largest campaign contribution I would ever get from anyone, and his personal services as the hardest campaign worker in history." Hoover declined the suggestion, but the File noted that he "was deeply touched by the wonderful confidence implicit in his offer."

Considering how Joe waxed friendly with Hoover, one startling fact about Joe's FBI file becomes less startling. There is not a single mention of Joe's adulterous affairs or any secret relationships or activities with those connected to the underworld despite the apparent knowledge both of Joe's bootlegging enterprises and affection for such underworld characters as Frank Costello, and, even more apparent, Sam Giancana. The files depict Joe as squeaky clean—a saint of sorts—his image sanitized with absolutely no skirmish or scandal concerning any of his credentials or dealings. This despite Seymour

Hersh's reporting that Cartha D. DeLoach, a deputy director under Hoover, had told him he knew Kennedy was a "prominent bootlegger during Prohibition" and that "he had associates in organized crime who respected him." Joseph Kennedy biographer Ronald Kessler included several references to Joe's bootlegging days, leading to the author's conclusion that "bootlegging on a sizable scale [accounted] for [Joe's] sudden and fabulous wealth." In a March 2013 *Vanity Fair* profile of former millionaire Hollywood producer Merv Adelson, he mentions Las Vegas mobster Moe Dalitz, saying, "He was a rumrunner. So was Jack Kennedy's father. In fact, Moe told me they were good friends." Adelson also divulges that one of his real estate projects, the Sunrise Hospital in Las Vegas, was financed through James Hoffa's Teamsters union pension fund. "Were the Teamsters mobbed up?" Adelson asks. "Oh God were they?"

Joe Kennedy's links to mobsters, the same ones Melvin Belli's friend Mickey Cohen was connected to for years on end, provided the prelude to soliciting their help during the 1960 presidential election. Author Ted Schwarz wrote, "As near as can be determined, Joe Kennedy had laid the groundwork for mob involvement in obtaining votes through the assistance of key leaders of organized-crime families. Joe supplied the money. The mob supplied the contacts and the organization, and they were responsible for the grassroots bribery."

When the state of Illinois became pivotal, the elder Kennedy requested assistance from Chicago mobster Sam Giancana according to Chuck Giancana, his brother, and Sam Giancana, Sam's nephew. The help was provided; JFK won the state. In the minds of the brother and nephew, there was immediate shock when JFK appointed his brother attorney general, confirmed by author Kitty Kelley's assertion that Bobby's being attorney general was the "last thing that anyone [in the mob] thought would happen." The appointment triggered feelings of betrayal, a nasty business within an underworld that had its own code of ethics and brand of loyalty connected with promises. Frank Ragano recounted in *Mob Lawyer* a conversation months after JFK's death when Giancana, who controlled the precinct captains in Chicago, joined Trafficante and him

Salvatore "Sam" Giancana handcuffed to a detective bureau chair after a 1950s arrest in connection with the murder of banker Leon Marcus. Dangerous Chicago don Giancana believed Joseph Kennedy reneged on a promise to never pursue him or Mafia brethren like Carlos Marcello, once JFK was elected, if the underworld helped secure the 1960 election for the Kennedys.   Credit: Corbis Images.

for dinner at a Florida restaurant. Ragano said Giancana "blustered in no uncertain terms that his organization won—or, rather, stole—the 1960 election for Kennedy by fixing votes for him in Cook County." (Special prosecutor Morris Wexler's report in 1961 discovered irregularities involving "substantial miscounts" in and around Chicago including "unqualified voters, misread voting machines and math mistakes." JFK won the state by 8,858 votes out of 4.7 million cast.)

On another occasion, Frank Ragano quoted Giancana, described by author Evan Thomas in his Robert Kennedy biography as one who had "hung people on meat hooks," as saying, "That rat bastard, son-of-a-bitch. We broke our balls for him [JFK] and gave him the election and he gets his brother [Bobby] to hound us to death." Sam's daughter, Antoinette Giancana, and coauthors John R. Hughes and Thomas H. Jobe, wrote, "When Sam learned that Robert F. Kennedy had been appointed attorney general, he felt it was a rabbit punch in the dark." Antoinette added that her father said, "Some day they are gonna get their lunch, in other words, somebody is gonna take after them and really destroy them, and it won't just be me, it's also going to be others that are going to lead to the Kennedy demise."

Mafioso Bill Bonnano wrote that the appointment was " . . . the shock of the winter. . . . If Kennedy had wanted to, he could not have sent a more alarming signal to our world." This reaction was based on Bonnano swearing that Joseph Kennedy, when asked before the election what Bobby's intended position was in the new administration, had responded, according to Bonnano, "The old man specifically told us that if Jack was elected, he was gonna make Bobby ambassador to Ireland or something like that." Bonnano also chronicled the friendship between his father Joe and Joe Kennedy while noting that in the mid-1950s, Joe Kennedy had begged Joe Bonnano to assist with newly-elected Senator John Kennedy's plans for the future. Bill Bonnano, who also noted Joe Kennedy's friendship with Frank Costello, wrote, "Joe [Bonnano] that day promised that he would do what he could to help Joe Kennedy when and if the time came. This was a pledge made out of friendship—but also out of something else. My father knew Joe Kennedy, knew enough about his past to feel confident that help offered would be returned. There was friendship—and a skeleton or two in the closet."

Bill Bonnano also swore in his book that Joe Kennedy was warned during the fall 1961 of impending trouble ahead if Bobby didn't forego his crusade against the Mafia. Bonanno wrote, "We sent . . . Smitty D'Angelo to Palm Beach to meet with [Joe] Kennedy and tell him about our concerns. He specifically told the old man that there were people in our world who felt betrayed, who had looked to him as a friend, only to be disappointed. Kennedy told him not to worry." Joe Kennedy's response, according to Bonnano: "There's nothing to worry about. The boys [JFK and RFK] will be home with me over Christmas. Wait until after Christmas." Bonnano then noted that "Christmas never came that year," since one week before the holidays Joe suffered a massive stroke, leaving him incapacitated. This permits speculation as to whether Joe Kennedy might have asked/ordered Bobby to back off his campaign to destroy the Mafia. But by the fall of 1961, RFK had already attacked the mobsters with a vengeance by deporting Marcello and charging him with conspiracy, hitting Trafficante with tax evasion charges, hounding Giancana, and escalating his crusade to imprison Hoffa. This makes it difficult to believe that Joe Kennedy could have persuaded the headstrong Bobby to forgo his obsession to rid the world of these men. Regardless, Joe, who also was aware of how the underworld took care of their enemies, should have realized that the warning from Giancana's henchman was real, and that if Bobby didn't back off, bad things could happen.

No one knows for sure whether Bobby would have heeded his father's advice if it has been passed along, especially since author Evan Thomas wrote, "Bobby had a deep respect for his father, tinged with fear." Regardless, "the mobsters continued to squeal that they had been double-crossed by the Kennedys," meaning that because Joe was warned and couldn't follow through due to his stroke, a chance to potentially fend off the president's assassination had been lost.

To those who are dubious of the proclamations by either Bill Bonnano or the Giancana family based on the potential for exaggeration, the stories they tell have a ring of truth to them based on Joe Kennedy's propensity to make promises and break them. Author Ted Schwarz wrote, "Joe's utilization of the mob was no different from the patron-client arrangement used in Sicily by men who formed the base of the American Mafia. Joe had done favors for which repayment was expected. He called them in to help his son win the presidential election." The author then added, "Jack misunderstood this, or his father did not explain the rules. He seems to have made deals on his own, never realizing that each favor granted was a favor expected." If Schwarz is correct, not only Joe Kennedy, but Jack, was beholden to the underworld for promises made. Perhaps this is why JFK was so reluctant to appoint RFK to be attorney general to begin with. Perhaps he knew of the risk, but with his father pressing the issue and failing to take "no" for an answer, the president had no choice in the matter.

What is important is that even if Bobby Kennedy did not believe it to be true, believed that he was simply enforcing the law as attorney general, what Sam Giancana, and by reference his associate Carlos Marcello and all of the Mafia dons, including Melvin Belli's client Mickey Cohen, being pursued had good reason to believe was that if they assisted with JFK's election, help put him in the White House, they would be left alone. This may have been pie-in-the-sky thinking, but the fact that the mafiosi *had the perception* that Joe Kennedy would order RFK to ease up caused the Mafia dons to believe Joe had made a promise, that he was indebted to them and should honor the promise. This line of thinking is bolstered by statements made by Tina Sinatra and a secret FBI wiretap conversation between Giancana and his underling, mobster Johnny Roselli.

In 2000, Tina, as noted, had told *Sixty Minutes*, as noted, that her father Frank had been the intermediary between Joe Kennedy and Giancana concerning the latter's help with the 1960 election. In 1961, after RFK continued to pursue the mafiosi, Tina described a conversation she had with her dad and how he had to placate the angry Giancana. "Sam was saying," Tina revealed, quoting Frank, "That's not right. You know he owes me." Tina then added, "He meaning Joe Kennedy."

The FBI tape was also quite revealing since it connected Frank Sinatra as well. Based on a transcript, the conversation in 1961 between Giancana and Roselli revealed that while Giancana believed Joe Kennedy was in debt to the mobster based on the favor Sinatra had asked of the Chicago don, Giancana, referring to his assistance with the election as a "donation," shouldn't expect too much. Roselli made this clear telling his boss,

" . . . they treat Frank like they treat a whore. You pay him and they're through," an indication that Giancana had been used and thrown away, a double cross. This caused research expert Larry Hancock to tell this author, "I certainly think the betrayal point is true; you only have to listen to the taped [FBI] conversations."[21]

That Giancana, Marcello, and the others who had expected to be left alone when JFK was elected felt betrayed ("You know he [Joe Kennedy] owes me.") was the key point, whether Joe believed he owed them something or not. Being double-crossed with no end in sight, based on RFK's obsessions, was the final straw for Bobby's enemies, one leading to JFK's assassination.

Joe Kennedy may have been guilty of many things in his life, including never letting his mob friends know he was a contact agent for the FBI, but double-crossing the Mafia was the fatal mistake. One may only speculate on what Joe Kennedy's mindset was when he forced JFK to appoint Bobby attorney general. Perhaps he had an ulterior motive, believing that with Bobby as attorney general, no one would dare investigate irregularities in West Virginia, Illinois, or any other state during the presidential election. Or perhaps, Joe, power hungry at every turn, wanted two sons at the head of government; one was not enough.

This explanation makes more sense when one considers further the context within which Joe ordered JFK to appoint Bobby attorney general. There is no doubt that Joe wanted to be president, his dream throughout his adult life. But those chances had all but disappeared through the messy ordeal he experienced as Ambassador to Great Britain. As David Nasaw wrote, Joe was "perpetually out of step with everyone around him" and this included his views about Adolf Hitler's intentions and American isolationism. Describing Joe's downfall, Nasaw believed that Joe wasn't a "team player" since he thought he was smarter than those above him. Therefore,

---

21 Author Curt Gentry alluded to the "donation" in his book *J. Edgar Hoover: The Man and his Secrets*, revealing that Hoover wrote to RFK, "[Giancana] made a donation to the campaign of President Kennedy but was not getting his money's worth." Gentry surmised, "the insult was palpable," before noting that in all likelihood Hoover was simply letting the Kennedys know he knew of their dealings with Giancana, something he could hold over their heads.

Nasaw wrote, Kennedy pursued his priorities but broke rules along the way "whenever he thought it necessary."

In October 1940, Joe Kennedy left his post to return to Washington. Bitter at being, for all practical purposes, recalled, he said he was "damn sore at the way I have been treated. I feel that it is entirely unreasonable and I don't think I rated it." By December, he had resigned but not without chewing at Roosevelt for what amounted to a dismissal. In turn, FDR told his son-in-law, according to author Nasaw, that Joe was "a temperamental Irish boy" who had become a "financial success," and though he was certainly patriotic, was also "thoroughly selfish . . . "

Joe Kennedy now had to decide whether any presidential ambitions were squelched through his unfortunate departure as ambassador. As early was 1938, there had been speculation. One article had appeared in the popular magazine, *Liberty*, asking the question, "Will Kennedy Run For President?" Further, author Ronald Kessler wrote, "Roosevelt said he knew Joe wanted to be the first Catholic president." Kessler further offered a quote from Joe's friend, Arthur Krock, that Joe "hoped to be nominated in 1940, without any question."

No nomination would ever appear due to the unkind characterizations of Joe Kennedy, especially in the media. The *New York Herald Tribune* wrote that the termination of Joe's "unfortunate" career as ambassador meant Americans "could breathe more easily." Author J. Randy Taraborrelli wrote, " . . . politically, Joseph was poison. He had completely destroyed his own political career and reputation by making negative comments about FDR and seeming to endorse some of Hitler's policies . . . "

Such notions, and Joe's knowledge that any presidential ambitions were history caused him to turn his attention to real estate development. But that didn't mean the Oval Office wasn't on his mind—if he couldn't be president then he was determined that one of his sons would be, thereby permitting him to live vicariously through them.

When his favorite son, Joe Jr., was killed when his plane exploded in midair over England during World War II, Jack was next in line. And it is not a far cry to believe that when Jack was elected president, Joe must have believed that when his two terms were completed there would be Bobby,

John Fitzgerald Kennedy/Joseph P. Kennedy/Joe Kennedy Jr.—When Joseph P. Kennedy's plans to become US president expired through his own misdeeds as Ambassador to Britain, he lived, as historian Doris Kearns Goodwin wrote, "vicariously through his children." This meant Joe Jr. would run for president, but when he died Jack was next in line.   Credit: Corbis Images.

the "assistant president," ready to carry on the Kennedy dynasty. Certainly Joe would have the last laugh over FDR and those critics who had made it, in Joe's mind, impossible for him to become the most powerful man in the world. Instead, the power-hungry Joe would, for all practical purposes, "be the president" without the title since he controlled both sons through his domineering presence. This was in line with observations made by Pulitzer Prize-winning and bestselling historian Doris Kearns Goodwin. While noting Joe Kennedy's unrest during his fall from grace as ambassador, she wrote, "Indeed, the more depressed he felt about his falling prestige, the more solace he found in his children's accomplishments. Little by little, starting slowly in this period and multiplying in the years ahead, [Joe] began to live vicariously through his children, counting their successes as his own, as if he were resurrecting his injured love of self through them."

To be certain, John Kennedy did not have to die but for the actions of Joe Kennedy, forcing JFK to appoint RFK attorney general, and then Bobby, continuing his personal crusade against those men he hated with even more vengeance than before. These actions sealed the president's fate: one unnecessary, one unwarranted, one that could have been avoided. JFK was definitely a flawed man but did not deserve to die because of the actions of his father, and brother Bobby.

Such common sense logic presents an interesting question, one that appears to never have been answered in any book or investigation to date: Who did Joe Kennedy believe assassinated his son? Introduction of "The Belli Factor" has pointed the finger square at Marcello as the one most likely to have masterminded the Dallas killings. But who was the most logical person or persons in Joe Kennedy's mind when he learned of the news that JFK had been killed?

Discovering the answer is difficult since from media reports and from Ted Schwarz's writings about Joseph Kennedy, it is known that "Joe was on a steady decline, no longer capable of making a sound." Other reports stated that the immobilized elder Kennedy could not write and only mumble the words, "no, no, no." This was due to the stroke that had occurred in December 1961, a blood clot in a brain artery, causing one to wonder whether Joe's acute medical condition that left him wheelchair bound and helpless was payback for his sins.

There were conflicting stories regarding how Joe learned of JFK's assassination. Some believed the telephone call was made by Lyndon Johnson. Another such story indicated that, with Eunice by his side, Ted told his father, "Dad, Jack was shot." Visualizing this sad moment, author Schwarz wrote, "Joe sat up in bed, was given a sedative, and read the story [in the *New York Times*]. He finished, swept the paper to the floor, and lay back down to sleep."

When he swept the newspaper to the floor, what was Joe Kennedy thinking? Did he get it? Did he realize instantly, as others had, among them his own son Bobby, who had uttered, "There's so much bitterness I thought they would get one of us, but Jack, after all he had been through, [I] never worried about it . . . I never thought it would happen. I thought it would be me."? Based on his knowledge of how revenge was an integral part of the Mafia operation, a given when they were double-crossed, Joe must have known, must have believed that his son's killers were easy to identify, easy to blame. If he did, then the guilt he felt must have been overwhelming, even stronger than that experienced by RFK. This was especially true since, according to Arthur Schlesinger, Joe told John Seigenthaler, "I don't want my enemies to be my son's enemies." But they were; and it is plausible to believe that Joe must have wondered whether JFK, as suggested above, had became a victim of Bobby's obsession with destroying James Hoffa and bloodthirsty mobsters.

In an ironic twist of fate, Joe outlived both Jack and Bobby. He endured the pain of losing both sons to assassins as his health deteriorated until his death in 1969, six years after the assassination of JFK.

Of Joe Kennedy, author Ted Schwarz wrote, " . . . He had spent his life hating the people he wanted to emulate, desperately seeking acceptance in all the wrong places . . . [he had] sold his soul in all the wrong places for all the wrong reasons. He had gained the world, and in the eight years between helplessness and death, he had seen it all fall apart." That Joe betrayed those he promised, especially the underworld figures who hated RFK, that he double-crossed them, should come as no surprise, for this was a man who had betrayed people who had trusted him his entire life.

With all due respect to any good Joe Kennedy accomplished in his life, he is the one man more responsible than any other for the death of his son, the president, the one who, figuratively speaking, killed John. Through the decisions Joe made before and after JFK was elected president, but especially by forcing Jack to appoint Bobby attorney general when he should have known the predictable consequences, Joe had caused a chain reaction to occur that could only end in tragedy.

Yes, Joe had taught Bobby everything he knew and JFK paid the price for their actions. In the epilogue to *Mob Lawyer*, Frank Ragano and Selwyn Raab wrote, "Within the close culture of the Mafia, a boss can never tolerate even the appearance of an insult. The Kennedys, unaware of the primitive mindset of these amoral mobsters, had insulted the grotesque pride of Santo, Carlos, Sam Giancana, and other overlords. Joseph Kennedy had made a commitment of his sons [no further harassment of these men] and they had violated it."

To be certain, father Joe, by being the chief enabler to the death of his son John, a tragedy that was preventable but inevitable due to Bobby's balls-out vendetta against very dangerous men, had truly reaped what he had sown, and more. His punishment: the debilitating stroke that left him incapacitated during the final years of his life when he suffered the loss of both John and Bobby. One may only imagine his mindset day after day sitting in his wheelchair with the knowledge that not one, but both beloved sons had been murdered.

Does this mean that the Kennedy family was truly cursed through Joe's wickedness? Former *New York Times Magazine* editor-in-chief and bestselling author Edward Klein believed so. He wrote, "The Kennedy Curse is the result of the destructive collision between the Kennedy's fantasy of omnipotence—their need to get away with things that others cannot—and the cold, hard realities of life." He added, "[The Kennedys] felt immune to mortal laws and somehow divinely protected from the inevitable consequences of their deeds and misdeeds. In their hunger of unlimited power, they saw themselves as superior beings who resided above the common herd. They felt special—omnipotent and worthy of being worshiped."

Based on what happened in Dallas, Joe, Bobby, and John Kennedy were proven wrong, they were not "immune to mortal laws," they were not "divinely protected from the inevitable consequences of their deeds and misdeeds," they were not untouchable, after flaunting their power in the faces of dangerous men. The actions of these men, ones who believed they were privileged, had consequences and the bad karma these actions triggered, the bad seeds sown into Bobby and John by Joe, had grown into tragedies of the highest degree when retaliation came knocking at the door.

In the final analysis, through knowledge of "The Belli Factor," through a new lens never before considered connecting him to organized crime, through a fresh perspective of the doomed assassin, Jack Ruby, and his trial, and through focusing on why Robert F. Kennedy *was not* killed instead of why JFK *was*, nails in the coffin are pounded home for those who most contributed to JFK's demise—Joe, the poison patriarch, the dominating father who infected his sons with venomous moral and ethical defects through his own arrogance and sinful behavior; Bobby, the ruthless law-and-order crusader who put his brother at risk; Carlos Marcello, the desperate mastermind of the assassinations; Santo Trafficante and James Hoffa, Marcello's allies in the battle to eliminate RFK from power; and Mickey Cohen, the instigator of a cover-up orchestrated by Melvin Belli in his defense of Jack Ruby.

Based on common sense and logic, in the end, JFK was a doomed president, a man whose fate was sealed, a man whose life was ripped more from the pages of a Greek tragedy than from the sweet story of Camelot. Through a series of deceptions, lies, and betrayals coupled with Bobby's personal vendetta against dangerous adversaries, Joe Kennedy, the powerful one who abused power at every turn, drove these men toward hatred, revenge, and murder pointing to an undeniable truth: John Fitzgerald Kennedy's senseless death could, and should, have been prevented. If not for the poison patriarch, his assassination in November 1963 would never have occurred.

Epilogue

Pointing the finger at Joseph Kennedy as being most responsible for his son John's assassination may strike some as cruel. After all, there is no question the elder Kennedy loved John very much. But in the end, the lessons passed from father to sons, from Joe to JFK and Robert, were ones that caused each to never understand that they could not simply do as they pleased, especially when it came to dealing with dangerous men with hate in their hearts and revenge on their minds. Yes, it was the poison patriarch who caused a series of events to occur leading to the death of the thirty-fifth president of the United States.

The strange saga that is Jack Ruby and Melvin Belli, the relationship bridging the gap, the one connecting, for the first time, RFK and JFK's enemies with Ruby through the Ruby/Belli/Cohen/Marcello link for the purpose of rendering RFK powerless, unwinds like a cheap dime novel, portraying the gangster, and the famous gangster lawyer sent to save him from the gallows. In these fantasy books, the lawyer wins; the gangster dies. Justice prevails; evil loses.

Did justice prevail in the Jack Ruby case? This is the question that propelled me to write this book, especially after I learned, during my research for my book, *Melvin Belli: King of the Courtroom*, of Belli's known connections to the Mafia casting a cloud over his illogical representation of Jack Ruby. Despite his having killed Lee Harvey Oswald, the man suspected of assassinating President Kennedy, I wondered if Ruby got a fair shake at trial or if he was the fall guy, the one who had to be silenced, portrayed as mentally unbalanced, the one eliminated so others could hide the truth.

A second reason for writing this book was my curiosity as to why no one, absolutely no one, had ever probed this critical area of interest. Based on this mindset, on and off over eight years, I did my best to uncover as much new information about Belli as possible while keeping in mind whose theories, either ones pointing to a conspiracy or lack thereof, made the most sense.

While establishing Belli's obvious links to the Mafia, I recalled firsthand how dangerous the underworld could be. While working as a correspondent for ABC's *Good Morning America* in the early 1980s, I was assigned to interview the attorney for Philadelphia gangster Angelo Bruno as part of a series on organized crime and its infiltration of the Atlantic City casinos. The program aired the interview and asked that I set up a second one. When I called the attorney's office the next morning, the receptionist was weeping. She told me the attorney had been killed the night before, the result of a bomb being placed in his car. This made me shiver with fright, wondering if I was in danger. When I started my car the next morning, my hands were trembling. Fortunately, no bomb exploded, but I never forgot that experience, that if one crossed the mob repercussions were expected. Joe Kennedy knew this; so did Bobby.

For those more interested in Melvin Belli's life and times, I recommend reading my 2007 biography, the only one written. I first met him in 1984 while overseeing a series of television segments entitled *The World According to Belli*, spotlighting his views on controversial subjects. Once production was completed, the rambunctious lawyer invited me to the Major League Baseball All-Star game at Candlestick Park. Under blue skies on a windy San Francisco day, we rode in his Rolls Royce convertible south on Highway 101 to the ballpark. Belli, married six times, the final one to a very caring woman named Nancy Ho who cooperated with me on the authorized biography, was in a jolly mood and he told fascinating stories as his snow-white hair fluttered in the air. We kept in touch over the years, and when the flamboyant lawyer died in July of 1996, I was greatly saddened, since one of the true icons of the legal profession had passed.

As this book progressed, and to gain a sense of the atmosphere and logistics surrounding the JFK assassination, I traveled to, and spoke at, the prestigious JFK Lancer Conference in Dallas. At twelve thirty in the afternoon on November 22nd, I stood in the infamous grassy knoll alongside hundreds paying tribute to the fallen idol. An eerie feeling prevailed as I glanced downward toward a white "X" painted on the street below where JFK's limousine had been when the fatal shots were fired. The Zapruder footage flashed in my mind and I could almost hear the pop, pop, pop of the gunfire that had changed history.

Minutes earlier, I had leaned against a window in the sixth floor corner of the Texas Book Depository facing Dealey Plaza. Next to me was the sniper's nest Lee Harvey Oswald allegedly employed in order to fire the bullets into JFK's brain. The severe angle to the "X" to my right and over tree limbs made me wonder whether it was possible to be such an accurate marksman from the location. This and other questions are raised and addressed in the building since it houses the Sixth Floor Museum at Dealey Plaza. Anyone can tour history to recollect the tragic events of 1963 in Dallas by purchasing a reasonably priced ticket.

Chronicling the plausibility of the events I believe took place fifty years ago, and placing blame where I believe it is deserved for them occurring while chastising others for their reckless theories and conclusions, is not meant in a spiteful manner. I recognize that I had a distinct advantage over investigators, authors, and experts since I knew, and wrote about Belli. But this does not lessen my belief that others should have picked up the trail long ago with questions about Belli's involvement in the Jack Ruby case, especially ones appearing *before* the Ruby trial. As noted, clues were hiding in plain sight regarding questions that should have been asked; but unfortunately, those probing the assassinations had their heads turned in the wrong direction by focusing on why JFK was killed instead of why RFK was not.

My intent in writing this book is certainly not to tarnish the reputation of Melvin Belli. I truly believe that his conduct in the Ruby case was forced upon him by outside pressures, that those pulling the strings, dangerous men such as Mickey Cohen and Carlos Marcello, ordered Belli to silence Ruby. This caused Belli, a brilliant but flawed man, to employ the insanity defense in an attempt to save his client. Hopefully the facts I have uncovered will trigger further research as to Belli's motives so that this book contributes to a true historical perspective of what occurred.

Mark Shaw

Sources

During the many years researching this book, more than one hundred individuals were interviewed. Forty-plus offered firsthand accounts of the assassinations of John F. Kennedy and Lee Harvey Oswald never published before. Each was an eyewitness to history; each had a different perspective on what occurred before, during, and after the Dallas killings fifty years ago.

Whenever possible, secondary sources (more than one hundred and twenty-five publications were reviewed) are only included when other information corroborated whatever facts were discovered. Certainly all information collected from FBI files is accurate based on the author having secured the files through the Freedom of Information Act.

Without question, readers are welcome to dispute the author's sources and any and all theories proposed in this book. The author welcomes both positive and negative feedback and will revise any further editions based on suggestions and corrections.

What follows is source material for each book chapter as well as the prologue and epilogue. I hope this information will serve as a guide when readers either want to fact-check the author's text, or learn more about specific areas of interest. Since instances where individuals spoke to the author are noted in the text, they are not listed here.

Prologue

Various accounts exist regarding the circumstances by which Robert Kennedy learned of the president's death. The quotes included are taken from author David Talbot's book, *Brothers: The Hidden History of the Kennedy Years* (2007). RFK's words to Justice Department spokesman Ed Guthman are sourced from that book and Guthman's own, *We Band of Brothers* (1971).

Book I

Chapter One

Descriptions of Melvin Belli and Jack Ruby are from Belli's books *My Life on Trial* (1976), *Dallas Justice* (1964) and *Time* and *Life* magazine. Basic facts about the assassinations are gathered from several sources including *The Death of the President* by William Manchester (1964). Description of Joe Tonahill from Elmer Gertz's book, *Moment of Madness: the People vs. Jack Ruby* (1968).

Facts regarding Oswald's post-arrest events, Ruby's activities after the arrest, and Oswald's shooting by Ruby have been documented in many books, including *The Plot to Kill the President* by G. Robert Blakey and Richard Billings (1981). Further information may be garnered by visiting the The Sixth Floor Museum at Dealey Plaza in Dallas, Texas.

Chapter Two

Descriptions of Jack Ruby and the Carousel, besides being garnered from *Jack Ruby's Girls* (1970), were collected from Seth Kantor's 1978 book *Who is Jack Ruby?*. It has stood the test of time as a true authority on the life and times of Ruby. Belli's background information is based on *Melvin Belli: King of the Courtroom* (2007) written by this author. Belli's focus on a civil law practice is taken from his book *My Life On Trial* (1976). ABA president-elect Edward Kuhn's statement is based on various newspaper accounts. Belli's conflicting explanations for initial representation of Ruby are collected from Belli's books *My Life on Trial* (1976) and *Dallas Justice* (1964).

Chapter Three

The description of the psychomotor epilepsy insanity defense is from Belli's *My Life On Trial* (1976). Belli's description of Judge Joe Brown is based on *Dallas Justice* (1964). Information on the prosecution team is from *My Life On Trial*. Belli's summary of his duty to Ruby and description of the jury pool are based on *My Life On Trial*, and regarding the latter, also on Gary Wills and Ovid Demaris's 1994 book *Jack Ruby*. Trial media information comes from various media sources. Ruby trial testimony is from court records and *My Life On Trial*. Ruby's comments regarding testifying are based on the 2004 book, *When The News Went Live*, written by television reporters Bob Huffaker, Bill Mercer, George Phenix, and Wes Wise. Jury foreman Max Causey's comments are from *The Jack Ruby Trial Revisited: The Diary of Jury Foreman Max Causey* (2000). Bill Alexander, Belli, and Henry Wade's final argument descriptions are taken from *Dallas Justice*.

Chapter Four

Max Causey's comments are from *The Jack Ruby Trial Revisited: The Diary of Jury Foreman Max Causey* (2000). Belli's recollections of the verdict are from *Dallas Justice* (1964). Belli's firing was reported in the *Dallas Morning News*. Information about the reversal of the Ruby verdict is based on court records. Accounts of Ruby's death and funeral are taken from the *Chicago Tribune* (January 1964).

Book II

Chapter Five

Facts and figures regarding the Warren Commission investigation are garnered from newspaper and magazine accounts and from the *Report of the President's Commission on the Assassination of President Kennedy* at the National Archives. G. Robert Blakey's quote comes from several email exchanges between this author and Mr. Blakey. Quotes about Belli and the Ruby case are taken from *The Trial of Jack Ruby* by John Kaplan and John R. Waltz (1965) and Garry Wills and Ovid Demoris's book *Jack Ruby* (1968). William Manchester's *The Death of a President* is the source for detailing Ruby's story regarding how he entered the Dallas Police Department basement. All information regarding the HSCA hearings are based on the *Report of the Select Committee on Assassinations U.S. House of Representatives*. The entire ABC interview with G. Robert Blakey may be found at abcnews.go.com/WNT/story?id=131462&page=1#. UHWPmVFFtJw.

Chapter Six

As noted, Seth Kantor's book, *Who Was Jack Ruby?* (1978), permits an inside look at Ruby like none before or since. Quotes from Diana Hunter and Alice Anderson are from their book, *Ruby Girls* (1970). In *The Plot To Kill The President* (1981) G. Robert Blakey provides more information about Ruby and his less than truthful disclosures. David Scheim's quotes are from *Contract on America: The Mafia Murder of John F. Kennedy*. Ruby's testimony before the Warren Commission is based on the *Report of the President's Commission on the Assassination of President Kennedy* at the National Archives.

Chapter Seven

Besides Frank Ragano's book, *Mob Lawyer,* and the eyewitness information provided to this author by his widow, Nancy Grandolff, biographical information about Santo Trafficante is based on several books including *The Silent Don: The Criminal Underworld of Santo Trafficante, Jr.* by Scott M. Deitche. Frank "The Irishman" Sheeran's account is chronicled in *I Heard You Paint Houses*, a 2004 book written by Charles Brandt. Author John H. Davis quotes are from *The Kennedy Contract: The Mafia Plot to Assassinate the President* (1993).

Chapter Eight

Various newspaper articles and multiple interviews with Nancy Ragano by this author provide insight into Frank Ragano. Gerald Posner's comments are from *Case Closed* (1993). Readers are encouraged to read Vincent Bugliosi's *Reclaiming History* (2007) so as to understand the former prosecutor's comprehensive arguments for the "Oswald Alone" theory as well as David Kaiser's *The Road to Dallas* (2008) to obtain the opposite viewpoint. Quotes from Frank "The Irishman" Sheeran come from Charles Brandt's book *I Heard You Paint Houses* (2004).

Book III

Chapter Nine

G. Robert Blakey and Richard Billings's comments are from *The Plot to Kill the President* (1981). Vincent Bugliosi's quotes are based on *Reclaiming History* (2007). Various newspaper accounts are taken from the *Dallas Morning News* archives. Judge Brown's comments are from Diane Hollaway's book *Dallas and the Jack Ruby Trial: Memoir of Judge Joe B. Brown, Sr.* (2001). Belli quotes are based on his book *Dallas Justice* (1964). Blakey and Billing's comments from their book *The Plot to Kill the President* (1981). The best references regarding stripper Candy Barr and the Candy Barr/Belli/Mickey Cohen link are the *Dallas Morning News*, Ted Schwarz and Mardi Rusam's 2009 book *Candy Barr: The Small-Town Texas Runaway Who Became a Darling of the Mob and the Queen of Las Vegas Burlesque*, Cohen's autobiography (*Mickey Cohen, In My Words*, 1975), and *Gangster Squad* written by Paul Lieberman (2012).

Chapter Ten

Information presented on Mickey Cohen is based on Cohen's autobiography noted above, Brad Lewis's book, *Hollywood's Celebrity Gangster* (2009), Warren Hinckle and Bill Turner's book: *Deadly Secrets, The CIA-Mafia War Against Castro and the Assassination of JFK* (1993), *Mickey Cohen: The Life and Times of L.A.'s Most Notorious Gangster (2012)* by Tere Tereba, *Gangster Squad* by Paul Lieberman (2012), and *The Enemy Within* by Robert Kennedy (1960). Information about Belli's links to mobster Mickey Cohen are based on Belli's book, *My Life on Trial* (1976), and FBI files obtained under the Freedom of Information Act. Information about Cohen's relationship with Carlos Marcello is excerpted from *Mafia Kingfish* by author John H. Davis (1989). Cohen's quote about visiting Carlos Marcello in New Orleans originates from *Mickey Cohen: In My Own Words* (1975). Comments by author Brad Lewis are from his book, *Hollywood's Celebrity Gangster: The Life and Times of Mickey Cohen* (2007).

Chapter Eleven

Besides the excerpts from Belli's FBI file (never published before), Belli's book *My Life on Trial* (1976), and this author's book, *Melvin Belli: King of the Courtroom*, are the sources for personal information about him. The interviews included about Belli first appeared in this author's Belli biography. Frank Ragano's comments about Belli are based on *Mob Lawyer* (1994) and eyewitness accounts by Nancy Grandolff, Ragano's widow. Author John H. Davis's observations are from *Mafia Kingfish* (1989).

Chapter Twelve

Earl Ruby's comments are from the *Warren Commission Report*. Eva Ruby's comments are excerpted from Frank Sinatra's FBI file secured by this author under the Freedom of Information Act. This author's interviews with Seymour Ellison were taped in San Francisco. The other Ellison comments are from Blakey and Billings's book *The Plot to Kill the President* (1981). Earl Ruby's comments to Curt Gentry are from Gentry's book *J. Edgar Hoover: The Man and the Secrets* (1981). Quotes regarding Nick Pileggi are from John H. Davis' book *Mafia Kingfish* (1989). Seth Kantor's quote is from *Who Was Jack Ruby?* (1978). Quotes from Bob Huffaker are excerpted from *When the News Went Live: Dallas 1963* (2007). Kelly Farris's comments to this author occurred during an interview in San Francisco. The source for Judge Joe Brown's quotes are from *Dallas and the Jack Ruby Trial: Memoir of Judge Joe B. Brown, Sr.* (2001) reprinted by author Diana Holloway. Belli's words about why he represented Ruby are from *My Life on Trial* and *Dallas Justice*. Interviews with Seymour Ellison and his wife occurred in their San Francisco home. The interviews with John Christian and Bill Turner occurred in Dealey Plaza, Dallas; the interview with Lily Woodfield took place at her home in Los Angeles. Vincent Bugliosi's quotes are from *Reclaiming History* (2007). Larry Hancock's quote is from his book *Someone Would Have Talked* (2010).

Book IV

Chapter Thirteen

The speculation as to Belli arriving in Dallas to see if he could represent Ruby is from Seth Kantor's book *Who was Jack Ruby?* The source for Blakey's comments is from *The Plot to Kill the President*. The BBC broadcast text regarding Don Ray Archer's comments about Ruby and Oswald are repeated by author Jim Marrs (*Crossfire: The Plot that Killed Kennedy*, 1989), and author Dick Russell (*On the Trail of the JFK Assassinations*, 2008). The Seth Kantor mention is from *Who Was Jack Ruby?* All of the quotes in this chapter from Judge Brown are from *Dallas and the Jack Ruby Trial: Memoir of Judge Joe B. Brown, Sr.* (2001). Gerald Posner's quote is from *Case Closed* (1993). Bob Huffaker's quotes are from *When the News Went Live* (2007). Elmer Gertz's quote is from *Moment of Madness: The People vs. Jack Ruby* (1968).

Bill Alexander's interviews occurred over the telephone from his Dallas office where he continues to practice law into his nineties. Ruby's comments to the Warren Commission are from the report noted above. Gertz's comment is from *Moment of Madness, the People V. Jack Ruby*. Belli's comments regarding Ruby are from *Dallas Justice*. Bob Huffaker's quote is from *When the News Went Live*. Tom Howard's comments are quoted from *Dallas Morning News* accounts. Author Curt Gentry's comment is from *J. Edgar Hoover: The Man and His Secrets* (2001). Ruby's comments to Chief Justice Warren are from the *Warren Commission Report* noted above. Jury foreman Wayne Causey is quoted from his book, *The Jack Ruby Trial Revisited*. Jon Waltz's quote is excerpted from John Kaplan and Jon R. Waltz's book *The Trial of Jack Ruby* (1965).

Chapter Fourteen

The Dorothy Kilgallen information is from Lee Israel's book *Kilgallen* (1979). Interviews with John O'Conner, Seymour Ellison, and other Belli associates and friends occurred in San Francisco. The interview with Rebecca Tonahill was by telephone from her home in the Dallas area. Lamar Waldron and Thom Hartmann's speculation that Belli was in Mexico after the Ruby trial is from Lamar Waldron and Thom Hartmann's book *Legacy of Secrecy: The Long Shadow of the JFK Assassination* (2008).

Book V

Chapter Fifteen

Readers are encouraged to watch *JFK: The Case for Conspiracy* produced by Robert J. Groden as it lays out the facts regarding the medical authority regarding JFK's death. The quote from Vincent Bugliosi is from *Reclaiming History*. Quotes regarding Mickey Cohen's hatred for RFK are from John H. Davis's book, *Kennedy Contract* (1993), and Tere Tereba's book *Mickey Cohen: The Life and Crimes of L. A.'s Notorious Mobster* (2012). The Justice Department quote regarding RFK is from *Mafia Summit* by Gil Reavill (2013). Quotes regarding possible Mafia involvement in the JFK assassination are taken from Vincent Bugliosi's book, *Reclaiming History* (2007). Frank Ragano's quotes are from *Mob Lawyer* (1994). Nicholas Katzenbach comments about RFK are from his book *Some of It Was Fun: Working with RFK and LBJ* (2008). RFK's quotes are from *The Enemy Within* (1960). Quotes about Hoffa and RFK are from author David E. Koskoff's book *Joseph P. Kennedy: A Life and Times* (1974). Quotes from author Evan Thomas are based on his book *Robert Kennedy: His Life* (2000). Hoffa's quotes are from *Hoffa, The Real Story* (1975). Bugliosi's comment is from *Reclaiming History* (2007).

Chapter Sixteen

Arthur Schlesinger words are from his book *Robert F. Kennedy and His Times* (1978). Bill Bonnano's comments are from *Bound By Honor: A mafiosi's Story* (1999). G. Robert Blakey's comments are from *The Plot to Kill the President* (1981). John H. Davis's comments are from his book *Mafia Kingfish* (1993). Sheeran's quotes are from *I Heard You Paint Houses* (2004) by Charles Brandt. *Mob Lawyer* (1994) is the source for Frank Ragano's comments. Marcello's legal scenario is based on court records and newspaper accounts. G. Robert Blakey's comments about the Marcello empire are from *The Plot to Kill the President* (1981). John H. Davis's comments on the Marcello trial are from his book *Mafia Kingfish* (1993). *Mob Lawyer* (1994) is the source for Frank Ragano's comments regarding Civello. Comments about the Apalachin Conference are from *Mafia Summit* by Gil Reavill (2013). Author Mark North's quotes are from *Act of Treason: The Role of J. Edgar Hoover in the Assassination of President Kennedy* (2011). David Heymann's quote is from *RFK* (1998). John H. Davis's comments are from his book *Mafia Kingfish* (1993). Bill Bonnano's comments are from *Bound By Honor: A mafiosi's Story* (1999). David Heymann's quote is from *RFK* (1998). Jack Newfield's comment is from *RFK, A Memoir* (1969).

Jeff Shesol's quotes about LBJ and RFK are from *Mutual Contempt: Lyndon Johnson, Robert Kennedy, and the Feud that Defined a Decade* (1997). Randall B. Woods's quotes are from his 2006 book *LBJ: Architect of American Ambition*. Richard J. Whalen's comment is from *The Founding Father: The Story of Joseph P. Kennedy* (1964). Gore Vidal's quotes about RFK are from *Gore Vidal: A Biography* (1999) by Fred Kaplan. John H. Davis's comments are from his book *Mafia Kingfish* (1993). Quotes from Vincent Bugliosi are from *Reclaiming History* (2007). Charles Brandt's comment is from his 2004 book *I Heard You Paint Houses*. Author Robert Sam Anson's quote is from *They've Killed the President* (1975). *Mob Lawyer* (1994) is the source for Frank Ragano's comments. Authors Lamar Waldron and Thom Hartmann are quoted from their book *Legacy of Secrecy* (2008).

Chapter Seventeen

RFK's comments to Ed Guthman and Guthman's description of RFK are from Guthman's book *We Band of Brothers* (1971). Guthman's statement is from David Talbot's book *Brothers: The Hidden History of the Kennedy Years* (2007). Quotes about RFK's description of the Mafia are excerpted from Bobby Kennedy's book *The Enemy Within* (1960). Evan Thomas's comments are from *Robert Kennedy: His Life* (2000). Quotes from Ken O'Donnell about RFK are excerpted from *Bobby and Jackie* by C. David Heymann (2009). Edward Klein's quote is from *The Kennedy Curse: Why Tragedy Has Haunted America's First Family for 150 Years* (2003).

David Heymann's comments are from *RFK* (1998). Randall B. Woods's words are from his book, *LBJ* (2006). Arthur Schlesinger's comments are from *Robert Kennedy and His Times* (1978). The comments from the HSCA are from its report (1979). Author Seymour Hersh's quotes are from his 1997 book *The Dark Side of Camelot*. Author Curt Gentry's comments are from his 1991 book *J. Edgar Hoover, The Man and the Secrets* (1991).

Chapter Eighteen

Listing of Kennedy family tragedies and further quotes from author Edward Klein are from his book *The Kennedy Curse* (2003). The account of Mimi Alford is from her book *Once Upon a Secret: My Affair with JFK*

(2012). J. Randy Taraborrelli's comments are from his book *Jackie, Ethel, Joan* (2000). Authors Gus Russo and Stephen Molton's comments are from their book *Brothers in Arms* (2008). David Heymann's quotes are from *RFK* (1998). Evan Thomas's quote is excerpted from *Robert Kennedy: His Life* (2000).

Richard D. Mahoney's quote is from his book *Sons and Brothers* (1999). Author David E. Koskoff's book *Joseph P. Kennedy: A Life and Times* (1974), is the source of his quote. Comments about RFK and civil liberties are from *Mutual Contempt* (1997) by Jeff Shesol.

Frank Sheeran's quotes are from Charles Brandt's book *I Hear You Paint Houses* (2004).

Chapter Nighteen

David Nasaw's comments are from his book *The Patriarch* (2012). Peter Collier and David Horowitz's comments are from their 1984 book *The Kennedys*. David Heymann's quotes are from *RFK* (1998). *The Dark Side of Camelot* (1997) is the source for author Seymour Hersh's comments. David E. Koskoff's quotes are excerpted from *Joseph P. Kennedy: A Life and Times* (1974).

Ronald Kessler's comments are from *The Sins of the Father* (1996). Author Christopher Bigsby's quote is from his biography *Arthur Miller* (2008). The quotes from David Nasaw about JPK's sexual proclivities are excerpted from *The Patriarch* (2102). Ted Sorensen's quote is from *Counselor: A Life at the Edge of History* (2008)

Author Seymour Hersh's quote is from his 1997 book *The Dark Side of Camelot*. Author Ted Schwarz is quoted from *Joseph Kennedy: The Mogul, The Mob, the Statesman, and The Making of an American Myth* (2003). Kitty Kelley's comment is from *His Way: The Unauthorized Biography of Frank Sinatra* (1986). Frank Ragano's quote is from *Mob Lawyer* (1994).

Antoinette Giancana and her fellow authors are quoted from the 2005 book *JFK and Sam* written by Antoinette Giancana, John R. Hughes, and Thomas H. Jobe. *Bound By Honor* (1999) is the source of mafioso Bill Bonnano's comments. Evan Thomas's quotes are from *Robert Kennedy: His Life* (2000). The quote from Ted Schwartz about JPK and the mob is excerpted from *Joseph Kennedy: The Mogul, The Mob, The Statesman and the Making of an American Myth* (2003). David Nasaw's comments are from his book, *The Patriarch* (2012).

Author Ronald Kessler's comments about Joe Kennedy and Gloria Swanson are from his 1996 book *Sins of the Father.*

Doris Kearns Goodwin's quote regarding JPK living vicariously through his children is from *The Fitzgeralds and the Kennedys* (2001). Ron Kessler's comment is from *The Sins of the Father* (1996). Arthur Schlesinger words are from his book *Robert F. Kennedy and His Times* (1978). Ted Schwartz's quote regarding JPK learning about JFK's death is from *Joseph Kennedy: The Mogul, The Mob, The Statesman and the Making of an American Myth* (2003). Frank Ragano and Selwyn Raab's comments about JPK and the mob are from *Mob Lawyer* (1994). Edward Klein's comment about the Kennedy curse is excerpted from Klein's book *The Kennedy Curse: Why Tragedy Has Haunted America's First Family for 150 Years* (2003).

Bibliography

Abell, Tyler. Editor. *Drew Pearson Diaries*. New York: Holt, Rhinehart, and Winston, 1974.

"The Kennedys": *American Experience*, PBS, *The Kennedys*. http://www.pbs.org/wgbh/americanexperience/kennedys/

Anson, Robert Sam. *They've Killed the President*. New York: Bantam, 1975.

Beauchamp, Cari. *Joseph P. Kennedy Presents: His Hollywood Years*. New York: Alfred A. Knopf, 2009.

Belli, Melvin, and Dany R. Jones. *Belli Looks At Life and Law In Russia*. Indianapolis, IN: Bobbs-Merrill, 1963.

Belli, Melvin M., and Maurice C. Carroll. *Dallas Justice*. New York: David McKay Company, 1964.

Belli, Melvin and Mel Krantzler. *Divorcing*. New York: St. Martin's Press, 1988.

Belli, Melvin. *Modern Trials*. Indianapolis, IN: Bobbs Merrill, 1954

Belli, Melvin. *My Life on Trial*. with Robert Blair Kaiser. New York: William Morrow and Company, 1976.

Belli, Melvin. *The Law Revolt*. 2 vols. Bellville, IL: Trial Lawyer's Service, 1968.

Belli, Melvin. *The Law Revolution*. New York: Sherbourne Press, 1968.

Belli, Melvin. ed. *Trial and Tort Trends*. (various volumes), Indianapolis, IN: Bobbs-Merrill, various years.

Bigsby, Christopher. *Arthur Miller*. London: Weidenfeld & Nicolson, 2008.

Bishop, Jim. *The Day Kennedy Was Shot*. New York: Funk and Wagnalls, 1968

Blakey, G. Robert, and Richard Billings. *The Plot To Kill The President*. New York: Times Books, 1981.

Bonnano, Bill. *Bound By Honor: A mafiosi's Story*. New York: St. Martins, 1999.

Bradlee, Ben, *A Good Life: Newspapers and Other Adventures*. New York: Simon and Schuster, 1995.

Brandt, Charles. *I Heard You Paint Houses*. Hansen, NH: Steerforth Press, 2004.

Bugliosi, Vincent. *Reclaiming History: The Assassination of President John F. Kennedy*. New York: W. W. Norton and Company, 2007.

Burrough, Bryan. "Remembrance of Wings Past" *Vanity Fair*, March 2013.

Canal, John. *Silencing The Lone Assassin*. St. Paul, MN: Paragon House, 2000.

Caro, Robert A. *The Passage of Power: The Years of Lyndon Johnson*. New York: Knopf, 2012.

Chicago Tribune—various articles, January 1963.

Christian, John G. and William W. Turner. *The Assassination of Robert F. Kennedy*. New York: Basic Books, 2006.

Clarke, Donald. *All or Nothing At All: A Life of Sinatra*. New York: From International, 1997.

Cohen, Mickey. *Mickey Cohen: In My Own Words*, New York: Prentice-Hall, 1975.

Cohen, Rich. *Tough Jews: Fathers, Sons and Gangster Dreams*. New York: Vintage, 1999.

Cole, Tom. *A Short History of San Francisco*. San Francisco: Lexikos, 1981.

Crichton, Robert. *The Great Imposter*. New York: Random House, 1959.

Davis, John H. *Mafia Kingfish, Carlos Marcello and the Assassination of John F. Kennedy*. New York: McGraw-Hill, 1989.

Davis, John H. *The Kennedy Contract*. New York: HarperCollins, 1993.

Deitche, Scott M. *The Silent Don: The Criminal Underworld of Santo Trafficante, Jr.* Fort Lee, NJ: Barricade Books, 2009.

Dempsey, John Mark, ed. *The Jack Ruby Trial Revisited: The Diary of Jury Foreman Max Causey.* Denton, TX: University of North Texas Press, 2000.

Denton, Sally, and Roger Morris. *The Money and the Power: The Making of Las Vegas and Its Hold On America.* New York: Alfred Knopf, 2001.

Douglass, James W. *JFK and the Unspeakable: Why He Died and Why It Matters.* New York: Orbis Books, 2008.

Flynn, Errol. *My Wicked, Wicked Ways.* New York: G. P. Putnam's Sons, 1959.

Garrison, Jim. *On The Trail of the Assassins.* New York: Sheridian Square Press, 1988.

Gentry, Curt. *J. Edgar Hoover: The Man and the Secrets.* New York: Norton, 1991.

Gertz, Elmer. *Moment of Madness: The People vs. Jack Ruby.* Chicago: Follett Publishing Co, 1968.

Giancana, Antoinette, John R. Hughes, and Thomas H. Jobe. *JFK and Sam.* Nashville, TN: Cumberland House, 2005.

Giancana, Sam and Chuck Giancana. *Double Cross: The Explosive, Inside Story of the Mobster Who Controlled America.* New York: Warner Books, 1992.

Goodwin, Doris Kearns. *The Fitzgeralds and the Kennedys.* New York: Touchstone, 2001.

Guthman, Edwin O. *We Band of Brothers.* New York: Harper and Row, 1971.

Graysmith, Robert. *Zodiac.* New York: Berkley Books, 1986

Groden, Robert. *The Case for Conspiracy.* DVD. Los Angeles: Delta Entertainment Corporation, 2003.

Hancock, Larry. *Someone Would Have Talked.* Dallas: JFK Lancer Publications and Productions, 2011.

Heymann, C. David. *RFK: A Candid Biography of Robert F. Kennedy.* New York: Dutton, 1998.

Heymann, C. David, *Bobby and Jackie: A Love Story*, New York: Atria Books, 2009.

Hersh, Seymour M. *The Dark Side of Camelot*. New York: Little, Brown and Company, 1997.

Hinckle, Warren, and Bill Turner. *Deadly Secrets: The CIA-Mafia War Against Castro and the Assassination of JFK*. New York: Thunder Mouth Press, 1993.

Hoffa, James. *Hoffa: The Real Story*. New York: Stein and Day. 1975.

Holland, Max. *The Kennedy Assassination Tapes*. New York: Alfred K. Knopf, 2004.

Hollaway, Diane. *Dallas and the Jack Ruby Trial: Memoir of Judge Joe B. Brown, Sr.* New York: iUniverse, 2001.

Huffaker, Bob, Bill Mercer, George Phenix, and Wes Wise. *When The News Went Live: Dallas 1963*. Lanham, MD: Taylor Trade Publishing, 2004.

Hunter, Diana, and Alice Anderson. *Jack Ruby's Girls*. Atlanta: Hallux, 1970.

Israel, Lee. *Kilgallen*. New York: Dell Publishing, 1979.

Jack Ruby On Trial. History Channel, Aired April, 2001.

Joesten, Joachim, *Oswald: Assassin Or Fall Guy?* London: The Merline Press, 1964.

Kaiser, David. *The Road to Dallas*. Cambridge, MA: The Belknap Press of Harvard University, 2008.

Kantor, Seth. *Who Was Jack Ruby?* New York: Everest House, 1978.

Kaplan, Fred. *Gore Vidal: A Biography*. New York: Doubleday, 1999.

Kaplan, John and John R. Waltz. *The Trial of Jack Ruby*. New York: Macmillan, 1965.

Katzenbach, Nicholas deBelleville. *Some of It Was Fun*. New York: W.W. Norton and Company, 2008.

Kelley, Kitty. *His Way: The Unauthorized Biography of Frank Sinatra*. New York: Bantam Books, 1986.

Kennedy, Robert F. *The Enemy Within*. New York: Harper and Brothers, 1960.

Kennelly, Thomas. *One More Story and I'm Out the Door*. New York: iUniverse, 2006.

Klein, Edward. *The Kennedy Curse: Why Tragedy Has Haunted America's First Family for 150 Years*. New York: St. Martin's Press, 2003.

Koskoff, David E. *Joseph P. Kennedy: A Life and Times.* New York: Prentice-Hall, 1974.

Kroth, Jerry. *Conspiracy in Camelot: The Complete History of the Assassination of John Fitzgerald Kennedy.* New York: Algora Publishing, 2003.

Kuntz, Tom, and Phil Kuntz. *The Sinatra Files,* New York: Three Rivers Press, 2000.

Kurtz, Michael L. *Crime of the Century.* Knoxville: University of Tennessee Press, 1982.

Kurtz, Michael L. *The JFK Assassination Debates.* Lawrence, KS: University Press of Kansas, 2006.

Lake, Steven R. *Hearts and Dollars.* Chicago: Chicago Review Press. 1983.

Lewis, Brad. *Hollywood's Celebrity Gangster: The Life and Times of Mickey Cohen.* New York: Enigma Books, 2007.

Lieberman, Paul. *Gangster Squad: Covert Cops, The Mob, and the Battle for Los Angeles.* New York City: Thomas Dunne Books, 2012

Livingston, Harrison Edward, and Robert J. Groden. *High Treason: The Assassination of JFK & and Case for Conspiracy.* New York: Carroll and Graf, 1998.

Mahoney, Richard D. *Sons and Brothers: The Days of Jack and Bobby Kennedy.* New York: Arcade Publishing, 1999.

Marrs, Jim. *Crossfire.* New York: Carroll & Graf Publishers, 1989.

Mills, Hillary. *Mailer.* New York: Empire Books, 1982.

Manchester, William. *The Death of a President.* New York: Harper and Row, 1964.

Meagher, Sylvia, *Master Index to the J.F.K. Assassination Investigations.* New York: The Scarecrow Press, 1980.

Moldea. Dan E., *The Hoffa Wars: Teamsters, Rebels, Politicians, and the Mob.* New York: Paddington Press, 1978.

Mustazza, Leonard. *Frank Sinatra and Popular Culture: Essays On An American Icon.* Westport, CT: Praeger, 1998

Nasaw, David. *The Patriarch: The Remarkable Life and Turbulent Times of Joseph P. Kennedy.* New York: The Penguin Press, 2012.

Nelson, Phillip E. *LBJ: The Mastermind of JFK's Assassination.* Xlibris Corporation, New York, 2010.

Newfield, Jack. *RFK: A Memoir*. New York: Thunder's Mouth Press, 1969.

North, Mark. *Act of Treason: The Role of J. Edgar Hoover in the Assassination of President Kennedy*. New York: Skyhorse Publishing, 2011.

North, Mark. *Betrayal in Dallas*. New York: Skyhorse Publishing, 2011.

O'Donnell, Kenneth and David Powers. *Johnny We Hardly Knew Ye*. New York: Pocket Books, 1973.

Oppenheimer, Jerry. *The Other Mrs. Kennedy*. New York: St. Martin's Press, 1994.

O'Reilly, Bill and Martin Dugard. *Killing Kennedy: The End of Camelot*. New York: Henry Holt, 2012.

Piper, Michael Collins. *Final Judgment: The Missing Link in the JFK Assassination Conspiracy*. New York: The Center for Historical Review, 1998.

Posner, Gerald. *Case Closed*. New York: Random House, 1993

Ragano, Frank, and Selwyn Raab. *Mob Lawyer*. New York: Charles Scribner and Sons, 1994.

Report of the President's Commission on the Assassination of President John F. Kennedy, Washington DC: Government Printing Office, 1964.

U.S. Congress. House. Select Committee on Assassinations. *Report of the Select Committee on Assassinations*. U. S. House of Representatives. 1979.

Reavill, Gil. *Mafia Summit: J. Edgar Hoover, the Kennedy Brothers and the Meeting that Unmasked the Mob*. Thomas Dunne Books, St. Martin's Press, 2013.

Rockaway, Robert A. *But He Was Good to His Mother: The Lives and Crimes of Jewish Gangsters*. New York and Jerusalem: Gefen Publishing, 2000.

Russell, Dick. *On the Trail of the JFK Assassins*. New York: Skyhorse Publishing, 2008.

Russell, Thaddeus. *Out of the Jungle: James Hoffa and the Re-making of the American Working Class*. New York: Alfred A. Knopf, 2001.

Russo, Gus, and Stephen Motton. *Brother In Arms: The Kennedy's, The Castros, and The Politics of Murder*. New York: Bloomsbury, 2008.

Scheim, David. *Contract On America: The Mafia Murder of President John F. Kennedy*. New York: Shapolsky Publishers, 1988.

Schlesinger, Jr., Arthur. *Robert Kennedy and His Times: Volumes I and II*, Boston: Houghton Mifflin, 1978

Schwarz, Ted, *Joseph P. Kennedy: The Mogul, The Mob, The Statesman, and the Making of the American Myth*. New York: John Wiley & Sons, 2003.

Schwarz, Ted and Mardi Rusam. *Candy Barr: The Small-Town Texas Runaway Who Became a Darling of the Mob and the Queen of Las Vegas Burlesque*. New York: Taylor Publishing, 2008.

Shesol, Jeff. *Mutual Contempt: Lyndon Johnson, Robert Kennedy, and the Feud that Defined a Decade*. New York: W. W. Norton and Company, 1997.

Shaw, Mark. *Melvin Belli: King of the Courtroom*. Fort Lee NJ: Barricade Books, 2007.

Sheresky, Norman. *On Trial*. New York: The Viking Press, 1977.

Sheridan, Walter. *The Fall and Rise of Jimmy Hoffa*. New York: Saturday Review Press, 1972.

Sneed, Larry A. *No More Silence*. Dallas: Three Forks Press, 1998.

Sorensen, Ted. *Counselor: A Life at the Edge of History*, New York: HarperCollins, 2008.

Sturdivan, Larry. *The JFK Myths*. New York: Continuum, 2005.

Summers, Anthony and Robbyn Swan. *Sinatra: The Life*. New York: Alfred A. Knopf, 2005.

Talbot, David. *Brothers: The Hidden History of the Kennedy Years*. Simon and Schuster, 2007.

Taraborrelli, J. Randy. *Jackie, Ethel, Joan*. New York: Warner Books, 2000.

Taraborrelli, J. Randy. *Sinatra: Behind The Legend*. New York: Carol Publishing, 1997.

Taraborrelli, J. Randy. *The Secret Life of Marilyn Monroe*. New York: Grand Central Publishing, 2009.

Tereba, Tere. *Mickey Cohen: The Life and Crimes of L.A.'s Notorious Mobster*. Toronto: ECW Press, 2012.

The Warren Commission Report, September 24, 1964.

Thomas, Evan. *Robert Kennedy, His Life*. New York: Simon & Schuster, 2000.

Vidal, Gore. *Palimpsest: A Memoir*. New York: Random House, 1995.

Waldron, Lamar and Thom Hartmann. *Legacy of Secrecy: The Long Shadow of the JFK Assassination.* New York: Counterpoint, 2008.

Wallace, Robert. *Life and Limb.* New York: Doubleday, 1955.

Whalen, Richard J. *The Founding Father: The Story of Joseph P. Kennedy.* New York: New American Library, 1964.

Willis, Gary, and Ovid Demaris. *Jack Ruby.* New York: The New American Library, 1967.

Woods, Randall W. *LBJ: Architect of American Ambition.* New York: Free Press. 2006.

Melvin Belli F.B.I Files (www.paperlessarchives.com/belli.html)

Frank Sinatra F.B.I Files (www.paperlessarchives.com/sinatra.html)

Frank Ragano F.B.I Files (www.paperlessarchives.com/ragano.html)

Robert F. Kennedy FBI Files (www.paperlessarchives.com/rfk.html)

Gerald R. Ford FBI Files (www.paperlessarchives.com/ford.html)

Sam Giancana FBI Files (www.paperlessarchives.com/giancana.html)

Joseph P. Kennedy FBI Files (www.paperlessarchives.com/JPK.html)

Viewpoint 88: The Men Who Killed Kennedy

"The Trial of Jack Ruby – Relssagen – Mod Jack Ruby" (see http://www.youtube.com/watch?v=7RSZDmlSr3o)

LBJ: American Experience. DVD. PBS, 2006.

Acknowledgments

N o book is possible without the cooperation of many people who aid the author's search for the truth. This is certainly the case with this book, one researched and written over the span of many years.

To those who read drafts of the manuscript and expressed their opinion about the book's content, among them my daughter Marni Morrison, Mark Gerzon, Hugh Campion, Darren Meahl, Duane Gliwa, Gilbert S. Purcell Sr., John O'Conner, Jerry Bales, Larry Glazier, Dave Foley, Seth Chernoff, Robert and Iza Peszek, Jenn Granat, Doug Olds, Becky Jones, Mike Goodin, Tom Day, Ken Birkemeier, G. Robert Blakey, Steve Smith, and John Seigenthaler: I say thank you. Thank you also to Gay Campbell, Mr. Seigenthaler's assistant, for her cooperation. Encouragement from Matthew Snyder at Creative Artists Agency was also appreciated, as well as the research work done by Martha Moyer, an expert on assassinations.

Nick Pileggi, the esteemed author of *Wiseguys*, was extremely helpful through the book's journey to publication with his wisdom and support. His endorsement and those of Bill Alexander, G. Robert Blakey, and John O'Conner, among others, is greatly appreciated.

Editing assistance was provided by Kristina Howard, June Cardinale, my wife Wen-ying Lu, and my daughter Marni Morrison. Greg Desilet proved to be a valued editor and offered substantial advice regarding the book text. Thank you all.

To those who permitted me to interview them—both those listed on a separate page, and those who wished to remain anonymous—I thank you for your assistance and for having the courage to speak about a most controversial subject.

To Frank Weimann, my literary agent, my heartfelt thanks for believing in me and the book. My thanks also to Tony Lyons at Skyhorse.

To my family support team—wife Lu, daughter Marni, son-in-law James, granddaughters Allison and Lucy—thank you for believing in me. To my beloved canine friend, black Labrador Black Sox, thanks for always being there during my lengthy writing hours.

To the Holy Spirit that guides my life on a daily basis, I say thank you, for nothing is possible in my life without your presence. I am truly blessed.

Mark Shaw

Index

Note: An 'n' following a page number indicates a footnote.